Tax Loopholes for eBay® Sellers

How to Make More Money and Pay Less Tax

Tax Loopholes for eBay® Sellers

How to Make More Money and Pay Less Tax

Diane Kennedy
Janelle Elms

McGraw-Hill
New York Chicago San Francisco Lisbon London
Madrid Mexico City Milan New Delhi San Juan
Seoul Singapore Sydney Toronto

Tax Loopholes for eBay® Sellers

2 3 4 5 6 7 8 9 0   CUS/CUS   0 1 9 8 7 6

ISBN 0-07-226242-7

Editorial, design, and production services provided by TypeWriting, Acworth, GA.

This publication is designed to provide accurate and authoritative information in regard to the subject matter covered. It is sold with the understanding that neither the author nor the publisher is engaged in rendering legal, accounting, or other professional service. If legal advice or other expert assistance is required, the services of a competent professional person should be sought.

From a Declaration of Principles jointly adopted by a Committee of the American Bar Association and a Committee of Publishers

McGraw-Hill books are available at special quantity discounts to use as premiums and sales promotions, or for use in corporate training programs. For more information, please write to the Director of Special Sales, McGraw-Hill, Two Penn Plaza, New York, NY 10121. Or contact your local bookstore.

Library of Congress Cataloging-in-Publication Data

Kennedy, Diane, 1956–
  Tax loopholes for eBay sellers : how to make more money and pay less tax / by Diane Kennedy and Janelle Elms.— 1st ed.
      p. cm.
  ISBN 0-07-226242-7
  1. Tax planning—United States—Popular works. 2. Income tax—Law and legislation—United States—Popular works. 3. Electronic commerce—Taxation—Law and legislation—United States—Popular works. 4. eBay (Firm) I. Elms, Janelle. II. Title.
  KF6297.Z9K426 2005
  658.8'7—dc22

                                                                2005022753

Dedicated to the next generation of entrepreneurs:

Especially Diane's son, David

And Janelle's nieces and nephews, Beckaboo, Tyler, Allie-bug, Zach, Avery, Niles, and Princess Laura

Contents

Foreword

Rules? You mean there are *rules*?

A lot of people buying and selling stuff online think they're living in an alternate universe, one where the normal laws of business don't apply. A Shangri-La where there are no rules, no laws, no regulations. A virtual Woodstock where people can bliss out and engage in capitalistic acts between consenting adults without fear, anxiety, or stress.

At a recent eBay University program on the West Coast, an audience member got up during the Q&A for my "eBay for Business" program and asked the following question: "Earlier this year I started selling stuff on eBay, mainly to clean out my attic. I ran out of attic stuff a while back, so I've started selling stuff for some of my friends and relatives. So far I've made about $50,000 after expenses. I don't really look at this as a business, but I'm being told that I have to pay taxes on what I'm making. Is that right?"

Let me get this straight…you've made $50,000 in just a few months and you're not sure if you have a business? Are you kidding?

A lot of people are surprised to find out that their cherished hobbies have somehow morphed into real businesses overnight without their knowledge. Your good-faith belief that what you are doing is "only a hobby" doesn't count for much when it comes to the Internal Revenue Service and your state and local tax authorities. Under current law, if you are making even as much as $1 doing anything, the tax authorities will view you as being self-employed, you will have to report your earnings as income, and you will have to pay taxes on that income. (If you are losing money, that's a different story, for you cannot deduct losses from a "hobby.")

Time to burst a big bubble, folks. When you are buying and selling stuff on eBay, on a Web site or blog, or indeed anywhere on the Internet, *if you are making money, you are in business*. Specifically, you are running a "retail" business, one that sells goods to the end consumer. As such, you are subject to the same federal, state, and local taxes that "brick and mortar" retail businesses in your community have to pay, and you must comply with the same laws, rules, and regulations that they do. There is no tax-free lunch on the Internet, and there never has been.

And it's getting worse, folks—as state and local governments are increasingly desperate for ways to raise revenue without raising people's income tax rates (a surefire way for politicians to lose at the polls), they are yielding to the overwhelming temptation to impose taxes on Internet commerce of all kinds, including eBay.

But now for some good news. Since you are now running a business, life is deductible! Well, at least some things in life are. If you are running a business, you are considered to be "self-employed" and can deduct a lot of things that people with hobbies just can't. According to IRS publications, self-employed people can legitimately take more than 1000 business, charitable, and "miscellaneous" other deductions on their tax returns. Not everything is deductible, though, and the rules don't always follow logical patterns.

So how do you deal with taxes and deductions now that you're an eBay entrepreneur? Well, you could buy a copy of the federal Internal Revenue Code and try to figure it all out yourself. The code currently runs to more than 10,000 pages of densely-packed text, with thousands more pages of U.S. Treasury Department regulations explaining each code section in great detail. If you've got a decade of your life to spend on this, you can probably figure out the taxes that apply to your business on eBay and fill out your own tax returns without paying a single penny in professional fees.

Or you could hire an accountant or CPA and have him or her explain all the deductions you can legally take. There's only one problem with that plan, though—accountants these days are nervous about volunteering information about what you can and cannot deduct on your tax return, and you can't really blame them. In a world where anyone can be sued for anything, they're worried about losing their license for "suggesting" that you can take deductions to which you're not legally entitled.

More than ever before, if you're buying and selling stuff online, the burden is on you to figure out how taxes work, learn what you can and can't legally deduct, and operate your business on eBay in such a way that Uncle

Sam gets as little as possible of your hard-earned cash.

While there is no shortage of self-help books for people who want to do their own taxes, there hasn't been a book specifically for eBay sellers on how to deal with tax problems. Until now.

Tax Loopholes for eBay Sellers is the first tax guide devoted entirely to helping eBay entrepreneurs cope with the U.S. tax system. The authors—tax authority Diane Kennedy and eBay expert Janelle Elms—have taken great pains to demystify our Byzantine tax system and boil it down to the essentials, so that even newbie eBay sellers can figure out what they should and should not be doing to keep the IRS away from their door.

As more and more people are buying and selling on eBay, they are going to have to learn to pay their dues and figure out creative ways to deal with taxes and government regulations. To those who grumble, I say, look on the bright side: Taxes are the best kind of problem to have when you're running your own business. My wish to all of my new small business clients is "May you have tax problems as soon as possible." Why? Because the only people who have tax problems are people who are succeeding and making money. If you were failing miserably, you wouldn't have to worry about taxes. No income, no taxes. So face it, folks—taxes are the government's way of telling you you've got what it takes to succeed, you're doing a great job, and you should keep it up.

Tax Loopholes for eBay Sellers should be in every eBayer's library. Heck, buy two copies—one for you, and the other for your accountant who's still using Number 2 pencils and thinks that eBay is Pig Latin for "bee."

Cliff Ennico
Attorney at Law and Legal/Tax
Expert for eBay University
CliffEnnico.com
Fairfield, Connecticut
August 2005

Introduction

Are you currently selling on eBay? Or, are you thinking about it but aren't quite sure how to get started, or whether you want to make that commitment? If you answered "yes" to either of these questions, then keep reading—because this book is for you.

If you've ever attended an eBay seminar, or taken a live or online course through eBay University, then you know that there is one question first and foremost on the minds of most eBay sellers. eBay instructors know this for a fact—they report that it is the single most frequently asked question of all. So, in this book we're going to answer it, along with a lot of other questions, and we're going to give you some other ideas to think about on how you can reduce or even eliminate those taxes.

But first, let's ask and answer the most frequently asked question of all time from eBay sellers:

Do I Have to Pay Taxes if I Sell on eBay?

Yep. If you are making money from selling merchandise or services on eBay, that money is taxable.

Of course, whenever eBay University instructors answer that question, the second most frequently asked question then comes up, which is, not surprisingly:

How Do I Do It?

We'll show you. In Parts I and II of this book, we take you through every-thing in step-by-step detail; from setting up your business, getting your business license and starting up a set of books, to valuing your inventory so you can determine your cost of goods sold and even sample bookkeep-ing entries. We also explain about sales taxes, state taxes, payroll taxes and income taxes, and have got charts, forms and resources to help you calcu-late and pay your taxes.

If you are already an eBay seller and just want to know about taxes, then you might want to start with Chapter 3 and go from there. But if you aren't operating your eBay business through some type of incorporated business structure, then we urge you to come back and take a look at Chapters 1 and 2, where we explain why operating through a business structure is a safer, and more tax-advantaged way to operate, and what are the best business structures to use for your eBay business. We also explain what the IRS is looking for when it is sorting out a real business from a hobby business, and why it matters. Even if you are already operating through a business structure it still might be worth taking a look at Chapter 2, to see if you are using the best business struc-ture for your eBay business.

> The most frequently asked ques-tions by eBay sellers are:
> 1. Do I have to pay taxes if I sell on eBay?
> 2. How do I do it?

So, now that we've explained the opening premise of this book, and asked and answered the two most frequently asked questions from all eBay University and seminar attendees, we have a question for you:

What If You Could Reduce or Even Eliminate the Taxes Generated By Your eBay Business (and Maybe Even More)?

The simple answer to the question of whether or not you have to pay taxes on eBay sales is "yes." But while that may be the simple answer, the more accurate answer is "it depends."

It depends, because if you sell something and make an income then, yes, you'll have to pay taxes. *But*, if you can offset that income against enough expenses and tax deductions, then no, you won't have to pay taxes. And, if you have excess expenses or tax deductions after you've offset all of that eBay income, then you can begin to offset the taxes you pay on your other income as well.

This is another reason why we wrote *Tax Loopholes for eBay Sellers.* First, we wanted to give you the rules about taxes and your eBay business, so you'll know when and how taxes are calculated and paid.

But we also wanted to show you how to use the tax rules to your advantage in the tax game. All games have rules, and the tax game is no different. In fact, if you play the tax game right, you should be able to lower, or even eliminate, those taxes. Now, how can you not want to win *that* game?

Think about this:

What could you do with an extra $100, $200 or even a thousand dollars or more each and every month? Even better what if you could take that money, put it in your pocket, and never worry about paying taxes on it? If we told you that you could do it, legally, ethically and morally, using this book and the power of the eBay online community, do you think you could find the time to learn how?

eBay Tonight, Pay Less Tax Tomorrow

For those of you who aren't already selling on eBay, believe it or not, the opportunity to earn more money and pay less taxes exists in a place you might not have considered—eBay. Yes, that's right—eBay.

Have you ever wondered why millions of other people are selling on eBay? For that matter, have you ever looked at all of the "How to" books on eBay selling that are available on the market today and wondered, "What's up with that?" And having said that, for those of you who are already selling on eBay, are you wondering right about now, "What's different about this book as compared to all of the others on the shelves?"

The difference between this book and all of the other books out there is that we aren't going to tell you that you can make millions selling on eBay or how to set up your eBay store. What we are going to tell you (and show you) is how to set up and operate your eBay business in the most tax-advantaged way possible, so that you can lower, or even eliminate taxes altogether. And if you do have to pay taxes on some of your income, we'll show you how to calculate and pay them.

> **TaxLoopholes Checklist to Paying Less Tax:**
>
> Step 1—Establish legitimate business
> Step 2—Identify legal business deductions
> Step 3—Change W-4 withholding certificate to reduce withheld taxes
> *eBay tonight … less tax tomorrow!*

How Are You Running Your eBay Business?

You see, although millions of people are selling things on eBay, many of them aren't selling in the most tax-advantaged way possible. These people are missing out on a wonderful opportunity to make more money and pay less tax at the same time! That's because they aren't taking their eBay business seriously, and running it as a business—they're running it like a hobby—and in the eyes of the IRS, there is a *big* difference between the two.

So that's the first thing we want you to think about, and get behind—that you can, with a few simple steps, turn your eBay activities into a legit-imate business, with all of the tax breaks and advantages that businesses enjoy. You can literally eBay tonight—and pay less tax tomorrow!

Throughout this book you're going to find checklists, diagrams and screen shots that will walk you through the process of setting up your eBay business the right way. Everything you will read in this book is legal, above-board, IRS-approved, and completely ethical. Believe it or not, the IRS wants you to succeed! Successful people pay taxes and contribute to the economy. Successful people operate successful businesses, which employ other people, who also pay taxes and contribute to the economy. The better off we each are individually, the better off America is as a whole. It's all a matter of understanding what the rules are, so that you can then use those rules to your maximum advantage.

eBay can be a virtual goldmine if you know what you're doing. You can make more money *and* pay less tax through legal tax loopholes, but first you'll need to learn the business and tax rules to fully take advantage of those loopholes. Whether you're just looking to sell your own personal items, want to unload some extra inventory, or if you're looking to build a profit-driven business that you can run from your own home, eBay can be the small busi-ness opportunity that makes a huge difference for your family.

Acknowledgments

The authors wish to acknowledge the expertise of two individuals who generously provided the wisdom from their years of business expertise.

Megan Hughes
Founder of Business First Formations, Inc.
You are the truly the queen of business formation, proper structuring, and management of business. Thank you for the hours you spent on this project.

Michael Savage, CPA
Manhattan Professional Group
Thank you for your help with the bookkeeping and accounting chapters. Your practical advice was invaluable.

Additionally, there are a lot of people that go into every book that is written. We thank Richard Cooley, Margie McAneny, Michael Nakamoto, and Larry Jellen for all of their help, support, and contributions.

Part 1

Taxes and
Business Structures

1

Why eBay Makes a Good Business

Do you ever feel like you're running in place? That no matter how hard you work, every step forward is all too often followed by one or more steps back? You get that promotion and the raise, only to see the extra money gobbled up in increased taxes or absorbed by an increased cost of living. You know there's got to be a way to get more without working two or three jobs and sacrificing your life entirely.

Do you ever look at the rich, wonder how they do it, and why they seem to get all of the tax breaks while you seem to be shouldering an ever-increasing tax burden?

Here's the first secret—in many cases, wealthy people *do* pay less in taxes. But that's not necessarily because they are given special tax breaks by Congress, or that the government protects its friends. What many of these people have that you might not have is *knowledge*—specifically, knowledge of how to reduce their taxes through government-sponsored tax loopholes and other tax reduction incentives.

For those of you who may not be completely clear, let's first define what a loophole is. A loophole is a government incentive to promote a specific public policy. It is *not* a tax dodge, or an illegal, immoral, unethical, elitist, anti-social, pro-corporate culture, forget-you-I've-got-mine action or attitude. In this instance, the public policy being promoted is the creation and operation of a business.

> A loophole is an incentive provided by the government to promote a specific public policy.

Jenny Makes a Plan

Jenny Guerro, a 38-year-old single mother of two boys, lived in Dallas, Texas. For several years, she worked as a legal secretary for a large downtown law firm, where she made a good living. She and her two kids lived a modest, comfortable lifestyle in a nice apartment in a good neighborhood at a rent she could afford.

Financially, Jenny was getting by just fine but concerned about the future. She kept her credit card balances down, because she knew all too well how quickly credit card debt can spiral out of control. And while she was not quite living paycheck-to-paycheck, realistically, Jenny knew she was only a few paychecks from the street.

When the boys were little it was easier—the future seemed much further off, and often it was enough simply to get the bills paid and food on the table. The boys' wants were easier, too—action figures and t-shirts were always welcomed. As they grew older—David was 12 and Roberto was 15—their tastes changed. T-shirts were replaced by Sean John gear, and action figures were traded up for MP3 players. Although the boys were financially realistic and understanding of the family finances, Jenny didn't like having to say no all the time. College was coming, too, with all of its associated expenses.

One evening, late at night, Jenny found herself awake, wondering how she would pay for the boys to go to college and try to save for her own retirement. Having enough money for "right now" wasn't enough anymore, and Jenny felt insecure about her financial future. She had dreamed about owning her own home one day, but as inflation and real estate appreciation continued to outpace her salary, that dream seemed further away all the time.

On that sleepless night, Jenny decided to get up and do a bit of online research into ways she could make some more money. She ran some searches on owning an online business and was overwhelmed at the thousands of hits that appeared. As she scanned through and looked at various opportunities, a few things became clear: (1) most of the opportunities involved franchising or some form of multi-level marketing and sales; (2) the majority of these opportunities looked too good to be true; and (3) often a significant outlay of cash was involved up front, with no guaranteed return whatsoever.

The problem with these ideas was that Jenny hated cold-call selling, and she certainly didn't have the cash resources to buy a franchise. Besides, she really didn't want to quit her existing job, as it paid well and provided her family with good medical coverage—a crucial requirement for Jenny.

At the same time, she recognized that more income-earning opportunities were available in sales than in other occupations. She could look for a weekend job working in a store, but retail certainly didn't pay the type of money she wanted to make, and the thought of spending another 16 hours a week at work was unappealing, to say the least.

The idea of having her own business sounded intriguing. One thing Jenny read over and over again on various Web sites was that business owners got great tax breaks and write-offs. She wondered what kind of business she could do that wouldn't interfere with her full-time job, didn't require her to do cold-call sales, and, most importantly, didn't require a huge amount of up-front cash. And, if she eventually decided to leave her job and operate her own business full time, she needed to make sure that her family's medical and dental care needs were covered at an affordable price.

Jenny thought about trying to get a real estate agent or a broker's license so that she could sell real estate or securities part time. That felt like a good fit—she could get behind the products, and her knowledge of securities law from work would come in handy. But, again, both of those ideas involved up-front cash to pay for courses, and eventually, if she was serious about pursuing either career path, she would need to leave her current job. Still, she wasn't willing to abandon the idea completely, so Jenny mentally filed it away for future exploration.

Feeling a bit discouraged, Jenny found herself browsing eBay in an attempt to clear her mind. She loved to shop on eBay—it was the only way she could afford better clothing and accessories for herself and the boys. She could buy anything on eBay, it seemed, and there seemed to be a buyer for anything a person wanted to sell.

Well, now, that was an interesting thought.

Jenny rolled the idea around in her mind. Like most families, Jenny and her kids had amassed quite a collection of things over the years, and their apartment was pretty full of stuff that no one was using anymore. Garage sales are tough to do from an apartment, so until now Jenny had decluttered by taking a few boxes at a time to the local Goodwill or Salvation Army donation centers. What if she sold their old stuff on eBay instead? Could she make enough money to make it worthwhile, and could it be operated like a business, so that she could take advantage of the tax deductions and tax breaks that businesses enjoyed?

She decided to give it a shot, so she went into the My eBay administration section on the eBay Web site. Although Jenny had a user account, she had never sold anything on eBay. When she had set up her original user account, all she had provided was her name, address, and telephone number. As a seller, she would need to add more information—most importantly, credit card and checking account details. This information ensures that eBay has a way to collect its listing fees and so that eBay knows that sellers are who they say they are.

Jenny also went into her PayPal account to see if she needed to make any changes to that. As an eBay user, Jenny had set up a PayPal account to pay for her purchases quickly and easily. It was also helpful for items that didn't arrive or for those that didn't arrive in the condition as specified, because PayPal worked in much the same way that a credit card did—she, as the buyer, could file a claim of nonreceipt and get her money back. She knew that PayPal was the preferred method of payment for buyers, and she wanted to make sure her items were easy for sellers to purchase.

When Jenny looked at how PayPal worked for sellers, she discovered that to be protected, she needed to make sure that she shipped only to the addresses buyers had on record with PayPal and not to any unconfirmed addresses. This was important, because PayPal protected only sellers who adhere to this policy.

It was easy to set up the seller's side of her account. Jenny provided the credit card and bank account information and was immediately ready to sell. Now all she needed to do was decide what she was going to sell. Jenny went back to bed, feeling much better than she had when she sat down at the computer.

Over the weekend, Jenny and her boys began to catalog what they wanted to sell, when they remembered buying each item, and approximately how much each item had originally cost. Jenny created an inventory list as they went along, and she and the boys each completed one, with each of them listing 10 things they wanted to sell. One of the things that Jenny made sure they each did was do a "completed items" search on eBay for each item they wanted to sell. This gave them an idea of what was selling, what wasn't selling, and how much items were selling for. Jenny's beginning list looked something like this:

Owner	Item Description	When Purchased	Purchase Price	Current Condition	Average Selling Price on eBay	"Best Practice" Starting Price*
Jenny	Coach purse, model 1463, red leather	2004	$225	Very good—minor wear consistent with light use	$100–150	$9.99
Roberto	PlayStation 1 system and six games	2000	$500	Used, but in good working condition	$80–125	$9.99
David	GameBoy Color with four games	2000	$250	Used, but in good working condition	$25–75	$9.99

*Although eBay users are free to set their own starting prices and manage all aspects of their sales, eBay does provide "Best Practice" recommendations on sales and marketing aspects to help new and experienced sellers achieve maximum results.

When Jenny and the boys finished their list and added up all of their items, they were looking at potential gross sales of about $800, just for the 30 items they had put together so far.

During the following week, Jenny and the boys cleaned up the first ten items they were going to sell and wrote accurate descriptions of the condition, wear and tear, and any problems. Jenny took pictures with a digital camera, so that she could show off the items to their best advantage. The following weekend, Jenny listed the first group of ten items on a seven-day auction. Eight of the ten items sold, and some of them sold at a higher price than Jenny had anticipated. According to their inventory list, these eight items had a combined anticipated maximum purchase price of $500, but they had sold for a total of $575!

> With her first profit in hand, Jenny and the boys began discussing what they might want to do with that money. But before they did anything, Jenny told them that she needed to figure out what the tax consequences of this extra money was going to be. She didn't want to be in a situation at the end of the year where she was being hit with an unexpected tax bill—especially after they had already spent all of their eBay profits. She told the boys that she was going to bank the money for a bit, while she figured out what was the best way to run their new operation.

Business drives the United States, along with most other countries. Businesses provide jobs and income for their workers. Businesses drive the economy by producing saleable goods and services that are bought, sold, and taxed. Economically, there is a direct correlation between business growth and economic growth as a whole. And the better the economic growth, the more jobs and money are available for everyone.

As a result, the government rewards businesses, and those who start them, with tax breaks. As a business owner, you hire employees, employ advisors, invest capital in your business, and generally stimulate the economy. The country is stronger because of strong businesses.

Now here's the second secret—tax breaks are for *all* businesses, not just the big ones. There's nothing in the tax code that says only businesses that have profits of $1 million or more get these breaks. And *that's* the secret that business owners know and one of the things that most wealthy people have in common—business ownership provides better tax breaks. So, if you want more out of your life, your first step is to start your own business, learn how set up a financial blueprint, and start reducing your taxes.

What Is a Legitimate Business?

Before we get too far into how eBay can work as a business for you, let's back up and explain the difference between a *true* business and a *hobby* business and why that difference is important.

A true, or legitimate, business (at least in the eyes of the IRS), meets nine IRS requirements (see the requirements in the accompanying box). As long as you follow these nine steps, you are considered a legitimate business and are entitled to all of the tax savings and deductions that are available for businesses.

The first item on the list is that your business be organized and operated with the intention of making money. But,

Tax Myth:
You have to make a profit to have a legitimate business.

Tax Loophole:
You can have a loss, which you write off against other income, year after year, as long as you can pass the IRS's "Nine Steps Test" to prove you have a business.

Make sure your Business measures up. Take "The 9 Steps to Business Test" found at **www.taxloopholes/ebaysellers**. We'll let you know how your business stacks up—*for free!*

believe it or not, making a profit is *not* an IRS requirement. New businesses aren't usually expected to make money for the first few years; in fact, the IRS estimates that many businesses will lose money for the first three to five years, and sometimes for much longer periods of time. Established case law reveals that even a business that has lost money for more than 20 years is still a proper business, despite the lengthy period of loss.

A great example of a business that lost money in spectacular fashion is Amazon.com. Amazon.com was formed in 1995 and lost millions of dollars each year until 2001, when it finally posted its first ever profit. In fact, at the time Amazon.com declared its first profit, it had accumulated losses of about $1.4 billion! Yet, because Amazon.com was following the rules and the nine IRS guidelines, it was treated as a business by the IRS—losses and all.

The next most important factor in proving your business's legitimacy is that you have a proper recordkeeping system in place and that you are operating like a business. That means you need to keep a proper set of accounting records in accordance with what's called *generally accepted accounting principles*, or *GAAP*, and you keep the business finances separate from your personal finances. For example, if you are operating your business through your personal checking account and aren't keeping anything but the most minimal of records, the IRS may determine that you aren't really operating a business, as much as you have a hobby.

Other ways to show the IRS that you are operating a legitimate business can be investing in education (a sales course, bookkeeping course, and

The IRS "Nine Steps to Business" Test
The IRS wants to see you take the following nine steps to prove you have a legitimate business:

1. You carry on the activity in a businesslike manner.
2. The time and effort you put into the activity indicate you intend to make it profitable.
3. You depend on income from the activity for your livelihood.
4. Your losses are due to circumstances beyond your control (or are normal in the startup phase of your type of business).
5. You change your methods of operation in an attempt to improve profitability.
6. You, or your advisors, have the knowledge needed to carry on the activity as a successful business.

7. You were successful in making a profit in similar activities in the past.
8. The activity makes a profit in some years (how much profit it makes is also considered).
9. You can expect to make a future profit from the appreciation of the assets used in the activity.

You can take the "Nine Steps" test for free at www.taxloopholes.com/ebaysellers, to see how your eBay business stacks up against the IRS guidelines. But don't panic if you don't meet the criteria for all of them. It doesn't mean the IRS will automatically disqualify you as a proper business. Just make sure that you are strong in the areas that are relevant to your eBay business operations.

so on), hiring advisors such as a CPA or a bookkeeper, joining mentor groups or other small business associations, and generally demonstrating that you are trying to improve your business.

Now here's the best news of all. You could take a course with eBay University or an eBay course at your local community college to jump-start your business idea. Your business would prosper, the cost of the course would be a tax deduction, and your taking the course helps prove that you are a legitimate business owner.

Here are some of the elements that make up each of the nine steps to a legitimate business.

1. Carry on in a businesslike manner:
   - Have a separate business bank account.
   - Keep bookkeeping records.
   - Have a filing system to keep copies of business-related receipts and records.
   - Make an effort to collect monies owed to you.
   - Review your business's financial statements.
2. Take time and effort to operate profitably:
   - Keep track of the time you spend each week in business activities.
   - Keep a schedule of business appointments.
   - Keep notes of conversations or communications with experts, advisors, and consultants on ways to improve your business.
   - Keep records of business-related seminars you have attended.
3. Depend on the income you make in your eBay business:
   - Use the income you make from your eBay business to meet your living expenses.
   - If you are currently working for someone else as an employee, consider eventually replacing your work income with your eBay business income.

4. Business losses are normal, or beyond your control. The factors the IRS is looking for here are
   - If your eBay business has sustained a loss, the reasons for the loss are documented.
   - The losses are normal for this type of business, especially in the beginning.
   - Others operating a similar business have also experienced these kinds of losses.
5. Operate or change operations in an effort to make money. The IRS wants to know that you are trying to make a profit, and are looking for evidence that
   - You have made changes to improve your eBay business operations.
   - You have looked at other ways to improve your business (such as purchasing business books, attending seminars or marketing courses, and so on).
   - You have talked to business consultants or other experts about ways to make your eBay business more profitable.
6. You or your advisors have the knowledge to operate a business profitably:
   - You have identified one or more experienced advisors who can help you.
   - Those advisors have related business knowledge so that they can offer you relevant assistance.
7. You have prior experience in running a profitable business:
   - You have run a business and were able to do it profitably.
   - You have run an eBay business or something similar.
8. The business has made a profit in the past:
   - Your eBay business has made a profit in at least some of the years it has been operating.
   - If it has made a profit, that profit was large enough to make it economical to continue the business.
9. You anticipate that the business will continue to make a profit in the future:
   - You anticipate that your eBay business will remain profitable.
   - You are using your eBay business profits to invest in appreciating assets that add value to the business.

The Most Important of the Nine Steps to Business

The one step that you must beware of, and that we can't emphasize enough, is that *your eBay business must be trying to make a profit*. A very unscrupulous group of people are operating on the Internet and elsewhere and will try and tell you (or, more likely, sell you) a set of "tricks," or "secrets the IRS doesn't want you to know," that also promise to save you taxes. Unfortunately, what these people are usually selling is a sham home-based business idea—for example, one infamous group said that by simply putting a filing cabinet into a room in your house, you have effectively turned that room into a home office and are now entitled to write off all costs associated with that room (such as furniture, a por-

> If you don't take your eBay business seriously, why should the IRS? Keep good records to show that you are serious about your business.

tion of the mortgage and utilities, and so on). But by adding a piece of office furniture, you are *not* operating a business with the intention of making a profit. Even worse, taxpayers who had paid money to these snake-oil peddlers wound up paying more than they bargained for, as the IRS came after them for not only the unpaid taxes, but for penalties and interest charges as well.

The IRS really hates home-based business scams and has acted aggressively to punish those who try and claim these false business-based deductions. Each year, the IRS publishes a list of its "Dirty Dozen" top tax scams; the sham home-based business was a perennial favorite. The IRS credits a decline in home-based business scams to its get-tough policy, but the agency continues to warn taxpayers that it is still checking up on them. But keep in mind that even if your eBay business doesn't meet all nine steps, as long as it is strong in the steps that it does meet, your business can easily qualify for all of the tax benefits of a home-based business.

The key is your *intent*. Even if you have a loss in the beginning (as most new businesses do), you can prove you are operating a legitimate business. And a legitimate business means you can write the loss off against other income.

What Is a Hobby Business?

A hobby business is a business that the IRS has determined doesn't pass its nine steps test for a true business. This is usually due to poor planning by the owner, who hasn't put the required elements into place to have a legitimate business. As mentioned, examples of this include not keeping proper accounting records, running business finances through your personal bank or checking account, and generally making no effort to make a profit. All of these things tell the IRS that you aren't really serious about operating as a business.

If the IRS determines that you are operating a hobby business rather than a legitimate one, watch out. The IRS has the right to tax your eBay profits while at the same time disallowing your business tax expenses and deductions. The IRS will allow you to deduct only some expenses—and even then, you can deduct only up to the amount of income you make. That means the best you can do is break even, and the worst you can do is pay more taxes than you would have otherwise.

Hobby or Business?

Be careful how you answer—there is a *huge* difference

	Hobby	Business
You make money—	Tax Due	Tax Loophole!
You lose money—	No tax-writeoff	Tax Loophole!

Figure 1.1   The tax difference between a hobby and a business.

If you make money, it doesn't matter whether you have a hobby or a business—you owe the tax (Figure 1.1).

Why eBay Works as a Business

So, now that you know what makes a business from the IRS perspective, let's talk about why eBay works as a business. eBay is the world's most popular and successful online auction web site. People from all over the world use eBay every day to search for, purchase, and sell items of all types—everything from toys to houses.

For some people, using eBay is simply a way to clean out the garage and make a little pocket change. At the far end of the spectrum are large companies looking to create online sales outlets, unload overstocked merchandise, and develop new channels of customers. And, somewhere in between, are the more than 430,000 people who are making their livings by selling merchandise on eBay. The ability to scale eBay activities to suit everyone's individual needs or lifestyles makes it work well as a business. Whether you are selling one or one thousand items per week, your eBay business is equally legitimate in the eyes of the IRS. Simply put, you can design and operate your eBay business in whatever way suits you best.

The power of eBay is in its diversity—you may have heard that *everything* has been offered up for sale at one time or another on eBay. In addition to acting as the world's online marketplace, eBay also serves as a valuation point and a research tool; for many people, eBay is the first place they turn when they are trying to locate a specific item or determine its market value. For example, many people who've experienced a fire or flood in their homes use eBay as a way to determine the current market value of the items that need to be replaced. It is much easier to prove current market replacement value of an item if you can show the insurance company what that item has been selling for on eBay.

Operating an eBay business isn't difficult, nor does it have to be time-consuming. It does take a little bit of work to get set up and to put the systems into place so that you'll need to meet the IRS business requirements.

How eBay Can Work for You

If you haven't yet started an eBay business, you're probably wondering what it would really take to do it. Maybe you've never had a business before, or you're hesitant about using the Internet, given the stories of fraud and identity theft that you've read about. Or maybe you thought you had to have an existing business or a supply of products to sell.

The fact of the matter is you don't need an existing business to get started. And, as for a beginning inventory of products, you already have this. Stop for a moment and think about the things you have stored in your attic, in your basement, in your garage or closet, or right under your nose.

At one time, many of these were desirable products; things you used for a while and put away or things you've simply outgrown—a doll collection, a child's toy cars, clothes, china, glass knickknacks, and even outdated textbooks. Anything you might sell at a garage sale or flea market, no matter how big or small, is ideal inventory for your eBay business.

Did you know that nearly 72 percent of all eBay sellers start out by selling what's in their own home? Old videotapes, furniture, pots and pans, shoes, purses, jewelry, and older electronics are always popular items—plus you'll find thousands of collectible items as well. Fast-food promotional toys, collectable stuffed animals, lunchboxes, salt and pepper shakers, old dolls, sports equipment, and even old computers and computer parts—virtually anything you can imagine selling at a garage sale or a flea market are fair game for eBay.

For those of you who already have a business and are looking for ways to increase your exposure, the eBay benefit to an existing small business is enormous. The Internet allows business owners to showcase their goods or services to more people and at a cheaper cost. If you are a business owner, you know the value of your marketing campaign relative to your business. With eBay, you've got a marketing team that is doing a lot of work for you—at minimal or no cost.

If you're like other successful small business owners selling on eBay, you might discover that you can sell your items for even more per unit, because more people are bidding on your items. Your items will sell faster, too, because you can now sell anywhere in the world; you don't need to wait for someone to show up in your store. And, because your need for retail space will decrease, or possibly be eliminated altogether, your costs will go down; your eBay store may become all the store you need.

Operating an eBay Business Can Save You Money on Taxes

With an eBay business, you'll start saving tax money, because once you have established a legitimate business, you can begin to take advantage of tax loopholes, business deductions, and tax credits that are available only to businesses. These loopholes can add up to significant savings.

Here are our three favorite deductions available to eBay business owners:

- Home office/inventory storage
- Travel
- Paying kids or other family members to help with your business

Using these three deductions, smart business owners can transfer a fairly significant amount of their monthly running costs to pre-tax dollars from their current status as after-tax expenses. For example, if you are using 20 percent of your home for your home office and inventory storage space, you can potentially deduct 20 percent of your mortgage interest and municipal utilities such as water and garbage pickup, gas, and electricity as a cost of doing business. If you travel around looking for merchandise to sell on eBay, your costs for each day you spend searching and your vehicle expenses are all deductible. (Imagine being able to deduct that trip to Vegas for the World Shoe Association trade show.) And if you engage family members or others in the business and pay them a reasonable salary for their time spent working, you can reduce your taxable income even more. These are just a few of the tax-saving strategies you'll find in Part 3 (Tax Loopholes for eBay Sellers). Before that, in Part 2 (Easy Accounting for eBay Sellers), we'll review the recordkeeping steps you need to take to make sure you get to keep the deductions, in case the IRS ever comes calling. Even better, we'll review what you can do to reduce the risk of an IRS audit from the beginning. That all comes after you've established that you have a legitimate business in the eyes of the IRS.

Do you see the potential to save money from just counting payments to your kids, home office expenses, and travel? Even if you work a regular, full-time job and are in a high tax bracket, your part-time eBay business can help to lower your tax bracket. That's because if your eBay business makes a paper loss (after taking all of the business deductions available to you), that loss can be applied against your salaried income, which will lower your overall tax bracket and thus the corresponding amount of tax that you pay. And these are just three loophole opportunities—there are literally *hundreds* more.

Here's another tax tip: If you are operating an eBay business that you know is going to sustain a loss, you can literally begin saving taxes tonight. By having your employer change your withholding amounts to reflect your new, lower taxable income, you can start paying less tax *now*, instead of waiting until springtime of the following year to have that excess tax money refunded to you. For those of you who set up your tax withholdings to ensure you overpay and

> Here's another tax tip: If you are operating an eBay business that you know is going to sustain a loss, you can literally begin saving taxes tonight.

receive a refund each year, we challenge you to explain how being deprived of the use of your own money each year is helping your overall financial picture. Most people don't overpay their cable bill or electricity bill, so why would you voluntarily want to overpay your taxes? Personally, we can appreciate that extra cash now, so that it can be working for us instead of for the government. Besides, by setting up your tax withholdings to ensure you get a large refund every year, what you are really doing is giving the government an interest-free loan, which is most certainly not a favor that will ever be returned!

> If you overpay your taxes each year, hoping for a big refund, you are actually just giving the government an interest-free loan.

Now is the time to cash in on one of the last, great money-making opportunities of our time: establishing your own legitimate eBay business to make more money and pay less taxes.

If You're Not Already Using eBay

If you haven't yet used eBay, a good way to get your feet wet is to become an eBay buyer. This allows you to learn and explore how eBay works, the tricks of the bidding process, and the ins and outs of payment and shipping. The more knowledgeable you are as a buyer, the more knowledgeable you can become as a seller. This is going to become important for several reasons: First, it will help protect you from buyer fraud, which is something that almost every eBay seller has or will encounter in an eBay business. Buyer fraud traditionally takes the form of a buyer claiming non-receipt of the goods and forcing the seller to provide a refund. In many cases, the buyer will request that an item be shipped to a nonregistered address or directly to a friend or relative as a gift. A new or naïve seller who accedes to this request (which is usually phrased in a friendly, reasonable fashion) runs the risk of losing payment for the item, all shipping and packaging costs, and the item itself.

The other crucial element that you gain from becoming a buyer is feedback. Both eBay buyers and sellers have the opportunity to provide feedback on how a transaction proceeds each time an item is

> Use the Buy It Now feature to purchase and pay for items. This will help you build up your feedback numbers quickly.

purchased and sold. Buyers provide feedback on shipping time, packaging, and the quality of the item purchased, while sellers generally provide feedback on payment time. Feedback can be positive, neutral, or negative, depending on how each party experiences the transaction. Negative feedback is something that generally both parties try to avoid, and eBay has several dispute-resolution mechanisms that parties can go through in an effort to resolve an argument without negative feedback.

Feedback can be the lifeblood of sellers in particular, because the better a seller's feedback, the more confident bidders are to purchase the seller's merchandise. Think about it for a minute—if you had a choice of two items, one of which was from a seller with hundreds or even thousands of positive feedbacks, and the other from a seller with only a few feedbacks (even if they were all positive), which do you think you would be more likely to trust?

As a general rule, a minimum of 20 positive feedback comments is a great place to begin selling, but if you don't have that many, don't despair. Just understand that you may find it easier to sell items as your feedback numbers increase.

> Feedback is the lifeblood of sellers. Build it. Watch it. Protect it.

Become an eBay Member

Registering to become an eBay user is simply a matter of providing your name, address, and credit card information; your membership begins instantly. There is no charge to join eBay, but credit card information is needed by eBay to charge listing fees (the small fee you'll pay each time you list an item for sale). eBay tracks your listings and once a month charges you a cumulative fee made up of a small insertion fee to have your listing viewed by 150 million people worldwide, optional listing fees, and a final value fee, which is a percentage of the final selling price. Buyers are never charged any fees by eBay.

> **Get Started with eBay:**
> 1. Go to www.ebay.com.
> 2. Provide your name, address, and credit card information.
> That's all there is to it!

Next Steps—Getting Started

Do the rich know a secret about money and taxes that others don't? You bet! They know that the secret to wealth is to create a successful business. The important part is that you've got to set up your business to take full advantage of all of the available tax benefits. If you are ready to think and act like a successful businessperson with your very own eBay business, make sure you follow these Next Steps to get started:

1. Start off your eBay business on the right foot by making sure that you meet the IRS guidelines. Take "The IRS Nine Steps to Business Quiz" in Appendix A.

2. If you haven't sold or bought anything on eBay, sign up and get started today. Go to www.ebay.com and check out items for sale. Make a bid and then watch it through the coming days.

3. While you're waiting to find out the results of your bid, go to eBay University at www.ebay.com/university to find a course near you or visit http://books.mcgraw-hill.com/ to buy one of these excellent resources for first-timers:

   - *eBay Quicksteps* by Carole Matthews and John Cronan
   - *How to Do Everything with Your eBay Business*, 2nd Edition, by Greg Holden
   - *How to Sell Anything on eBay . . . and Make a Fortune!* by Dennis Prince
   - *eBay Your Business* by Janelle Elms, Michael Bellomo, and Joel Elad

4. If you have bought but never sold on eBay, start small. What do you have *right now* in your home or garage that you could sell? Write up a description of the product, take a picture, figure out how you will be paid (PayPal and/or credit card or some other means), and post your own auction.

5. If you have already sold on eBay and are ready to move to the next step, read on to the next chapter. There, you'll learn how the tax man views your business, how to use eBay reports and other resources to meet the recordkeeping requirements, and special tax advantages available for an eBay business.

2

Designing Your eBay Business

I n Chapter 1, we talked about what makes eBay a good business and why an eBay business works so well to reduce your taxes, even if you already have a full-time job and don't plan to quit anytime soon. In this chapter, we'll take a deeper look at what happens after you begin your eBay sales business. Remember that the first step is to make sure you have a business and are operating it in line with the nine steps outlines in Chapter 1 and Appendix A.

Introduction to Business Structures

One of the first decisions you need to make is what type of business structure you're going to use for your eBay business. If you don't make this decision, the IRS will make it for you—and that might not be the best idea. For example, if you own the business yourself, the IRS may decide that your business is a *sole proprietorship*, or Schedule C, business. You'll learn in the next few pages how that structure can be the worst business structure you can have—it puts all of your assets at risk and costs you more in taxes. If you have a partner, the IRS will determine that you're operating as a *general partnership*, which means you have to split the

> To learn more about the filing requirements for corporations in your home state, visit our companion web site, www.taxloopholes.com/ebaysellers.

> **Why a Sole Proprietorship Is Dangerous**
> - *Everything* you own is at risk from a business lawsuit.
> - You'll pay more taxes.
> - You have a higher risk of an IRS audit.

income and double the risk. Plus, you're going pay still more in taxes. You need to determine whether the cost of a business structure is really work the extra hassle and money.

Business Types

You can choose from among four business types when structuring your eBay business:

- C Corporation
- S Corporation
- Limited liability company (LLC)
- Limited partnership (LP)

The first decision you'll have to make is which is more important to you: ease of use or paying less taxes. If you're okay with paying more taxes, secure in the knowledge that you won't have to prepare a lot of paperwork, the LLC is probably your best bet. On the other hand, if you're ready to make the commitment to follow a short checklist of To-Do items, a corporation is the best bet.

Let's start off with the LLC first, because that's a quick answer for people who are willing to pay a little more in taxes. The LLC is actually *not* a taxing structure. You can select how you want to be taxed, or, if you don't, the IRS will select for you. If you file as an LLC, don't select how you want to be taxed, and you're designated the only owner—you are automatically filing as a *sole proprietorship*, also known as a *Schedule C filer*.

Generally, we advise strongly against the sole proprietorship structure (or rather lack of structure), because it doesn't provide asset protection and it costs more in taxes. However, if you form an LLC and then default to the sole proprietorship tax structure, you will receive asset protection, but you're going to pay more in taxes.

Before you make up your mind about default LLC or corporation, we encourage you to read on to discover what it really means to have a corporation. Then, after you have all the facts, you can make the best decision for your circumstances.

> **It's Up to You:**
> Default LLC—Less work, more tax Corporation—More work, less tax

Two of these business types, the C Corporation and the S Corporation, are ideal for use in your eBay business. The other two, LLCs and LPs, work really well in other situations—particularly for businesses used to hold appreciating assets, such as real estate or stocks and bonds. We talk more about LLCs and LPs in Chapter 12. For our purposes now, we can say that C Corporations and S Corporations offer the best combination of protection and tax savings.

Note: If this is all new to you, don't worry. We'll break it down for you and make it easy to understand. At the end of this chapter, we include some information and resources about how to get help determining what is the best structure for you and getting it set up.

What Is a Corporation?

Corporations have existed in some form since ancient Rome. The oldest commercial corporation supposedly came into being in Sweden in the 14th century. In the early 17th century, corporations were designed (such as the Dutch East India Company) to protect investors in the maritime shipping and exploration trade. Until that time, if a group of investors got together, bought a ship and supplies, hired a crew, and sent the ship off to some far land, and the ship either sunk or was raided by pirates, those investors were on the hook for everything—the cost of the ship, the cost of the cargo, compensation to the families of the sailors lost at sea, and more. Investors often wound up losing not only all the money they originally put into the deal, but also thousands of extra dollars (or the currency of the day). Investors were going broke or just

> A corporation is, in the eyes of the law, a separate and distinct being. It pays its own taxes (at least C Corporations do) and in most states is governed at least in part by its own laws.

weren't willing to risk any more money, and the financial situation was getting dismal for the shipping business. To fix the problem, corporations were created to protect investors.

You could think of a corporation as being similar to a child—while it has parents (in this case, the investors and the people who run it) who watch over it, a child also exists independently of those parents. And, as those of you who are parents already know, sometimes that independence means getting into trouble. For a corporation, that trouble might mean taking on more debt than it can repay, for example. But unlike the traditional parental role, in the case of a corporation, the investors (also called *shareholders*) are not held legally responsible for the acts of the corporation. So, if a corporation goes bankrupt, for example, the most that any shareholder can lose is the amount of money paid for shares. No creditor can come after shareholders personally for the debts owed by a corporation.

The same also applies (in most cases) to the people running a corporation, who are called the *officers* and *directors*. As long as these people have not used the corporation to carry out any illegal activities or to get rich personally at the expense of the shareholders, they cannot be held personally responsible for the debts of the corporation (Figure 2.1).

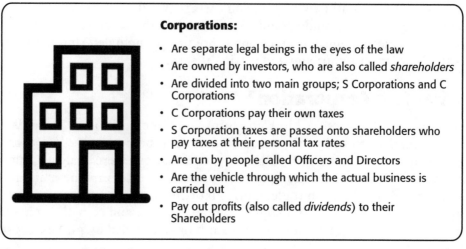

Corporations:

- Are separate legal beings in the eyes of the law
- Are owned by investors, who are also called *shareholders*
- Are divided into two main groups; S Corporations and C Corporations
- C Corporations pay their own taxes
- S Corporation taxes are passed onto shareholders who pay taxes at their personal tax rates
- Are run by people called Officers and Directors
- Are the vehicle through which the actual business is carried out
- Pay out profits (also called *dividends*) to their Shareholders

Figure 2.1   Definition of a corporation.

Now that you have an idea of what a corporation is, let's take a look at the pieces that make up a corporation. Then we'll take a look at what each piece means and how it fits into the overall picture (Figure 2.2).

First, a quick vocabulary lesson: Corporations (C or S) are owned by shareholders. If you invest in the stock market or you have a mutual fund or a 401(k) plan, chances are you are already a shareholder in one or several different corporations (Figure 2.3).

Ownership units are called *shares*. S Corporations have only one kind of share, called a *common, voting share*. That means that every share in an S Corporation is equal, and every shareholder can vote with his or her shares for or against certain business decisions. So, if you have 55 shares, and someone else has only 50 shares, you can outvote that person because you have more shares. On the other hand, if three shareholders own shares and you have less shares than the other two people have together, then there is a chance that the other two could vote together and outvote you (Figure 2.4).

C Corporations can have different types of shares. Some types of shares may not be able to vote but may get a larger share of the profits as compensation. Typically, only larger, public C Corporations have different types of shares, and this isn't something we'd recommend for most eBay businesses.

Both C and S Corporations are run by their *officers* (the president, vice president, and so on), who are in turn overseen by their *directors*. Officers and directors may or may not also be shareholders, depending on what the shareholders decide when they set up the corporation. Ownership units are called *shares*, and C corporations may have one or more *classes* of shares (Figure 2.5).

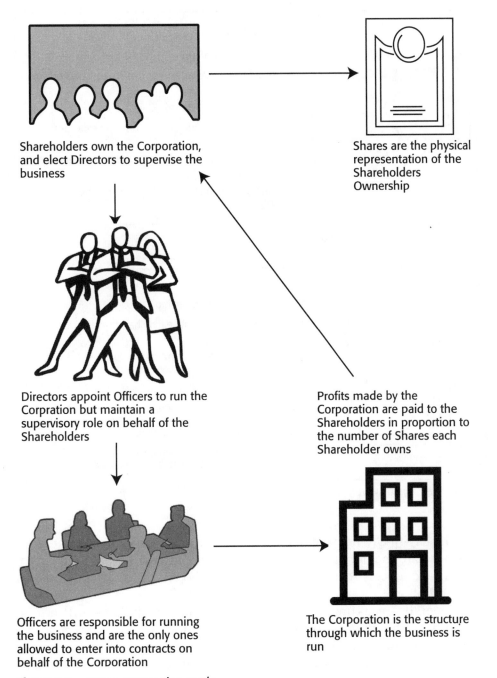

Shareholders own the Corporation, and elect Directors to supervise the business

Shares are the physical representation of the Shareholders Ownership

Directors appoint Officers to run the Corpration but maintain a supervisory role on behalf of the Shareholders

Profits made by the Corporation are paid to the Shareholders in proportion to the number of Shares each Shareholder owns

Officers are responsible for running the business and are the only ones allowed to enter into contracts on behalf of the Corporation

The Corporation is the structure through which the business is run

Figure 2.2   How a corporation works.

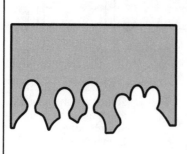

Shareholders:

- Own the Corporation
- Have Shares that represent their overall percentage of ownership
- Elect the Directors of the Corporation
- Share in the Corporation's Profits in proportion to their ownership percentage
- Do not participate in the day-to-day operations of the Corporation
- Can't be personally sued by people suing the Corporation

Figure 2.3   What a shareholder is.

Shares:

- Individual pieces of ownership
- Taken together, represents each Shareholder's ownership percentage
- Are voted for or against Corporation business actions, usually a simple majority wins
- All the same kind in S Corporations
- Can be different in C Corporations (i.e., voting or not-voting. Non-voting shares usually have preferential profit payout over other share types)
- Large or publicly traded companies tend to use different share classes more than small businesses do

Figure 2.4   What shares are.

The day-to-day management of a corporation is carried out by its *officers*, who are the only people allowed to sign contracts or bind the corporation. The officers report to the directors, who report to the shareholders (Figure 2.6).

Generally speaking, officers, directors, and shareholders will not be found liable for the acts or debts of the corporation. The most a shareholder can lose is his or her shares, while directors and officers must either do something illegal or allow other officers and directors to commit illegal actions before they will be found liable for any acts or debts of the corporation.

Table 2-1 summarizes all of these terms into a quick reference guide for you. This may all seem confusing, but remember that a corporation needs

Directors:

- Are directly elected by the Shareholders

- Select the President, Vice-President, and other Officers

- Supervise the Officers while they carry out Corporation business

- Act in a supervisory role only—don't directly manage corporation business

- Cannot directly enter into contracts in the name of the Corporation (although they can tell the Officers to enter into those contracts)

- Can't usually be personally sued by people suing the Corporation, unless the Directors are using the Corporation or the Officers to engage in criminal acts

Figure 2.5   What a director is.

Officers:

- Are appointed by the Directors

- Have the responsibility for the day-to-day operations

- Are the only people who can sign contracts and authorize the Corporation to go into debt

- Can be shareholders (but they don't have to be)

- Can't usually be personally sued by people suing the Corporation, unless the Officers have been using the Corporation to engage in criminal acts

Figure 2.6   What an officer is.

to be flexible—it can be a one-person operation, or it can have thousands of people running it. But it can be very simple, too.

In practical terms, as an eBay business owner, it is quite likely that you will wind up being the officer, director, *and* shareholder of your corporation. But even if you are a one-person corporation (which is *not* the same thing as a *corporation sole,* for those of you who have heard that term), as long as you aren't using your eBay business corporation to carry out any illegal activities—such as money laundering, for example—you won't be found personally liable for anything that your corporation does or owes.

If you're working with a spouse or one or more other partners, that person or persons may also be an officer, director, and shareholder. On the other hand, if your uncle lends you some money to get started, he might

Microsoft or Mom-n-Pop?

When it comes to the ability to take advantage of tax loopholes and tax deductions, the IRS treats all corporations the same.

Table 2.1   Business Structure Vocabulary

	C Corporation	S Corporation
Owners	Shareholders	Shareholders
Ownership Units	Shares	Shares
Management Structure	Directors and officers	Directors and officers
Management Duties	Officers carry out business operations and report to directors, who report to shareholders. Only officers can enter contracts and bind corporation.	Officers carry out business operations and report to directors, who report to shareholders. Only officers can enter contracts and bind corporation.
Management Liability for Business Debts or for Actions Against the Structure	None, unless management commits or allows illegal actions by or on behalf of the corporation.	None, unless management commits or allows illegal actions by or on behalf of the corporation.
Flow-Through Taxation	No	Yes
Tax Quirks	Profits are taxed at corporate level and then again at shareholder level, where they show up as dividends or distributions.	Medical premiums are considered a taxable benefit to shareholders owning more than 2 percent of the corporation. In a C Corporation, owner/shareholders do not pay taxes on medical benefits received.
Availability of Tax Deductions and Loopholes	Best	Good
Creditor Protection	Owners cannot be sued for business liability. Owners may lose control of corporation shares (and assets) in a personal lawsuit.	Owners cannot be sued for business liability. Owners may lose control of corporation shares (and assets) in a personal lawsuit.

ask to be made a shareholder instead of just a loan holder. However, unless he's going to be actively involved in running your business, you wouldn't necessarily want to make your uncle an officer or director, even if he did lend you some money.

Corporation: Better than a Sole Proprietorship or a General Partnership

For a lot of people getting started in business, the costs to form a business structure and then maintain it might seem too high and offer little value for money. "I can still write off my expenses on a Schedule C form when I do my personal income taxes," they may say, "and I don't need to waste what little profit I may be making on legal fees." In other words, they prefer to stay with the default business structure, which really means no business structure.

Several things are wrong with that plan. First, your ability to write off expenses is going to be more limited in a Schedule C business than it would be in an incorporated business. Second, although you will be spending more money to incorporate, all of those costs can be expensed from your business earnings, which will help to lower your overall tax burden. Third, any savings you might experience from not incorporating are going to be offset by the extra self-employment taxes you'll be paying on all of your eBay earnings. That extra tax will cost you an additional 15.3 percent in taxes (as of 2005). Fourth, as a Schedule C business, you are a more likely candidate for an IRS audit. The IRS is more likely to determine that you aren't operating a legitimate business but a hobby business, which will further reduce your ability to save taxes by taking advantage of legitimate business loopholes.

Finally, any legitimate business has an element of risk. Maybe you obtained credit in the name of the business and are now having financial difficulties that delay or prevent the repayment of the debt. Or maybe you were driving across town to pick up some merchandise or supplies when you inadvertently caused a car accident. In both of these situations, if you are operating your eBay business directly and not through a corporation, you have absolutely no protection from a creditor or an injured person if they decide to sue you personally. You cannot protect your personal assets or the assets of your eBay business in this situation. If, however, you were operating your eBay business through a corporation, the risk can be minimized. While your eBay business assets may be exposed to creditors or to an injured party, unlike a Schedule C business, your personal assets—your house, your boat, your car, and your savings account—will remain safe and untouchable in the event of a lawsuit.

If you have taken the less-paperwork route of forming an LLC and then take the default tax route of a sole proprietorship, you'll have the protection of a business structure. You will be more likely to be audited, and you will pay more tax for making the choice of doing less paperwork.

This lack of personal protection combined with the tax disadvantages are, to us, enough to make the use of a Schedule C business a scary propo-

> A sole proprietorship is more likely to be selected for audit than an incorporated business.

America is the most litigious society in the world, and Americans are more likely to be sued personally than people in any other country. Why risk everything you own if you don't have to? Use a business structure to protect what's yours.

sition for a beginning business owner. That's why, for the remainder of this book, we're going to work from the position that you have chosen to incorporate a business structure through which to operate your business, and we'll provide the accounting and tax information on that basis. However, even if you have decided to be a Schedule C business, you will be able to take advantage of a number of the strategies in this book (Figure 2.7).

C Corporation versus S Corporation

Both C Corporations and S Corporations work really well for eBay businesses. The type you choose for your eBay business will be dependent on a couple of things usually related to tax treatment.

C Corporations prepare and file their own tax returns and pay taxes at different (often lower) rates than personal income tax rates. S Corporations, on the other hand, also prepare and file their own tax returns, but the net profits (or losses) are not paid at a corporation level but are passed on to the individual shareholders, who each pay taxes on their share at their own personal rates.

C Corporations have the most tax deductions available of any business structure, including the ability to operate a medical plan covering the officers and employees. In a C Corporation, all costs associated with the med-

---

Good Idea, Bad Idea, or *Really* Bad Idea?

Good ideas:
- C Corporation (has the most tax benefits and can choose when to pay taxes)
- S Corporation (can split its income into tax-advantaged streams)
- Limited Liability Company (can pick how it wants to be taxed)

Bad idea:
- Sole Proprietorship (pays 15.3% extra tax and has no asset or liability protection)

Really bad Idea:
- General Partnership (carries twice the risk of a Sole Proprietorship, but only pays half as much and still pays 15.3% extra tax)

Figure 2.7   Three business ideas and their consequences.

ical plan are expensed by the corporation, as well as being considered a tax-free benefit to the employees. S Corporations, on the other hand, can also put a medical plan into place and expense the costs, but any employees who own more than 2 percent of the corporation's shares are required to report the value of their medical plan coverage as a taxable benefit. So, if you don't currently receive medical coverage through another source (such as your employer or your spouse's employer), operating your eBay business through a C Corporation would allow you to implement a medical plan and deduct all of your medical expenses. Depending on the monthly sales volume of your eBay business, you may also be eligible to purchase certain health insurance benefits through eBay, which has a health care program set up for

PowerSellers. If you were to employ your children, you could also cover them under the medical plan, even after they got too old to be covered under your dependent coverage. This can be a great way to make sure your kids have adequate medical coverage when they are away at college.

> You can learn more about the health insurance benefit plan offered through eBay to PowerSellers at http://pages.ebay.com/services/buyandsell/powerseller/healthcareprog.html.

S Corporations have some great advantages, too, and may work best for startup businesses with low profits and lots of expenses. Because C Corporations pay taxes at their own level, owners who want to take money out of a C Corporation must use one of two methods: either taking a salary and paying taxes on it or taking a distribution, or *dividend*, out of the corporation's profits. The problem with the second method is that the corporation has to pay taxes on the profits before they are distributed, while the owners receiving the distributions must also pay capital gains tax on those distributions. That's called *double-taxation*, and it has been a longstanding issue for C Corporations. In other words, the corporation pays tax on the profit (tax #1) and then the owner pays tax when he gets the dividend (tax #2); put them together and you've got double taxation. While changes to tax law concerning capital gains have reduced the impact of this double-taxation, it still exists as of 2005.

S Corporations experience no double-taxation issue, because all of the net profits (or losses) are distributed to the owners, who pay the taxes at their own rates. S Corporation owners can also take a salary and pay taxes on it—in fact, we don't recommend that you, as an S Corporation owner, take money out only in the form of a distribution. That's because, if you took money out of your S Corporation only as a distribution, you wouldn't be paying any Social Security or FICA taxes on your earnings, and the IRS doesn't want that. As a rule of thumb, depending on the amount of money that your S Corporation makes each year, you should try to keep your salary withdrawals and your

S Corporations Are Great for	C Corporations Are Great for
People who provide a service	People who provide a professional service according to the IRS (doctors, lawyers, engineers, accountants, and so on)
People who anticipate that their eBay business will be their primary source of income	People who have a high employment income (more than $50,000 per year) and who don't need all of the profits from their eBay business immediately
People who are earning $50,000 per year or less	People who want to provide a medical plan for themselves and their families and want the maximum available tax loopholes and deductions to offset their expenses
People who anticipate that they will have a lot of startup expenses in the early years of their eBay business	People who want to grow their business to have 100 or more shareholders
Once you know you have a business	It's time to look at how you will operate it. One of the smartest first steps you can make to reduce your risk from excess taxes and lawsuits is to make sure you have the appropriate business structure. Then, keep that safety net in place by making sure you are properly maintaining the structure. You'll likely discover many new things as your run your business. Those new discoveries mean you save tax.

profit distributions fairly even and not overly skewed toward distributions only. This isn't as crucial in the early stages, as your business is expected to lose money and business owners often don't take a salary, but it does become more important as your business progresses (Figure 2.8).

Choosing the Best Corporation Type for Your Business

When you're trying to decide which type of corporation will work best for you, the first thing to consider is which one will be most beneficial to you from a taxation standpoint. This is a good time to start getting your advisors in place. Nobody—and we mean *nobody*—can do and know everything alone. If you don't ask for help in planning and setting up your

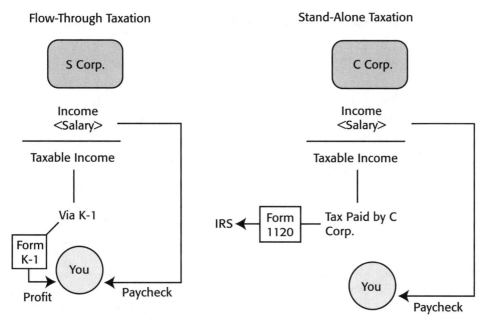

Figure 2.8 S Corporation versus C Corporation.

structure, you're asking for more frustration and possible mistakes in setup that can wind up costing you time, energy, patience, and *money*. The wrong structure (or bad advice) can cost you more tax than you legally need to pay.

Here are a few tips to get you started:

- S Corporations are great for early stage businesses, where you are anticipating sustaining losses for the first few years.
- C Corporations are great if you have a very inventory-rich business or you are already a high-income earner and don't want to take all of the profit out of your business each year.
- C Corporations are great if you want to install your own medical or dental plan.
- S Corporations are great if your eBay business will include such things as consulting and listing goods for others on consignment, or charging a fee for your time and energy.
- It is easier to begin as an S Corporation and change to a C Corporation later than it is to start as a C Corporation and change to an S Corporation.

> **Corporation Sole:**
> Not all corporations are created the same. The term *corporation sole* is used to describe a type of business structure that is red-flagged by the IRS for automatic audit. We do not recommend this type of so-called corporation under any circumstances.

Setting Up and Maintaining Your Corporation

Setting up your own corporation can be fairly simple. If you are experienced and comfortable with the process, you may be able to set up and maintain it on your own. If you aren't experienced and comfortable, you should look for some outside assistance. Your advisors can help you here, and plenty of low-cost incorporation services are available in every state to help you get started. We've also listed a couple our favorite incorporators on the companion web site. These service providers are fast and accurate, and they provide great value for the money.

You will also have annual maintenance to consider. Almost every state requires some form of annual report to be filed by corporations each year, and in most states C and S Corporations are required by law to hold annual meetings. If the IRS or someone suing you wants to claim you weren't operating as a legitimate business, a complete board meeting minutes book, with one year or more of board minutes, will go a long way toward discrediting those claims.

> Visit the companion web site at www.taxloopholes.com/ ebaysellers to find a referral list of experienced incorporation service providers who can help you get incorporated and running in your state.

Most states require that you have a resident agent, or a registered agent, for your corporation. A *registered agent* is someone who accepts service of legal documents that may be filed against your corporation. While you can often serve personally as your corporation's resident agent, we don't recommend this for two reasons: first, it means that you must have your home address on display in the public records for your corporation, which can impact your privacy; second, it may impact on your ability to travel, as you need to be around to accept service. You wouldn't want someone to come to your house and drop off a complaint or other legal filing while you were on vacation or on a merchandise-buying trip, because you might not even find out that a problem existed until it was too late to do anything about it.

At a bare minimum, you will need to prepare, or have prepared, the following documents for either a C Corporation or an S Corporation:

- Articles of incorporation, bylaws, organizational resolutions for directors and shareholders, and share certificates.
- A business license registration (you may need more than one—some states require you to license at the state, county, and/or city levels). Every state's requirements are a little different, and your incorporator should be able to help you with this.
- Certificate of acceptance of resident agent, which confirms that your corporation has a registered office and a registered agent in the state where it is being formed.

- Form SS-4—"Application for Employer Identification Number" with the IRS. All businesses incorporated or operating in the United States must obtain an EIN, also called a *tax ID number*. You will need this number to open a bank account for your corporation, to file federal and state tax and license returns, and for other purposes. The good news is you can complete this application online—in fact, we provide a copy of the form you need at the companion web site.
- S Corporations need to do an extra filing with the IRS, called a Form 2553, where the corporation elects to be taxed on a flow-through basis. *Be careful here*—this form must be filed within 75 days of the incorporation to be effective for that tax year. Missing this filing means that you may default to C Corporation taxation for the first year of operation or longer. You'll find a sample of this form on the companion web site.

I Just Want to Run My Business

An attorney we know was teaching a class to a group of new entrepreneurs. During the class, he talked about business structures and the importance of having a structure whenever you have a business. "Never," he firmly stated, "have a business just in your own name. It's not a question of how much you make through your company. It's a question of how much you have to lose. If you get sued through the business, and you don't have the protection of a business structure, you can lose everything you own."

After the class, a woman in her mid-40s came up to speak with him. She explained that she had just sunk every dime she had into a new business. He asked what type of business structure she was using, and she told him she just didn't have the extra money to form a business structure. He cautioned her not to operate without a business structure, but she was firm that nothing bad would happen and she needed to get the business up and going. She said she'd call him in three months.

Two months later, the woman called. Our friend was delighted, as he assumed that she had finally heeded his advice and was going to form a business structure.

"Not exactly," she answered to his excited inquiry. "You see, I'm being sued. What can I do now to protect myself?" she asked.

"Absolutely nothing," he responded. She had risked everything and lost everything by operating her business without having a business structure in place.

Getting Help

If you're serious about setting up your eBay business to succeed, you're going to need some help. Nobody can be expected to be an expert in everything, and the harder you try to be the know-it-all, do-it-all person, the more likely you are to fall behind on one or more areas of your business.

And remember that talking to advisors is one of the IRS's nine steps to proving you have a business.

The trick is, of course, to find someone who is good at what they do and familiar with eBay and eBay businesses in general. Fortunately, as eBay becomes more popular, more people are available to help you. The eBay member boards are a great place to connect to like-minded people and ask for referrals in your area. Your local chamber of commerce may have suggestions for attorneys and accountants in your area who are familiar with small businesses and eBay home-based business operations. Word of mouth is always effective—ask your neighbors or local small business owners who does their books—at the very least, you'll find out who *not* to do business with. Sometimes, bad references travel even farther than good references.

You can also visit the companion web site to get information on incorporation service providers as well as accounting and bookkeeping services. Remember that in this electronic age, you don't necessarily have to be down the street from your bookkeeper. One of our bookkeeping service providers is based in Dallas, Texas, yet they work with clients across the United States.

> The three most expensive words in the English language can be *do it yourself.* Get qualified advisors to move your business forward.

Next Steps—After Incorporation

Catching Up with Jenny

Jenny was feeling pretty excited about how her auctions had gone in their first week on eBay. By selling just a few items, she had made a pretty significant chunk of money, and she had no reason to think that the family couldn't continue this happy trend. However, Jenny also realized that she'd better find out what the tax consequences of her eBay sale were going to be, so she didn't wind up with a nasty tax bill at the end of the year. Fortunately for Jenny, she had Tia Olivia.

Tia Olivia was Jenny's aunt and, luckily, a practicing CPA. Jenny gave Olivia a call and arranged to meet over lunch later that week to discuss Jenny's business idea and how to proceed. Olivia asked Jenny to bring the inventory list she had made with the boys, including the spreadsheet with all of the completed item sale prices and the shipping costs. She also told Jenny to make a list of everything she had used in the business so far (tape, boxes, packing materials, and so on) and a list of all of Jenny's out-of-pocket expenses to date.

When they met for lunch, Olivia looked over Jenny's paperwork and agreed with Jenny that this was a pretty exciting idea. Then she asked Jenny how serious she wanted to get with her plans. She explained that Jenny had a great opportunity to make some money and save on taxes, but that she'd need to do a bit of work first and spend some money to make that happen. If she wasn't serious, Olivia told her, and didn't plan on continuing this eBay business past the first year or so, or however long it took her to sell the items on her inventory list, there was a simpler way to proceed, but it wouldn't save her any money.

Jenny asked her aunt what the difference was. "It's really a matter of economics," Olivia explained. "If all you want to do is clean out your apartment, you might just be better off declaring the money you earn on your tax return at the end of the year and paying the tax you'll owe on it. It's no different from having a garage sale." Believe it or not, the money you make throwing a garage sale is taxable income in the eyes of the IRS. In reality, most people don't declare the money they make on a garage sale, and, frankly, the IRS has bigger fish to fry. But that doesn't mean they *can't* come after people for that garage sale money, because they have the legal right to do so.

"If you are operating as a temporary business, the money you'll spend setting yourself up as a tax-advantaged business will probably eat up your profits. If the money you spend is more than you'd pay in taxes on the goods you sell, it isn't worth it," Olivia said. "But, on the other hand, if you are planning to continue selling things on eBay after you've cleaned out your apartment, you might want to spend the extra money and set yourself up as a business. Because you're now going to be a continuing business operation, you'll have more opportunities to take advantage of the tax deductions and tax loopholes available to businesses, and your long-term savings will more than offset the costs you spend setting things up."

Olivia explained that starting as a real business has an advantage over starting out as an unincorporated business. She explained that although Jenny would have lots of expenses in the beginning, she could write them off against her profits, and after that, against her regular employment income; but converting from an unincorporated business at a later date means she could lose the ability to write off all of those early stage expenses against her regular employment income, because she might be considered just a hobby business by the IRS. "So if you have profits of $2,000 and startup expenses of $2,500, that extra $500 is wasted, because you can't offset anything other than the direct income. At the end of the day, it really comes down to whether or not you're in this long term."

Jenny weighed her aunt's words carefully. Although it was tempting to go for the short-term gain and not bother setting up a full business, that wasn't what she had been thinking about the night she found eBay. She had been looking for a long-term solution to her financial position and a way to save for the future, not just make a few dollars for the here and now. But what *would* she sell after the apartment had been cleaned out, and was it important that she answer that question right now?

"Olivia, if I set up a business now, what happens when I finish selling the things in my apartment? Does my business cease if I stop selling things?" she asked.

"No, not at all! Your business exists for as long as you want it to, regardless of whether it is always active. You see, new businesses are expected to spend time exploring options to make themselves profitable—in fact, that's something the IRS especially wants to see. So, the time you spend researching merchandise or test marketing different products on eBay is all a part of that process. Your business may make no money—in fact, it may lose money—but it's still a valid business in the eyes of the IRS and entitled to take advantage of everything a business has to offer."

Jenny thought that sounded pretty good. Besides, she reasoned, she could be researching new products while she was selling her existing stuff, and it would be good practice for her future business efforts. She told Olivia that she was all for saving money, even if she had to spend a little bit to do so.

Olivia then suggested to Jenny that she incorporate her company and operate it as an S Corporation. She explained the two ways for corporations to be taxed, and that at this early stage, Jenny was better off taking the S Corporation route and having all of the business's profits flow through to her at her personal tax rate. Although Jenny was making a good living, she still wasn't at the highest end of the tax bracket, so there wasn't much point at this early stage in going through the extra work involved in operating a C Corporation. "Besides," Olivia told Jenny, "you can always change it later by filing a simple one-page form with the IRS."

Incorporating did a couple of things for Jenny. First, it allowed her to meet the IRS guidelines for operating a legitimate business by acting like one. Jenny's business would have its own bank accounts and would buy and sell items through those accounts—not through Jenny personally. The business could also do other things, such as arrange for its own cell phone service, Internet access, and other business-related expenses. When Jenny protested that she would be using these things anyways, her aunt agreed but asked Jenny which would be better—having her company pay these bills from its before-tax profits, or having Jenny pay these bills from her after-tax paycheck. "The difference is," her aunt explained, "that every pre-tax dollar spent will go toward reducing your net income at the end of the day, and that in turn will reduce your tax rate. You'll be making the same amount of money from your work as always, plus you'll have the extra money from your eBay business," she said. "But now you won't necessarily need to budget those expenses into your paycheck, because your company will be paying for them instead."

Jenny thought that sounded good, though, she said, "I feel like somehow I'm cheating the system by writing off all of these things. I'd be using the Internet anyway, even without the business. How can the IRS not see that as abusing the system?"

"It's simple," Olivia explained. "The IRS allows business expenses that are 'reasonable and necessary' in connection with the production of income." How reasonable would it be to expect Jenny to operate a eBay business without spending money on Internet access? The same was true for her cell phone service. If Jenny was out looking for merchandise to sell on eBay, she might need to contact the boys to look up the value of something for her. Or, if she wanted to get fancy, Olivia suggested that she might even consider a palm device or a phone with Internet access, so Jenny could quickly research an item herself—wherever she was. "Not only that," Olivia continued, "but if you wanted to engage the boys in the hunt for saleable merchandise, they'd need phones of their own." None of these costs were unreasonable—in fact, they were all quite necessary and proper for Jenny to be able to operate her business in the most efficient and profitable way possible.

Now Jenny was getting excited. She asked Olivia for ways that she could move other family expenses to the business and was amazed when Olivia asked her how much of her rent and utilities would she like to write off as a business expense each month. "You've got to be kidding, Olivia. This is too good to be true."

"Not if you do it properly," Olivia replied. "If you set up a true home office, then all of the expenses associated with that home office also become deductible. Again, you're going to apply the 'reasonable and necessary' definition here, plus you're also going to follow a few simple rules. First, the area that you set aside for your home office can only be used for that purpose. You can't stick a computer on your dining room table and write off that room, especially if you are also using the table for eating. You can't stack your entire inventory up against a wall in your living room and write off the living room space. Neither of those things meet the IRS home office requirements. But if you convert a bedroom into an office where you keep your desk, computer, and shipping supplies, that would count. If you used the closet space in that room to keep your inventory, that would also count. If you needed more inventory storage space, you could use other closets and those would count—as long as all those closets held was inventory."

Olivia explained that first Jenny would need to measure the room she was going to use, including closet space, so she had an accurate square footage amount. She would then move everything out of the room that wasn't connected with the business, so it met the IRS requirements for a home office. Then Jenny would bill her company once a month for rent. The rent would be for the same percentage of Jenny's rent, electricity, heating costs, condo fees, and other expenses, that her home office took up. If Jenny's home office was 300 square feet and that made up 25 percent of Jenny's overall living space, the rent Jenny would charge her business would be 25 percent of Jenny's overall housing costs each month.

At the end of their lunch, Jenny's head was spinning. Olivia laughed at her stunned expression, and said, "Welcome to the business world." She then noted that Jenny had paid for their lunch, and added, "I hope you kept the receipt. We discussed business over lunch and that means the cost of that lunch has now become a deductible expense. One of the things you're going to have to get used to, as a business owner, is keeping track of these things and remembering to get receipts. Don't try to take expenses that you can't substantiate with a receipt—because that is something the IRS will see as abuse. Oh, and one more thing—how far did you have to drive to meet me here today? Make sure you note that on the way home, because there is a way to deduct business-related mileage. In fact, you might want to throw a little notebook or sticky pad into the glove compartment and keep it there to record mileage from now on."

The last thing Olivia did was to give Jenny a "getting started" package. It included a test to make sure that Jenny was going to be operating her business as per the IRS guidelines, an incorporation checklist for Jenny to complete and give back to her aunt, and a sheet for Jenny to write down the items and approximate value of all furniture, computer equipment, and supplies that she was going to be transferring into the business. Once everything was complete, Jenny would fax the papers to her aunt, who would take care of the incorporation and prepare the required transfer documents.

As Jenny headed back to work, she felt eager to finish her workday and get started on her new business plan.

Once you know you have a business, it's time to look at how you will operate it. One of the smartest first steps you can make to reduce your risk from excess taxes and lawsuits is to make sure you operate your eBay business through and have the appropriate business structure. Then keep that safety net in place by making sure you are properly maintaining that structure. You'll likely discover many new things as your run your business. And when those new discoveries mean you save tax, that's the best of all worlds!

Next Steps—Incorporating and Setting Up Your Business

There is a lot of information in this chapter, and accordingly there are a lot of next steps for you to take. But don't let that overwhelm you. You can keep things easy by going slow, and by breaking these steps down into three major decision categories: (1) determining the business structure that is best for you; (2) forming that business structure; and (3) taking the after-formation steps to get your business ready to operate.

Deciding on a Business Structure

1. Review the information in this chapter regarding business structures and become familiar with the different entity types and their pros and cons.
2. Select the appropriate business structure to set up. You may want to work with a qualified advisor who understands your personal and business goals and circumstances and can help you to determine what business structure will work best for you.

Forming a Business Structure

1. Go to www.taxloopholes.com/ebaysellers and click through to the link for information on setting up business structures in your state. You'll also find other resources at our web site, including people who can help you to get your business formed and ready to operate.
2. Locate a resident agent and arrange for resident agent service.
3. Prepare and file the incorporation paperwork to form the appropriate business structure, following the easy checklist included in the "getting started" package, which you'll find at the companion web site.
4. Once your business has been formed, file for its federal Tax ID number with the IRS.
5. File any other IRS documents such as a Form 2553 that may be required for your business structure.
6. Prepare the post-formation documents that are appropriate for your business structure.
7. Open a business checking account.

8. File any state-level business registrations required to register your business for state business tax, Unemployment Insurance, and Workers' Compensation.
9. Check with your local municipal office to see if you need a business license to operate a home-based business in your town.

Getting Ready to Operate Your Business

1. Do a valuation of your inventory for transfer into your corporation, using the form found on the companion web site.
2. Do a valuation of office equipment, computer equipment, or any other items, such as office furniture and packing supplies, that you need to transfer into your corporation, using the forms found in Appendix B.
3. Prepare the transfer documentation to document the transfer of inventory and personal property from yourself into your corporation and how you will be compensated for the sale. You can use the documentation we've provided in Appendix C for this purpose.
4. Purchase any additional computer software, office furniture, equipment, or supplies that you'll need to set up and begin your eBay business properly.
5. Measure your home office and inventory storage space so you can determine what percentage of your overall residence will be taken up with your eBay business.
6. Make a list of all of your current expenses for comparison against our "300+ Business Deductions" list that you'll find in Appendix G (you can also download your own copy from the companion web site), so that you can determine what you will be able to deduct or write-off from your eBay business.
7. Set up a bookkeeping and recordkeeping system, and enter all of your opening balances. Check our web site to download the "QuickBooks Chart of Accounts" that we provide specifically for people with eBay businesses.
8. Get a small notebook to keep in your car that you can use to track all business-related mileage.
9. Educate yourself. Learn about the tax laws in your state. Some states require you to charge sales tax only on new items you are selling, while others want you to charge sales or use tax on used items as well. Find out if you will need a reseller's certificate, which allows you to buy items for resale in your business without paying sales tax.
10. Finish reading this book to determine the rest of the steps.

3

The Taxman and eBay

What taxes do I need to pay for my eBay business? That is the Number 1 question posed by many starting eBay sellers. Truth is, the IRS will tax each of us on the income we make. The beauty of starting an eBay business, however, is that even though you have money you put in your pocket each and every month from your eBay sales, you can actually show a loss on paper; and if you show a loss, you won't pay taxes. In this chapter, we show you just how this works. We also take a look at some other business taxes that may be relevant to you.

Making a Profit (but Showing a Loss)

You might be asking yourself how it is possible, or legal, to put money in your pocket yet tell the taxman you have a loss. It is possible and legal, though, because the taxable profit is determined using the following formula:

Sales price

Less: Cost of Sales (eBay fees, shipping, and the like)

Less: Basis

Less: *General Expenses*

Equals: **Taxable Income**

The *Sales Price* and the *Cost of Sales* are fairly self-explanatory. Chances are, though, the *basis* needs some explanation—read on.

Valuing Your Inventory

If you bought an item and then sold it, the *basis* for the item is the price and other costs associated with that purchase. However, if you bought something years ago for personal use and are now selling it, figuring the basis is a little trickier. In this case, the basis is actually the value you assigned that item when you "contributed" the asset to your company. In other words, the toaster oven that you paid $50 for two years ago now has a fair market value of only $30. It has depreciated, or gone down in value, by $20. You know exactly how much the fair market value is now because that's how much you sold it for on eBay.

The basis formula for this product would look like this:

Sales price of item:	$30.00
Less basis:	–30.00
Equals taxable income:	$0.00

Now subtract your general expenses, which are the hidden business deductions you'll discover in Chapter 7. You'll end up with a loss—on paper. But you actually just put $30 in your pocket.

This can get a little tricky. If the IRS ever asks, you must be able to *prove* you have that amount of basis and those expenses. Otherwise, the IRS will just see the $30 for a sale of a product and tax you on the sale. Good records will save you hundreds, maybe even thousands, of dollars in taxes. That's why it's so important to value your inventory before you begin.

One good way to value your initial inventory is to research the average selling price for your items on eBay. You may even want to print some completed listings to have some backup documentation that the value you have assigned your inventory was based on fact, not fiction or speculation. You could also check your items against the valuation page on the Salvation Army's web site, at www.satruck.com/ValueGuide.asp.

Your choice:
No Records
= More Tax
or
Good Records
= More Money

Let's Talk about Taxes

As with everything else, taxes are going to figure into your eBay business equation. The question is, how can you organize your business to make sure that taxes have the smallest impact on you?

As an eBay business owner in the business of selling items on eBay, you're going to have to think about three types of taxes: income taxes; sales and use taxes at the federal, state, and municipal level; and payroll taxes. Depending on where you live, you may not have to worry about some of these taxes. For example, Nevada has sales and use tax, but no state income tax; therefore, Nevada residents and businesses pay only federal income taxes. California businesses pay all of these taxes, while Texas businesses pay sales and use taxes and a modified form of income tax called a franchise tax.

We'll take a quick look at what these taxes actually mean to you as an eBay business owner, but first let's talk about nexus, so that you know where you'll be taxed (and taxing).

Determining Nexus

Nexus is a fancy term that means "where your business is located." From a tax perspective, nexus is your geographical taxing district. You might ask, why should I care what my nexus is? It's important to know because two types of taxes are determined based on where your nexus is—state income tax and sales tax.

If you live in Chicago, and your eBay business was incorporated in Illinois, your business nexus is Illinois. That means you'll be subject to Illinois tax law when it comes to your eBay sales. Typically, this means that you'll have to charge other Illinois residents state sales tax and collect and remit that tax to the local government. You'll also have to pay Illinois state income tax.

What if you incorporate in another state? Does that mean you can avoid the state income and sales tax issues for your home state? Not at all. One of the great home-business scams that proliferates on the Internet and elsewhere claims that you can avoid state taxes by incorporating your business in a tax-advantageous state such as Nevada or Wyoming. In fact, some hucksters will go so far as to try and sell you a "virtual office," with a telephone number and mailing address within that state, and will encourage you to open a bank account within that state as well. They'll also say something like, "If you use this Nevada or Wyoming address for your invoices and make sure that all of your banking is done through your Nevada or Wyoming bank, then you'll be a Nevada or Wyoming business in the eyes of the taxman."

Nice try, but that's not even close to being true. First, *every* business pays federal taxes, regardless of where it was incorporated or where it's operating. Second, when it comes to trying to avoid state tax, the problem is that you are still sitting and working in Chicago, Illinois. That's where you look for merchandise, that's where you package the merchandise, and that's where you ship it from. In the eyes of most states, your physical presence and work in the business is enough to be considered doing business in that state, and that means you must register in the state—which then means you're back in the very state tax system you just tried to avoid by incorporating elsewhere. And if you don't register your business in your home state, some unpleasant things can happen, such as fines and penalties. Most states also tie your business's ability to sue an individual or business to your registration in that state. In other words, if you don't register your business in Illinois and someone from Illinois fails to pay for his or her eBay merchandise, or if a business with which you contract to develop your web site, do your bookkeeping, or perform other services doesn't do the job—that's too bad. You have no legal standing in that state and therefore no right to sue for any damages.

If you have fallen into this trap, all is not lost. You can register in your home state and then apply to move your business jurisdiction from the original incorporation state. That way, you avoid paying the unnecessary extra state fees, along with the equally unnecessary inflated costs that the virtual office incorporation service has likely sold you.

Alright, enough about nexus. Let's talk about taxes.

Sales Tax

Sales tax is assessed against all sales of tangible, or real, personal goods. It doesn't matter whether or not the goods are brand new or used. If they are being sold, they become subject to sales tax (that is, if your state charges sales tax; some don't).

When you pay sales tax on an item, you are usually paying a blended overall tax that covers your state, county, and city. What you pay at the register is the total of all of these tax percentages. For example, in California the (2005) state tax rate is 6 percent, but county and municipal rates push the overall California sales tax rate to about 8 percent on average. In Texas, those rates are around 6 percent and 9 percent, respectively.

As a seller, you are responsible for assessing the correct amount of tax and collecting it on each sale that you make. You are responsible for holding these funds until it is time to send them in to your local tax authority, which is done on a weekly, biweekly, or monthly basis, depending on your state's regulations. You are also usually responsible for preparing and submitting a report detailing the total amount of your sales in each county and/or city, so that tax collectors can confirm and verify that you have charged enough tax and have submitted the entire amount due. If you make a mistake and charge too little sales tax, you will wind up paying the balance, so it is in your best interests to make sure that you know the rules for your state.

The good news is that plenty of software programs are available to help you calculate sales and use taxes. In fact, eBay can help out with special software. When you are setting up your eBay sales descriptions, you can choose to turn on the sales tax module, and by selecting the state where your business is located, you can ensure that the proper tax is calculated for purchasers who also live in your state.

Table 3-1 sets out the current state and combined sales tax rates payable in each state. (This chart was prepared at the time this book was being written—fall 2005—so bear in mind that it might not be up to date.) Taxes change frequently,

> Sales tax is paid on all items sold—even used personal property is potentially subject to sales tax if you sell to someone in your state. For particulars, check with your tax advisor or state tax agency; rules vary from state to state.

and unfortunately the way the system is set up, you as a seller are responsible for keeping up to date on current rates in your state. To give you a head start, we provide a link to each state's Department of Revenue web site at www.taxloopholes.com/ebaysellers.

An argument has been raging for years about whether Internet sales should be subject to state sales taxes. Tax opponents say that cyberspace belongs to no state, and therefore no taxes should be paid on Internet sales. Tax proponents, on the other hand, say that not charging tax on Internet

Table 3.1 Current Combined Average Sales Tax Rates in the United States

State	Combined Average State, City, and County % Rates	State	Combined Average State, City, and County % Rates	State	Combined Average State, City, and County % Rates
Alabama	7.95	Kentucky	6	North Dakota	5.5
Alaska	1.05	Louisiana	8.55	Ohio	7.15
Arizona	7.65	Maine	5	Oklahoma	8.1
Arkansas	7.95	Maryland	5	Oregon	N/A
California	7.95	Massachusetts	5	Pennsylvania	6.25
Colorado	6.15	Michigan	6	Rhode Island	7
Connecticut	6	Minnesota	6.7	South Carolina	5.55
Delaware	N/A	Mississippi	7	South Dakota	5.25
District of Columbia	5.75	Missouri	6.8	Tennessee	9.4
Florida	6.7	Montana	N/A	Texas	7.9
Georgia	6.8	Nebraska	6.3	Utah	6.45
Hawaii	4	Nevada	7.35	Vermont	6
Idaho	6.1	New Hampshire	N/A	Washington	8.35
Illinois	7.5	New Jersey	5.95	West Virginia	6
Indiana	6	New Mexico	6.5	Wisconsin	5.4
Iowa	6.6	New York	8.4	Wyoming	5
Kansas	6.75	North Carolina	7.05		

sales hurts the brick-and-mortar stores in that state who don't have a choice over whether or not they collect sales taxes.

Note: eBay does not have a specific policy with respect to collecting and remitting sales tax. Instead, eBay simply recommends that eBay sellers contact a tax professional to determine whether it is necessary to charge sales tax on your eBay sales. eBay does not provide tax advice, nor does it warrant that its sales tax features will address all tax requirements.

Use Tax.   The *use tax* is an odd little tax imposed by most states to discourage shopping in more tax-advantageous states. Basically, use taxes make up for the sales taxes you would have paid in your home state. They are levied on goods that you purchase in one state and then bring back home to use. For example, assume you are a Californian who traveled up to Oregon to purchase goods (Oregon has no state sales or use tax) and then took those goods back to California. You would owe a use tax equal to the amount of sales tax you would have paid in your home state of California.

> Use tax is a "gotcha" most frequently imposed by state auditors when they are checking out businesses. If the business bought items out of state and didn't pay a sales tax, they're going to have to pay use tax.

Use tax may also be imposed if you buy goods using a wholesale or resale certificate for resale by you, and then you wind up keeping and using the items yourself. For example, if you sold Canadian chocolate on eBay and held a valid resale license, you could buy your merchandise from another eBay seller who wholesales Canadian chocolate or a brick-and-mortar food wholesaler who sells Canadian chocolate without paying sales tax on your purchase. That's because when you resell that chocolate on eBay, either live or through your eBay store, you will be collecting the sales tax (from buyers who live in your state) at that time and remitting it to the state authorities. *However*, if you were to hold back a case of Canadian chocolate from your wholesale purchase for yourself, you would owe use tax on that case of Canadian chocolate.

In most states, the use tax rate is the same as the sales tax rate, because effectively the use tax is going to replace the sales tax that would otherwise have been charged. It is usually calculated and reported on the same form that you use to calculate and report your sales tax, and it would be paid at the same time.

Sales Tax on Consignment Sales.   Some people expand their eBay businesses to sell items for other people. People who sell on consignment in eBay are deemed *trading assistants* or *trading posts*. People and companies with merchandise to sell who don't want to sell it themselves can contact a trading assistant or trading post and arrange to have their goods listed and sold by that person. We talk more about how to become a trading assistant and how a trading post works in Chapter 11; you can also find out more about this program through the companion web site.

As a trading assistant, you can deal with clients in or outside your state. Practically speaking, you'll most often wind up dealing with clients who live close to you, as this is going to make dealing with the merchandise easier. (Actually, for tax purposes you may well be better off dealing with clients only in your home state. We explain why in the next section.) You could arrange to ship the item directly from your client's place, but this can be tricky and risky for you. If a buyer experiences a problem with the merchandise, or it is lost in transit, you will ultimately wind up dealing with the upset purchaser and potentially exposing yourself to receiving bad feedback for the transaction.

In terms of tax issues, consignment sales are usually treated the same as if you owned the merchandise personally. If you sell the merchandise to someone in the same state as your eBay business, you will be required to collect and remit sales tax on the sale. If you sell to someone outside your state, you won't need to collect sales tax, but you should carefully document the sale to prove that you were not required to collect or remit the tax. In either case, you, not the original owner, are responsible for paying any sales tax that arises.

Sales and Use Tax on Out-of-State Sales.   Generally speaking, you are not required to collect or remit sales or use tax on items that you sell to eBay buyers who don't live in the state where your eBay business is incorporated. However, you must keep good records. If you are audited by your local authorities, this is an area that *will* be targeted for focus to ensure you are in compliance.

This is another good reason to act as a trading assistant only for clients who live in your state. Under current law, you usually pay sales tax only when you have a business presence in the state where the goods are being both sold and delivered. But if you live in Colorado and the products are being sold from a consignment client's house in New Jersey to someone else who lives in New Jersey, you'll probably have to pay sales tax in New Jersey. That's because you will be considered as having a business presence in New Jersey, as both the goods being sold and the purchaser are in that state.

> Be careful if you drop ship directly from a consignment client to a seller—you don't want to find yourself in a position of having to remit and pay sales taxes in your consignment client's state because that is where the goods were sold.

Note: Make sure you sign up at www.taxloopholes.com/ebaysellers for the latest updates on sales tax issues. The jurisdiction for sales tax collection continues to be a hot issue for eBay sellers.

As a purchaser, on the other hand, you are required to declare and pay use taxes if you buy goods from an Internet retailer or a brick-and-mortar retailer in another state and use those items. So, if you purchase packaging supplies over the Internet from California and use them to ship goods from your eBay operation in Illinois, theoretically you should be reporting the cost of those supplies on your sales tax return each month and paying Illinois use tax. The good news is that it's a deductible expense—you can deduct all use taxes that you pay for items that you use in your eBay business.

On page 49, you'll find a handy chart that you can refer to when the question of sales tax arises.

Reporting and Paying Sales and Use Taxes.   The monthly sales volume from your company and your state's requirements will determine how often you will need to complete sales and use tax reports. Reporting could be required monthly, quarterly, semiannually, or annually. To give you an idea of the types of information you will need to provide, check out the copy of Jenny Guerro's first return (Figure 3.1). You can also find copies of the sales reports for a few other states in Appendix D and current web links to all 50 state taxation authorities at the companion web site.

Payroll Taxes

If your business operates as an S or a C Corporation, you will need to set up a payroll for yourself. An LLC that has either elected to be taxed as a partnership or has not elected a tax structure is not allowed to pay a salary to owners. All income will be subject to self-employment tax. The 2005 rate for this extra tax is 15.3 percent.

S Corporations have a couple of choices when it comes to paying shareholders. If you, as an owner and employee, perform work, you will receive a paycheck. The paycheck will be subject to payroll taxes. An S Corporation also pays shareholder distributions. The distributions are not subject to payroll taxes.

This question often comes up: Why not simply take all the money as distributions and avoid payroll taxes? Unfortunately, the IRS will not be happy with you if you try this. If you have an S Corporation, we recommend that you divide up your salary and distributions on about a 50/50 basis. If your business has a taxable income of $40,000, that means you'll have a salary of $20,000 and then take distributions of $20,000. In addition,

When Do I Pay Sales Tax?

If You	You Pay
Buy office supplies in your home state	Sales tax in your home state
Buy office supplies in another state that charges sales tax	Sales tax in the state where you buy your supplies
Buy office supplies in a state that doesn't charge sales tax	Use tax in your home state

If You	You
Sell goods on eBay to a purchaser who lives in your state (goods are shipped from your location)	Charge sales tax on the purchase price (before shipping and handling charges are added) and remit to your state tax authorities
Sell goods on eBay to a purchaser who lives in another state (goods are shipped from your location)	Are not required to collect or remit sales taxes on the sale
Sell goods on eBay as a trading assistant, where both the original owner and the purchaser live in your state (goods are shipped from your location)	Charge sales tax on the purchase price (before shipping and handling charges are added, in most states) and remit to your state tax authorities
Sell goods on eBay as a trading assistant, where the original owner lives in another state and the purchaser lives in your state (goods are drop-shipped from original owner's location)	Are not required to collect or remit sales tax on the sale
Sell goods on eBay as a trading assistant, where neither the original owner nor the purchaser live in your state (goods are drop-shipped from original owner's location)	Might have to collect and remit sales tax, if the original owner and purchaser live in the same state
Sell goods on eBay as a trading assistant, where the original owner lives in your state and the purchaser lives in another state (goods are shipped from either your or original owner's location)	Are not required to collect or remit sales tax on the sale

if you are going to be employing your children or other dependents, you'll need to get a payroll system in place for them as well.

Payroll can be tricky, but it doesn't have to be the bane of your existence. This is where your advisors really come into play. A good bookkeeper can help you with getting your payroll set up and explain to you how to

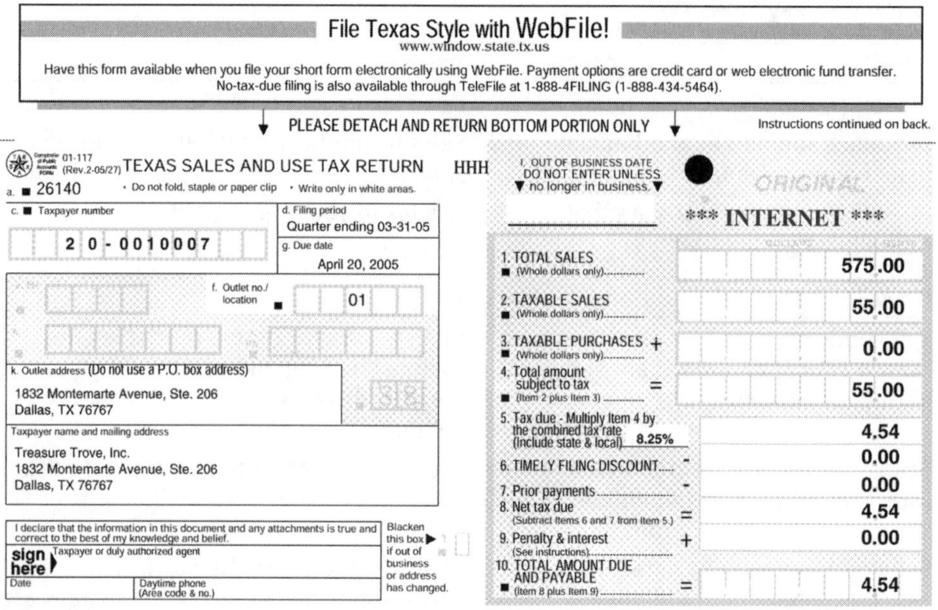

Figure 3.1   Jenny Guerro's first sales and use tax return.

write yourself checks and make sure you are taking the right deductions, or you can have the bookkeeper do this for you. Intuit's accounting software package, QuickBooks, includes a payroll module that will make all of these calculations for you, along with helping you make sure you send in the proper payments and prepare the forms at the appropriate times. You can also use an online or brick-and-mortar payroll service to manage your payroll. Payroll services can be a great resource for small businesses that employ only a few people and don't have the knowledge to do it in-house.

You need to be concerned with four main components of payroll taxes:

- Personal income tax withholding
- Social Security and Medicare premiums
- Unemployment insurance
- Workers' compensation

Personal Income Tax Withholding

The amount of income tax that should be withheld can be calculated in all sorts of different ways—daily, weekly, biweekly, monthly, quarterly, semi-annually, and annually. Depending on how often you decide to pay yourself, you can choose whatever method suits you best. You can either calculate the amount of income tax manually, using IRS Publication 15

(Circular E, "Employer's Tax Guide"), or, if you're using software such as QuickBooks, it can calculate the tax withholding for you.

Income tax is paid by you personally and is deducted from the gross amount of your check. Your corporation will hang onto this money until it is time to send it in to the state and/or federal government. If you live in a state that also assesses an income tax, you will need to make extra withholdings for that. Again, when you are getting started, it may be easier to find a bookkeeper to help you set up your records properly.

Social Security and Medicare Premiums

The Social Security and Medicare premiums are calculated based on the gross amount that you have paid yourself for each pay period. As of 2005, the Social Security premium is set at 12.4 percent of your gross pay, with 6.2 percent coming from you and the other 6.2 percent being expensed to your corporation; the Medicare premium is set at 2.9 percent, again with half coming from you personally and the other half being an expense to your corporation.

As of the 2005 tax year, you are required to pay Social Security premiums only on the first $90,000 you earn (which works out to a maximum payment of $5,580.00). The Medicare premium has no limit—the more you make, the more you pay.

Reporting and Paying Payroll Taxes and Withholdings.   For most eBay business owners you'll be paying the federal combined income tax, Social Security, and Medicare withholding payments quarterly. If the accumulated amount due is more than $2,500 per quarter, you will need to make a monthly (or more frequent) deposit. You will need to file IRS Form 941 on a quarterly basis, reporting the Social Security, Medicare, and the federal tax amount withheld.

If the combined payroll tax amount for you and any dependent employees you have is more than $2,500 per quarter, you'll need to pay the amount owing on a monthly basis, on the 15th day of each month. These monthly payments are usually made at your bank, which forwards the money to the IRS. Not all banks provide this service, so check ahead when you open your business account. In addition, when you make these monthly payments, you need to send along a small form called a Form 8109. You'll find these forms in the yellow booklet you got from the IRS about two to three weeks after your corporation's tax ID was issued.

On the other hand, if you don't take any salary for a month, you don't have to send in any payroll tax amount. This can be a really useful loophole if you are trying to schedule when you pay taxes. If you alternate between taking distributions one quarter and salary the next quarter, you

Table 3.2   Bookkeeping Entry to Record Joe Morgan's Monthly Payroll Expenses

Date	Account	DR	CR
06/30/05	Joe Martin Salary Expense	4,668.00	
	Social Security Tax Expense	248.00	
	Medicare Tax Expense	58.00	
	Unemployment Insurance Expense	15.00	
	Workers' Compensation Expense	22.00	
	Cash (checks 1208, 1220, 1227)		4,000.00
	Social Security Tax Liability		248.00
	Medicare Tax Liability		58.00
	Joe Martin Income Tax Liability		362.00
	Joe Martin Social Security Tax Liability		248.00
	Joe Martin Medicare Tax Liability		58.00
	Unemployment Insurance Liability		15.00
	Workers' Compensation Liability		22.00

can reduce the number of times per year that you have to file the Form 941 and remit payroll taxes two times per year instead of four times per year.

If you live in a state that assesses income tax, you will also have to file a state-level withholding report and send in the income tax you've deducted from your payroll checks as well.

Confused? It does sound difficult to track, but actually the reporting isn't so bad, as long as you have a bookkeeping system in place that is helping you withhold and track the payroll deductions. Many of the forms are little more than restatements of these amounts. In fact, to show you what we mean, we've reproduced a fictitious monthly payroll entry for Joe Martin at Table 3.2 above, along with his quarterly IRS Form 941 (Figures 3-2 and 3-3) and California Quarterly Wage and Withholding Report (Figure 3-4). It's not so bad! (You'll meet Joe later in this chapter—he owns and operates a used computer equipment shop in California and used eBay to broaden his sales base.)

Unemployment Insurance Premiums

Unemployment insurance premiums are calculated based on the same pay period structure as your other payroll taxes and should accrue in a separate account. At the federal level, you report and pay this total accrued amount, less state premiums, once a year (within one month of your corporation's fiscal year end). State premiums are calculated and paid on whatever schedule your state uses, which is typically monthly. This is an expense to your corporation only—you won't be deducting these premiums from your paychecks.

Form **941 for 2005:** **Employer's Quarterly Federal Tax Return**   9901
(Rev. January 2005)   Department of the Treasury — Internal Revenue Service   OMB No. 1545-0029

Employer identification number   2 0 — 1 2 3 4 5 6 7

Name (not your trade name)   Geekman Enterprises, Inc.

Trade name (if any)

Address   23645 Orange Boulevard, Ste. 109C
          Number   Street   Suite or room number

          Cupertino   CA   92929
          City   State   ZIP code

Report for this Quarter ...
(Check one.)

☐ 1: January, February, March
☑ 2: April, May, June
☐ 3: July, August, September
☐ 4: October, November, December

Read the separate instructions before you fill out this form. Please type or print within the boxes.

Part 1: Answer these questions for this quarter.

1 Number of employees who received wages, tips, or other compensation for the pay period including: *Mar. 12* (Quarter 1), *June 12* (Quarter 2), *Sept. 12* (Quarter 3), *Dec. 12* (Quarter 4) 1 | 1

2 Wages, tips, and other compensation . . . . 2 | 4668 . 00

3 Total income tax withheld from wages, tips, and other compensation . . . . 3 | 362 . 00

4 If no wages, tips, and other compensation are subject to social security or Medicare tax . . ☐ Check and go to line 6.

5 Taxable social security and Medicare wages and tips:

	Column 1		Column 2
5a Taxable social security wages	4668 . 00	× .124 =	578 . 83
5b Taxable social security tips	0 . 00	× .124 =	0 . 00
5c Taxable Medicare wages & tips	4668 . 00	× .029 =	135 . 37

5d Total social security and Medicare taxes (*Column 2*, lines 5a + 5b + 5c = line 5d) . 5d | 714 . 20

6 Total taxes before adjustments (lines 3 + 5d = line 6) . . . . 6 | 1076 . 20

7 Tax adjustments (If your answer is a negative number, write it in brackets.):

7a Current quarter's fractions of cents . . . . | 0 . 00

7b Current quarter's sick pay . . . . | 0 . 00

7c Current quarter's adjustments for tips and group-term life insurance | 0 . 00

7d Current year's income tax withholding (Attach Form 941c) . . | 0 . 00

7e Prior quarters' social security and Medicare taxes (Attach Form 941c) | 0 . 00

7f Special additions to federal income tax (reserved use) . . . . | 0 . 00

7g Special additions to social security and Medicare (reserved use) | 0 . 00

7h Total adjustments (Combine all amounts: lines 7a through 7g.) . . . . 7h | 0 . 00

8 Total taxes after adjustments (Combine lines 6 and 7h.) . . . . 8 | 1076 . 20

9 Advance earned income credit (EIC) payments made to employees . . . . . . 9 | 0 . 00

10 Total taxes after adjustment for advance EIC (lines 8 – 9 = line 10) . . . . . . 10 | 1076 . 20

11 Total deposits for this quarter, including overpayment applied from a prior quarter . . . 11 | 0 . 00

12 Balance due (lines 10 – 11 = line 12) Make checks payable to the *United States Treasury* . . 12 | 1076 . 2-

13 Overpayment (If line 11 is more than line 10, write the difference here.) | . | Check one ☐ Apply to next return. / ☐ Send a refund.

Next ➡

For Privacy Act and Paperwork Reduction Act Notice, see the back of the Payment Voucher.   Cat. No. 17001Z   Form **941** (Rev. 1-2005)

Figure 3.2   Form 941 for the three-month period April 1–June 30, 2005, page 1.

9902

Name *(not your trade name)*	Employer identification number
Geekman Enterprises, Inc.	20-1234567

Part 2: Tell us about your deposit schedule for this quarter.

If you are unsure about whether you are a monthly schedule depositor or a semiweekly schedule depositor, see *Pub. 15 (Circular E)*, section 11.

14 ☐ C ☐ A   Write the state abbreviation for the state where you made your deposits OR write "MU" if you made your deposits in *multiple* states.

15 Check one: ☑ Line 10 is less than $2,500. Go to Part 3.

☐ You were a monthly schedule depositor for the entire quarter. Fill out your tax liability for each month. Then go to Part 3.

Tax liability: Month 1 [.   ]

Month 2 [.   ]

Month 3 [.   ]

Total [.   ] Total must equal line 10.

☐ You were a semiweekly schedule depositor for any part of this quarter. Fill out *Schedule B (Form 941): Report of Tax Liability for Semiweekly Schedule Depositors,* and attach it to this form.

Part 3: Tell us about your business. If a question does NOT apply to your business, leave it blank.

16 If your business has closed and you do not have to file returns in the future . . . . ☐ Check here, and

enter the final date you paid wages [/ /] .

17 If you are a seasonal employer and you do not have to file a return for every quarter of the year . . ☐ Check here.

Part 4: May we contact your third-party designee?

Do you want to allow an employee, a paid tax preparer, or another person to discuss this return with the IRS? See the instructions for details.

☐ Yes. Designee's name [   ]

Phone ( ) – Personal Identification Number (PIN) ☐ ☐ ☐ ☐ ☐

☑ No.

Part 5: Sign here

Under penalties of perjury, I declare that I have examined this return, including accompanying schedules and statements, and to the best of my knowledge and belief, it is true, correct, and complete.

X

Sign your name here [   ]

Print name and title [Joe Martin, President, Geekman Enterprises, Inc.]

Date [05 / 26 / 05] Phone (012) 345 – 6789

Part 6: For paid preparers only *(optional)*

Preparer's signature [   ]

Firm's name [   ]

Address [   ] EIN [   ]

[   ] ZIP code [   ]

Date [/ /] Phone ( ) – SSN/PTIN [   ]

☐ Check if you are self-employed.

Page **2** Form **941** (Rev. 1-2005)

Figure 3.3 Form 941 for the three-month period April 1–June 30, 2005, page 2.

EDD Employment Development Department
State of California

QUARTERLY WAGE AND WITHHOLDING REPORT
PLEASE TYPE THIS FORM PER INSTRUCTIONS ON REVERSE
You must FILE this report even if you had no payroll. If you had no payroll, complete Items C or D and P.

Page number _____ of _____

QUARTER ENDED 06/30/2005   DUE

DELINQUENT IF NOT POSTMARKED OR RECEIVED BY

00060198

YR	QTR
05	2

EMPLOYER ACCOUNT NO.
12345678

DO NOT ALTER THIS AREA

P1	C	T	S	W	A

EFFECTIVE DATE
Mo.   Day   Yr.   WIC

Geekman Enterprises, Inc.

A. **EMPLOYEES** full-time and part-time who worked during or received pay subject to UI for the payroll period **which includes the 12th** of the month.

1st Mo.	2nd Mo.	3rd Mo.
1	1	1

B. ☐ Check this box if you are reporting ONLY Voluntary Plan DI wages on this page. Report PIT Wages and PIT Withheld, if appropriate. (See instructions for Item B.)

C. ☐ NO PAYROLL   D. ☐ OUT OF BUSINESS/FINAL REPORT
Date _____

E. SOCIAL SECURITY NUMBER	F. EMPLOYEE NAME (FIRST NAME)	(M.I.) (LAST NAME)	
680243987	Joseph	M Martin	
G. TOTAL SUBJECT WAGES	H. PIT WAGES	I. PIT WITHHELD	
4668.00	4668.00	323.00	

E. SOCIAL SECURITY NUMBER	F. EMPLOYEE NAME (FIRST NAME)	(M.I.) (LAST NAME)
G. TOTAL SUBJECT WAGES	H. PIT WAGES	I. PIT WITHHELD

E. SOCIAL SECURITY NUMBER	F. EMPLOYEE NAME (FIRST NAME)	(M.I.) (LAST NAME)
G. TOTAL SUBJECT WAGES	H. PIT WAGES	I. PIT WITHHELD

E. SOCIAL SECURITY NUMBER	F. EMPLOYEE NAME (FIRST NAME)	(M.I.) (LAST NAME)
G. TOTAL SUBJECT WAGES	H. PIT WAGES	I. PIT WITHHELD

E. SOCIAL SECURITY NUMBER	F. EMPLOYEE NAME (FIRST NAME)	(M.I.) (LAST NAME)
G. TOTAL SUBJECT WAGES	H. PIT WAGES	I. PIT WITHHELD

E. SOCIAL SECURITY NUMBER	F. EMPLOYEE NAME (FIRST NAME)	(M.I.) (LAST NAME)
G. TOTAL SUBJECT WAGES	H. PIT WAGES	I. PIT WITHHELD

E. SOCIAL SECURITY NUMBER	F. EMPLOYEE NAME (FIRST NAME)	(M.I.) (LAST NAME)
G. TOTAL SUBJECT WAGES	H. PIT WAGES	I. PIT WITHHELD

J. TOTAL SUBJECT WAGES THIS PAGE	K. TOTAL PIT WAGES THIS PAGE	L. TOTAL PIT WITHHELD THIS PAGE
4668.00	4668.00	323.00

M. GRAND TOTAL SUBJECT WAGES	N. GRAND TOTAL PIT WAGES	O. GRAND TOTAL PIT WITHHELD
8500.00	8500.00	623.00

P. I declare that the information herein is true and correct to the best of my knowledge and belief.

Preparer's Signature _____   Title Owner _____   Phone (012) 345-6789   Date 07/15/2005
(Owner, Accountant, Preparer, etc.)

DE 6 Rev. 4 (2-04) **(INTERNET)** MAIL TO: State of California / Employment Development Department / P.O. Box 826288 / Sacramento, CA 94230-6288

Figure 3.4   Joe's quarterly California Quarterly Wage and Withholding Report.

Even if you are a one-person corporation, you will still need to register and pay unemployment insurance. That's because if you work for the company, you're an employee. As an employee, the company must provide unemployment insurance.

Workers' Compensation

Most states have privatized workers' compensation insurance and allow you to purchase it through a private insurance agency. Usually, workers' compensation arrangements are put in place and you begin making payments within a short time after your first payroll quarter has ended. In some states, you'll need to have these arrangements in place before your corporation's business license can be issued. As with unemployment insurance, workers' compensation premiums are an expense to your corporation and aren't deducted from your paychecks.

The benefit of workers' compensation is that it covers medical expenses and in some cases will even replace lost wages if you or your employee is injured on the job. As much as we don't like to think about it, injuries do happen. It's nice to know that there might be a little extra insurance to cover your costs if it happens to you.

Reporting and Paying Unemployment and Workers' Compensation Premiums.   In most states, you are required to register and begin making contributions to unemployment insurance and workers' compensation programs after your first payroll has been made. The amount you pay will be determined by the state in which your business resides, the number of employees you have, and the amount of your payroll. You can find more details in Appendix E, where we provide a list of state departments of labor and other employment-related web sites, so that you can determine the steps your business will need to take.

W4, W2, and 1099 Forms

Each employee of your company needs to complete a Form W4 each year. You'll need the information contained in these forms to calculate the payroll tax deductions properly. Even if you're the only employee of your company, make sure you prepare a Form W4 for yourself and keep it on file. Do your first one after incorporation, and then make you and your employees complete a new one every January after that.

Payroll tax:
- Must be paid for all employees

It includes:
- Workers' compensation
- Unemployment tax
- Social Security tax
- Medicare tax

At the beginning of each calendar year you'll also need to prepare a Form W2 for every employee summarizing their total earnings for the preceding year, along with the total amounts that you have withheld for income tax, Social Security, Medicare, and anything else. You need to file one copy of these forms with the IRS and give a copy to your employees by the last date in February. If you file your Form W2s online, you can extend the filing deadline to March 31st, but you still need to distribute your employee copies by the last day in February.

Also, if you pay anyone for casual labor as an independent contractor, make sure you issue him or her a Form 1099 at the same time you prepare and issue your Form W2s. You must also file your Form 1099s with the IRS at the same time you file your Form W2s.

If you pay independent contractors more than $600 per year, they must declare and report that income on their own returns and pay their own taxes on those monies. It's actually more effective and requires less bookkeeping in the long run to employ your children and other dependents, rather than paying them as independent contractors and issuing a 1099.

If you're wondering where to find these forms, they're available online from the IRS (www.irs.gov) or from your local IRS field office. If you use QuickBooks (more on that in Chapter 6), you can use that program to prepare and print the forms. Or, if you simply do a Google search for either form, you'll find hundreds of places where you can download them from the Web. You'll also find places that will help you prepare the forms quickly and easily, simply by answering questions and entering the figures from your accounting records. These businesses can be great time-savers, as many also offer a feature that both files your Form W2s and 1099s with the IRS and then also mails the documents out to each employee or independent contractor.

The chart on page 58 helps you to remember what happens, and when.

Business Income Tax

Well, after all the confusion with sales and use taxes and payroll taxes, we've got some good news. Business income tax is *much* easier to figure out than sales tax.

Business taxes are typically paid yearly, at the time you prepare and file your business tax return. Whether or not your business will also pay tax at the state level will depend on your state. State-level taxes are often referred to as *franchise taxes*.

This is an area where a C Corporation can be very helpful. A C Corporation is allowed to set its own year-end date. S Corporations, though, need to stay with a year-end date of December 31 to keep pace with personal returns. So, if you are thinking about operating your eBay business

How and When to Pay Federal Payroll Taxes

When do I deduct payroll taxes from my employees' checks?	When do I send that money to the government?	What form(s) do I use	Where do I pay my company's payroll taxes?
Before you issue payroll checks—biweekly, monthly, and so on	If your total payroll taxes (income tax, Social Security, and Medicare) are less than $2,500 per quarter, you pay quarterly, by the end of the month following your fiscal quarter. For other small payrolls (under $50,000 payroll taxes per year), you pay monthly, on the 15th day of the month.	If your total payroll taxes (income tax, Social Security, and Medicare) are less than $2,500 per quarter, file IRS Form 941. For other small payrolls (under $50,000 payroll taxes per year), use the yellow coupon book, Form 8109 for your monthly deposits, and then file IRS Form 941 each fiscal quarter.	If your total payroll taxes (income tax, Social Security, and Medicare) are less than $2,500 per quarter, you can submit the money with Form 941. For other small payrolls (under $50,000 payroll taxes per year), you are required to deposit payroll taxes at your bank along with a Form 8109 coupon from the yellow coupon book. (If you don't have a yellow coupon book, use a Form 8109B, available from the IRS office.)

through a C Corporation, consider a June 30 year-end date. This way, you'll have an extra six months to play with your tax money—and wouldn't you rather keep your money for as long as possible? This ability to stagger when taxes are paid is called *leveraging* your taxes, and it has a lot of benefits.

Reporting and Paying Business Income Tax

At the federal level, C Corporations file IRS Form 1120, while S Corporations file Form 1120S. S Corporations also prepare a schedule called a Schedule K-1, showing each shareholder's portion of the net profit or loss that needs to be declared on his or her personal return.

The information on the forms you will be filing at the state level may be similar to the information you provide on your federal tax return, or it may be a simplified return. You'll find Jenny Guerro's Form 1120S and her Franchise Tax Return in Appendix F, to give you an idea of what information is required in Texas. We also provide you with a list of web site links and required forms for C and S Corporations in all 50 states at the companion web site, so that you can see what will be required for your eBay business.

Table 3.3 shows corporation tax return year-end dates, due dates, and extension dates.

> A major cause of IRS audits is improper business classifications. The IRS is expecting you to have certain expenses based on your business type. Choosing the wrong classification can lead to problems. For example, an eBay seller should generally report as a retailer. That means that the IRS expects an amount entered on the tax return for ending inventory each year. Miss this one and you could be looking at a full-blown audit.

Helpful Resources

Feeling a little confused? Taxes and tax reporting requirements can do that to just about everyone. This is one of those areas where you probably will be spending a bit of money, either to educate yourself as to the reporting and filing requirements in your state or in paying someone to help you set up your books and other records or organize your books and records for you. Taxes are so important that you do need to get help. There is nothing worse than fumbling your way through all of these issues and then finding out a year or two later that you didn't do things properly and now owe the IRS or a local state agency a bunch of money.

Table 3.3   Corporation Tax Return Due Dates

	Year End	Due Date	Can Extend To
S Corporation	12/31	3/15	9/15
C Corporation*	1/31	4/15	10/15
	2/28	5/15	11/15
	3/31	6/15	12/15
	4/30	7/15	1/15
	5/31	8/15	2/15
	6/30	9/15	3/15
	7/31	10/15	4/15
	8/31	11/15	5/15
	9/30	12/15	6/15
	10/31	1/15	7/15
	11/30	2/15	8/15
	12/31	3/15	9/15

*Remember that a C Corporation may choose any month as its year end, whereas an S Corporation must use the calendar year-end of December 31 to receive its beneficial tax treatment.

How eBay Helped Joe Martin's Business

Joe Martin locked up the shop doors about 5:30 p.m. and headed out into a hot California afternoon. The asphalt surface was radiating heat upward, making for a long, hot walk across the parking lot to his car. Joe noticed the heat, but his attention was fixed on more important matters—such as the declining state of his business.

Joe owned a computer shop situated in a small strip mall in Sunnyvale, California, deep in the heart of Silicon Valley. He offered a full range of services and components—he'd build the customer the computer of her dreams or sell her the components to build it herself. When he'd opened the shop, it was a great time to be in computers. The dot-com boom was in full swing, and everyone needed the newest, latest, fastest computers and components to create their software master-pieces. Joe's knowledge and friendliness were well-known in the computer commu-nity, and his shop had been tremendously successful. But that was before the dot-com craze very definitely ended. Joe was losing ground rapidly to big-box retailers and to the online computer-making powerhouses, whose bulk buying power ensured they could always produce a cheaper product than Joe could.

Joe was a resourceful fellow and had turned his knowledge to other directions. Rather than competing with dealers who sold new computers, Joe had scaled back his production of new equipment and moved toward selling refurbished high-end equipment. Lots of merchandise was available—every time another dot-com closed its doors, its computer equipment came into the market at liquidation prices. On this level, Joe could compete—the equipment he was selling was high quality and still relevant to gamers and other computer users who were looking for performance and quality, two things that Joe thought was missing from a lot of the mass-pro-duced, cheap computer equipment currently on the market.

Joe made sure his shop was kept clean, and the equipment on display was kept clean, polished, and looking as new as possible. Joe also made sure that his work-bench and storage area were well out of customer sight to keep his shop looking as sleek as possible. Still, even with all of his efforts, Joe was beginning to struggle. It seemed that everyone had all the computers they needed, and their attention was on other things. Customer visits were tapering off, and sometimes hours passed between in-shop customer visits.

Joe believed a market for used, high-quality computer equipment still existed, but that Sunnyvale and the surrounding areas were probably saturated with shops like his. He needed to find a way to broaden his potential market outside the Silicon Valley area, but on an economical basis. TV, radio, and print advertising were expen-sive, and he wasn't convinced that the cost of advertising in an industry-specific magazine was going to work, either. The folks Joe wanted to reach were those in charge of purchasing and maintaining office equipment across the country, such as office managers and IT consultants—in other words, people who had limited budg-ets and enough knowledge to understand the value that used high-end equipment represented.

And that's where eBay entered Joe's business equation. Looking through com-puter equipment listings, Joe discovered what many other small business owners had already discovered—a ready market for the equipment and a lively sales rate, especially if the price was right.

Joe took his digital camera to work and took pictures of some of his inventory. After reviewing his eBay seller options, he decided to open an eBay Store. He liked the idea of having a static inventory that he could list for longer periods of time—he wouldn't spend all of his time listing or relisting items. He also learned that according to eBay best practices, he could use an auction-style format for his listings that was designed to encourage purchasers to visit his store to browse his full inventory.

Joe also liked the marketing and product placement opportunities that eBay offered to the second- and third-level store categories—for a reasonable price, he could have a much wider exposure than advertising in local newspapers. Since stores, if set up correctly, are search-engine optimized for free, an eBay Store would give him more exposure than a web site at a much lower cost. He also appreciated being able to link his existing store web site to his eBay Store—he had more space to explain who he was, what he did, and his selling philosophy.

Within two to three months of opening his eBay Store, Joe noticed a definite upward trend in his monthly receipts. He was beginning to move merchandise more quickly, and his positive feedback numbers were growing. Joe was even hunting around the valley more aggressively for merchandise to sell and began making a habit of scanning the classified sections of area newspapers looking for bankruptcy sales and liquidation auctions. He noticed that a lot of his sales were from out-of-state customers, which was just fine with him, as he wasn't required to collect sales tax on the items he sold. In fact, things were looking so good on eBay that Joe wondered whether he should keep his storefront open at all—what he really needed was more storage space, rather than display or retail space, and he thought if he could find some low-visibility warehouse space at a cheaper cost, his profit margin would improve even more. Joe made a note in his calendar of when his lease was up and when he had to give notice of either his intent to renew or move out. He decided to take a closer look at his options when he was 60 days out from the notice period.

Next Steps—Getting Ready to Start Your Business Operations

Incorporation is the first step, but certainly not the only step! This is where a lot of new business owners get stuck.

Our recommendation is to simply take things step-by-step. That's why we've created the Next Steps at the end of each chapter. If you're working with a business or tax advisor, this is a great time to get them involved to make sure you complete all of these steps along with any other steps your state requires.

1. Determine the nexus for your business.
2. Go to www.taxloopholes.com/ebaysellers to look at the filing requirements for your state.

3. Set up a sales tax account with your state to collect sales tax.

4. Set up payroll accounts with your state. Most likely, this will include state income tax withholding, unemployment insurance, and workers' compensation insurance.

5. Prepare a Form W4 for yourself and make sure that every other employee prepares one as well. Keep all of the signed Form W4s in your payroll file and prepare new ones each January.

6. Set up a schedule to remit the withheld and deposited amounts for sales and payroll taxes.

7. File reports as required on a monthly and/or quarterly basis. These reports will include the following:
   - Sales tax report
   - State unemployment report
   - Workers' compensation report
   - State income tax withholding report
   - Form 941 (IRS—Social Security, Medicare, and income tax withheld)

8. Calculate and pay your eBay business's estimated income taxes from business income as required for state and federal authorities.

9. At the beginning of each calendar year, prepare Form W2s and Form 1099s for each employee and independent contractor. Give these forms out to your employees and independent contractors by the last day in February. Make sure to file a copy of all W2s and 1099s with the IRS by the last day of February (if you're mailing them) or by March 31st (if you use an electronic filing system).

Part 2

Easy Accounting
for eBay Sellers

4

Basic Recordkeeping

Keeping records can either be the bane of your existence or a simple part of your day-to-day business activities. (Guess which one we prefer?) Recordkeeping is like anything else; it's easier to maintain than to begin fresh. If you spend a few minutes each day maintaining your business records, it's pretty easy to keep up. If you spend a couple of days sorting out your records once every few months, it's like starting over every single time. And, doing it that way is time consuming, frustrating, and easy to put off until it becomes a massive task. You also run the risk of missing out on important tax deductions.

In this chapter, we discuss the types of records you need to keep, and why. We also take a look at some useful tools from eBay that can help business owners with this part of their operations.

Why Recordkeeping Is Important

A main reason why recordkeeping is important is because it makes the IRS happy. And a happy IRS is something that *all* business owners and taxpayers can appreciate.

The IRS uses a "carrot-and-stick" method to get what it wants. We've already talked about why the IRS is so happy to give businesses and small business owners great tax breaks. That's the carrot. Businesses, and the people who run them, keep the U.S. economy going, just as they do in most other countries around the globe. But the IRS (or any other country's taxing authority) also has to make sure that businesses stay accountable and don't try to take advantage of a good thing. So forcing business owners to keep records under threat of losing all those business deductions, and possibly paying penalties, is the stick.

Keeping good records allows you much more control over your business operations. If you know where your business stands financially at any given point, you're in a much better position to take advantage of a great deal coming your way. You'll also learn more about how to read financial statements so that you can see the story in other people's financial statements immediately; this is important if you're thinking of acquiring another business or joining forces with another business.

Good Records Equal Great Business Opportunities

One of the biggest hidden benefits of having your own business is that you get on-the-job training for how to be a fantastic investor. For example, one of Diane's clients turned his ability to keep good records for his business into a huge business opportunity.

An experienced business owner, he had recently transitioned into buying real estate. Most of the properties he bought and sold were large commercial properties. He knew that often commercial buyers never even looked at the physical property before the purchase. All they cared about was the return they got on their investments. The only research they did was to look at the financial statements. And because of his experience in recordkeeping with his business, that was one thing he knew.

He developed a computer program that could quickly sort through the financial statements for commercial properties, and he looked for anything that was not average. In fact, he even looked for properties with expenses that were too high. He knew that properties like that usually sold for a multiple of what the income from the property was (for example, the purchase price was equal to two times the income potential). If the expenses were too high, the profit was low, and that meant the price would be low.

One day, Diane's client came up with a property with expenses that seemed too high. He started investigating and found that the seller had made a big mistake on his financial statements. In fact, he had overstated his property taxes by $50,000. The building was selling for a multiple of 10 times earnings (in real estate terms, this is called the *capitalization rate*). Diane's client bought the property, waited six months, and corrected the financial statements. The new, corrected financial statements meant that his profit was increased by $50,000. With a multiple of 10 ($50,000 times 10), he pocketed $500,000 after just six months of ownership.

How many opportunities like this are out there waiting for you to discover? The opportunity wasn't in the property. The real value came from being able to read the story of financial reports.

Good Records Equal Staying Safe from an Audit

In the United States, the words *IRS audit* are pretty intimidating. Everyone's heard of someone who ran afoul of the IRS and wound up in a tough audit situation.

But it doesn't have to be that way. In an audit, the IRS is mainly looking to see records. They want detailed business and financial records to back up the deductions a business has claimed. Throughout this book, we teach you about the hundreds of perfectly legitimate business deductions available to business owners. So, why would the IRS deny your business those deductions? Simply giving the IRS copies of your paperwork may be enough to satisfy their questions and end the entire audit process. In fact, you'll find that people who've had trouble with an IRS audit usually have one thing in common: poor, outdated, or incomplete records.

If your records are out of date or incomplete, it's going to be difficult to meet an IRS challenge to one or more of your business deductions. And if you can't meet the challenge, the chances are those deductions will be disallowed. This can throw your entire business tax return out of order, and you may wind up owing money on a profit, instead of using the loss to offset your other income. Take that one step further, and you could wind up paying penalties for taxes that you wouldn't have had to pay if you had kept complete and accurate records.

Sometimes the IRS Are the Good Guys

Did you ever think that an IRS audit could actually make you money? One of Diane's new clients told her this story of what had led him to her CPA firm.

Bill was an absentee owner of a bar. He didn't pay a lot of attention to financial statements from the bar, but he did know that he didn't make nearly as much money as he had hoped to make. One day he received notice of an IRS audit.

The auditor met with Bill and visited the bar to do a little observation. The auditor was concerned that the numbers didn't make sense. The IRS keeps a lot of statistics on businesses, and they often are the best predictor of what profits should be from a company. Something just didn't make sense with this business.

After the bar visit, the auditor met again with Bill and asked to see the "Z tape" again. The Z tape is a printout of the day's receipts from a cash register. Bill produced two sets of Z tapes for the day in question. The auditor reviewed them and then asked for the Z tape from third register. "Third register?" Bill asked, puzzled by the question. "But there are only two registers."

"No," insisted the auditor. "There are three registers."

> And, guess what? There *were* three registers. The bar manager had added in a third register and pocketed all of the cash from that register every day.
>
> That was one audit Bill was glad to see! The IRS had paid closer attention to the numbers from his business than he had. And the IRS discovered the embezzlement.

Good Records Equal Real Business

Good records are another key aspect of what makes a "real" business. The IRS has certain expectations of your business if it is to be treated as a legitimate business rather than a hobby. Good records show the IRS that you are serious about your business and aren't just trying to create a tax write-off. In fact, keeping complete, accurate, and up-to-date records are one of the IRS's nine steps to business that we talked about earlier in the book.

Have you ever cleaned out a bunch of old receipts from your purse or wallet and tried to remember what they were for? Plenty of retail stores use old cash registers that don't print the name of the store—or much of anything else, beyond the amount of the item and your change. That's not really going to help your business, especially if the IRS is reviewing those receipts. On the other hand, having a receipt attached to a note that details the date, store, and item bought will go a long way toward helping you make sure that your expenses get properly recorded and to show the IRS that you're not just playing around at business.

Good Records Equal Enhanced Business Growth Potential

If you want to expand your business and are looking for a line of credit or some other type of financing from outside investors, the first thing a bank or investor will want to see is your business's financial records. Having current and complete financial statements can allow a bank or other investor to evaluate how you operate your business and what kind of a risk you and your business may be. The better your records, the more accurate a picture they present, and this could make the difference between getting a loan or being refused.

Think about it this way: Suppose you're approached by two friends or relatives with business opportunities and no money to get started. One is filled with enthusiasm, waving his arms around and telling you about all of the great things he's going to do once he has the money to begin. Your other relative or friend gives you a written business plan with financial forecasts, a marketing plan, and some market data that shows you both the demand for her business idea and how she will succeed. Which person is most likely to get your money?

About 10 years ago, a client of Diane's came to her to review a possible investment opportunity in a manufacturing company. The financial statements were a bit of a puzzle, because the records showed that after the sales commissions were subtracted for the sale of each unit, the company actually lost $10 for each sale it made. No wonder the company needed cash—it was losing money hand over fist.

The clients couldn't believe what the numbers revealed. They went back to the naïve new owner of the manufacturing company and asked him how he planned to correct this problem. "What problem?" the owner exclaimed. "We'll just make it up in volume!"

This sounds like a comedy skit, but it really did happen. The manufacturing company went bankrupt a few months later. Luckily, Diane's client didn't lose any money; unfortunately, other people lost a lot of money.

Understanding financial statements and the story they tell can make you money and save you even more.

What Records Should You Keep?

According to the IRS, a business is responsible for "keeping proper records in order to prepare and support its annual tax return." There's a reason for the vagueness of this statement—it allows the IRS a lot of room to review business records to make sure things are complete and in order.

Most bookkeeping and business records are made up of receipts, bills, invoices, bank statements, check stubs, deposit slips, purchase orders, sales and use tax reports, payroll reports, credit memos, lease agreements, and loan documents. In the language of accountants and bookkeepers, these documents are collectively known as *source documents*.

Because these documents back up your expenses and deductions, they are important to your eBay business. So, one of the first things that you need to do is to set up a filing system to track, record, and store your business's source documents. Creating a file folder for each of these categories is a great way to start. In fact, we suggest that you do this each year, so that you can pack away your business's financial data for safekeeping one year at a time. That helps to keep your files better organized and a manageable size.

Generally speaking, source documents will fit into one of the following categories: income, expenses, inventory purchases, asset purchases, and permanent files.

The best place to get help with your recordkeeping requirements is from your advisors. Your bookkeeper, tax preparer, CPA, attorney, business mentor, and banker can all help you with this important part of your eBay business setup. You can also find some folks who can help on the companion web site, www.taxloopholes.com/ebaysellers.

Income

Every sale you make to a customer should be backed up with an invoice. eBay is helpful here, because it assists you in preparing an invoice as a part of the sales transaction.

Your invoice should include all of the pertinent information regarding the sale, including the date of sale, amount, sales tax (if any), shipping costs, terms of payment, and the purchaser's name and address. Your eBay invoices will usually provide all of this information. Make sure you keep a copy of every eBay invoice for your records. If you are keeping them in electronic form only, make sure that you back up your data regularly. One lost, damaged, or stolen hard drive, and your entire eBay business could come crashing down around your ears.

> **Good Records Equal Good Deductions**
>
> Receipts for items you pay for should include:
> - Date
> - Amount
> - Item purchased
> - Taxes
> - Shipping
> - Terms
> - Person or company from which you bought item

Expenses

In a perfect world, every penny that you spend on behalf of your eBay business would come with an accompanying receipt. As with your invoices, all of your expense receipts should have the date of purchase, amount of purchase, item description, any applicable taxes and shipping charges, terms of payment, and the name of person or company from which you purchased the item. If your purchase receipts don't have this information, add it in yourself.

A purchase receipt could take several forms. Credit card or debit card statements, cancelled checks, cash register receipts, copies of accounts and bills that you've paid, supplier invoices, and account statements are all great examples of purchase receipts.

Inventory Purchases

Every time you buy something you are planning to resell on eBay, you are making an inventory purchase. These purchases could also include the cost of parts and raw materials for manufactured products or things that you buy to add to your existing products (such as batteries or cables).

Your inventory purchases are typically backed up with the same type of source documents you receive for your expenses purchases. And that's to be expected—after all, they're still purchases.

Special Inventory Purchase Issues for eBay Sellers. A question that comes up all the time from eBay sellers is how to document things they buy at garage sales, church rummage sales, and other informal sales environments. (When was the last time you went to a garage sale and got a receipt?) But, at the same time, without some paper documentation from your sale, you may have a problem proving that sale to the IRS if they ever come looking.

> If you think that any of your source documents are incomplete, don't be afraid to add information or explanatory notes. The more detail you have in your records, the less chance the IRS will disallow the deduction.

If you are at a garage sale or other informal sale and the seller doesn't provide receipts, try writing out a quick sales slip on a piece of paper, showing the date, amount, and location of your purchase and ask the seller to sign it. Or, if you can, pay by check, and use your cancelled check as a receipt. If you took money out of the ATM on your way to the garage sale, you could try attaching a list of items you purchased with those funds to the ATM withdrawal receipt.

If all else fails, at least make a note of what you purchased and where and how much you paid, and put that in your records. It's better than nothing.

Asset Purchases

The assets your eBay business purchases also need to be carefully documented. That's because these items are subject to depreciation (a great tax-reducing write-off).

To make sure that your assets are properly documented, keep track of the usual points (date of purchase, goods purchased, purchase price, tax and shipping charges, warranty charges, name of purchaser, and any terms of payment). You also need to track any costs of upgrading or maintaining your assets, so that if you have your computer overhauled and new components installed, you would need to keep records of what was done, when, by whom, and for how much money.

If your business is buying a vehicle, large items of equipment, or real estate, you may also receive a closing statement or mortgage documents. Take especially good care of these records.

Permanent Files

Earlier in this chapter, we told you to keep your business's records in file folders and to create new files each year. Most of the time that's good advice. But a few types of records should be kept in permanent files that you don't close off and put into storage at the end of each year.

Your *permanent files* have asset purchase information and any long-term liabilities, such as bank loans, car loans, and other debts, that will take longer than one year to repay. Another example of a permanent records file would be your corporation's minutes book, which will have your eBay business's annual minutes, annual reports, and its founding corporate documents such as the articles of incorporation, bylaws, and shareholder register.

As a rule, if the source document relates to something that will be a part of your business for more than one year (such as an insurance policy, a lease, a mortgage, and other similar documents), keep it in your permanent files. Once you sell an asset that you have been maintaining in your permanent records, you can move that information to your temporary files for the year that asset was sold.

How Long Should You Keep Your Business's Records?

Pretty much every CPA or other financial advisor has an opinion about how long you should keep your business records. Generally, you'll find a lot of differing opinions out there.

As a CPA, Diane recommends that you keep your temporary files for at least five years after the tax return for that year has been filed. You might need to keep the records for any long-term assets you've sold for a bit longer than five years, though. If you're in doubt, check with your CPA or legal or financial advisor. Some records need to be kept for years!

The IRS has some additional requirements that we've set out in Table 4.1.

Table 4.1   IRS Record Retention Requirements

If you	Then you must keep records for
File a claim for refund or credit after the original return has been filed	Three years, or two years after tax was paid
File a claim for a loss from a bad debt or worthless securities	Seven years
Owe additional tax and the following three situations do not apply	Three years
Have not reported income that you should have reported and that income is greater than 25 percent of the gross income you set out on the return	Six years
File a fraudulent return	An unlimited period
Haven't filed a return for one or more years	An unlimited period

eBay Recordkeeping Tools

eBay offers several great ways to help you track and manage your inventory and sales. Many of those systems are designed to interact with certain popular accounting programs, such as QuickBooks, which can allow you to download data into your accounting files.

One of the first things you'll notice when you begin looking around the seller section of eBay is the tremendous amount of seller tools available to business owners. My eBay, Mpire, Sales Reports, Selling Manager, Selling Manager Pro, and Accounting Assistant are just six of many tools you can use. Following is a brief summary of the key features of each of these six programs, but we encourage you to explore these tools to see how they can fit into your eBay business plans.

My eBay

The My eBay section of eBay is personalized to each user and is password-protected so that your data stays safe. My eBay is a wonderful, centralized access point from which you can access all of your account and service subscription details.

In addition to basics for buyers, such as tracking your purchases, payments, and feedback, My eBay offers several helpful seller-related features. For example, you can easily view your current eBay fees as they are invoiced by eBay. Or, if you work using a different calendar schedule (for example, although you and eBay keep records on a calendar-month basis, eBay's calendar month usually does not begin and end on the first and last day of the month), you can define your dates and view your exact eBay fees for your calendar month. In addition, you can use the eBay archives to view past eBay fee invoices for up to 18 months, which can be helpful if you are trying to re-create proper records for your eBay business.

You can also review your sales in four different ways: listings that are scheduled but haven't yet started, listings in progress, listings of completed items that have sold, and listings of completed items that did not sell. You can easily send invoices and payment reminders directly from My eBay. In addition, you can access all of your subscriptions from the My eBay portal—if you subscribe to Sales Reports or any of the other programs we discuss here, for example, you can quickly access them through the My eBay interface.

Sales Reports

The Sales Reports feature is free to eBay sellers and provides basic information about your eBay sales each month. At a glance, you can see your total number of sales, successful auctions, and average selling price per listing. The Sales Report will also provide you with a summary of your total listing fees and PayPal service fees.

The Sales Report is set up on a monthly cycle that is linked to eBay's billing cycle. This means that it won't always match your records, as your month will begin on the first day, whereas eBay's first day will begin when you sign up and begin selling. Nevertheless, this is great basic information.

While the Sales Report is a nice, simple way to see your eBay progress at a glance, from a bookkeeping perspective it is of limited use, as the amounts it provides are totals and can't be broken down individually. The Sales Reports Plus program is more useful, but it is a subscriber-based service, meaning that you'll have to pay to access the information. You can learn more about this feature by going to http://pages.ebay.com/salesreports/salesreports.html.

Sales Reports Plus

The Sales Reports Plus feature provides all of the same information as the regular Sales Report but also allows you to break out information individually. This could be a great resource for tracking your individual eBay listing fees and PayPal user fees, as you can view them per-transaction, allowing you to enter that information into your books.

The Sales Reports Plus program offers useful features that we appreciate. You can track your buyers to see who are your repeat clients and what they are purchasing. You can also track your sales by merchandise type, and again, get a handle on what people want (so you can sell it to them). Or, you can track your sales by auction type, and find out whether a product sells better through an auction-style format, a Buy It Now fixed-price sale, or through your eBay Store. Finally, using Sales Reports Plus, you can track your unpaid items easily, which will help you to establish the appropriate credits in your books, so you aren't carrying any phantom income or expenses that haven't been offset by a corresponding credit. You certainly don't want to be paying any taxes on income that you haven't received.

Although this program is fee-based, you may find it a small price to pay for the detailed information Sales Reports Plus provides. It's free to all users for the first 30 days, and if you open an eBay Store, you get this service for free. To learn more, visit http://pages.ebay.com/salesreports/salesreportsplus.html.

Selling Manager

The next level of seller tools are the Selling Manager and Selling Manager Pro features. Both tools are designed to help busy eBay business owners manage their sales and inventory more efficiently, by automating many features. Both tools will help you to automate invoices, shipping labels, feedback, and contact with your buyers. You can also manage your relistings quickly with the bulk relisting option. Selling Manager also allows you to download your sales history in an Excel format.

Here are some of the automation features offered in Selling Manager:

- **Status Columns**—Show which post-sales activities you've completed and what you still have to do
- **E-mail and Feedback Templates**—Use customized E-mail templates and stored feedback to help you manage feedback more efficiently
- **Bulk Relist**—Relist multiple sold and unsold listings at once
- **Invoices and Shipping Labels**—Print labels and invoices directly from sales records
- **Download Sales History**—Export your sales records to keep files on your computer
- **Bulk UPI and FVF**—File, track, and manage multiple unpaid items and final value fee requests
- **Bulk Feedback**—Send feedback to multiple buyers all at one time

Selling Manager Pro

Selling Manager Pro has some great additional features. Like Sales Reports Plus, Selling Manager Pro allows you to view detailed sales and merchandise reports to see which items sell and which don't. Selling Manager Pro allows you to track your inventory more efficiently and provides you with alerts when any inventory items are running low. Selling Manager Pro also lets you see details of all of your eBay and PayPal fees, so that you can keep your books up to date.

Both Selling Manager and Selling Manager Pro are subscription-based services, but both are helpful in teaching new eBay business owners how to automate their businesses as much as possible. The more automated your business, the easier it will be to manage, and that in turn will give you more time to spend on marketing and expanding your business. Selling Manager is free for the first 30 days, and a monthly fee is charged after that. Selling Manager Pro is also free for the first 30 days with a monthly fee thereafter. However, eBay Store owners receive Selling Manager for free, and eBay Featured and eBay Anchored Store owners receive Selling Manager Pro for free.

Accounting Assistant

Accounting Assistant is another great eBay seller tool, especially where your accounting records are concerned. While the other programs we've discussed so far provide you with visual information, Accounting Assistant allows you to download that information into your own QuickBooks file. This is a great time-saver, as it will save you from having to re-enter transaction data, and it should prevent common accounting mistakes such as transposing digits.

eBay is still developing this program, but its current version offers these features:

- Easy downloading of eBay and PayPal transactions and fees
- An easy-to-use wizard that lets you tell eBay how you want your data entered into QuickBooks
- The ability to assign eBay sales transactions to existing customers and items in QuickBooks
- Automatic matching of eBay sales transactions to existing customers and items in QuickBooks to minimize data entry time; over time, eBay Accounting Assistant will get smarter about how to match this data to reduce your time spent doing data entry
- The ability to apply QuickBooks classes to segment your eBay sales transactions from other types of sales you may have in QuickBooks
- The ability to export your data to QuickBooks in its complete form so that you don't have to do additional work within QuickBooks

You must be using Selling Manager, Selling Manager Pro, or have an eBay Store to use Accounting Assistant, as it is designed as an add-on feature to these programs, but you don't have to pay extra for the programs. eBay offers Accounting Assistant free to these subscribers (as well as subscribers of some other programs). You must also be using certain versions of QuickBooks to use Accounting Assistant. To learn what versions of QuickBooks are currently being supported, visit eBay's Accounting Assistant web page at http://pages.ebay.com/accountingassistant/.

If there is a shortcoming with the Accounting Assistant program, it would be that it doesn't deal with payments made by anything other than PayPal. So, you will need to track and enter payments manually from customers who send in checks or money orders, or who pay with other online payment services such as BidPay. However, as the majority of online auction payments are made using PayPal, any additional work won't be significant. Besides, eBay sellers are always free to insist that all payments be made through PayPal, which would eliminate that problem entirely.

One other thing to keep in mind is that Accounting Assistant is still a test-stage program, and as such is a bit limited in the applications it currently works with. Here is a list of applications with which it *isn't* compatible (as of fall 2005):

- QuickBooks (any version) for the Mac
- The Canadian, English, Australian, or any other international version of QuickBooks
- QuickBooks Pro, Premier, or Enterprise prior to release year 2002
- QuickBooks Online

- QuickBooks Simple Start
- Quicken
- PeachTree
- Microsoft Money

At the time of writing (fall 2005), eBay indicates that it may develop Accounting Assistant to support some of these applications, depending on user demand. You can also check out PayPal's download feature, which is similar to Accounting Assistant and may work with some of these other software programs.

PayPal Reports

PayPal offers an entire set of tools to help eBay business owners track sales and completed payments. Because PayPal is an eBay company, all of these tools are designed to blend seamlessly with your eBay seller tools.

With PayPal Business user reports, you can do the following:

- View an online record of payments sent and received through the History Log
- Download your transaction history into Quicken or other formats
- View and print up to three past months of transactions on your account. Each month's statement provides totals of payments received, fees, and other credits and debits for each day, so that you can more easily track your transactions
- Receive real-time notifications as payments are processed with instant payment notification
- Use multi-user access to add multiple logins and access levels for your employees, so that they can complete necessary tasks without having access to extraneous features

Visit PayPal's web site at www.paypal.com to learn more about its wide range of features. Although you can use PayPal in all sorts of business environments, it really shines in its partnership with eBay and will undoubtedly become one of your favorite eBay business tools.

Mpire

Mpire is a new tool being developed for eBay sellers that combines all of the other programs we've discussed. With Mpire, you can manage your listings, consignment sales, and financial data, as well as import and manage your eBay and PayPal fees. Mpire also has tools to help you track your shipping and receiving functions and to analyze sales trends, so that you can see what's moving in your inventory and what isn't.

Although Mpire's financial tools section is primarily a checkbook function, it has add-on features that allow it to function at a much higher level and more similarly to a proper accounting program. Plus, its ability to integrate your eBay sales, costs, sales tax, and shipping data automatically could make Mpire a good solution for your eBay business.

You can learn more about Mpire's features and subscription costs at www.mpire.com.

Next Steps—Recordkeeping for Your eBay Business

Perhaps the single most important aspect of your business is the part that no one ever sees—unless you do it wrong. That part is the accounting and record-keeping. Good accounting means that you can take full advantage of all of the legal tax loopholes available to you, become a better business person, and sleep well at night. Bad accounting could mean you run the risk of forgetting deductions and, worse yet, losing deductions if the IRS chooses to audit you.

1. Identify your file storage area.
2. Label file folders for the year.
3. Set up permanent record folders for such items as these:
   - Your corporate records (Articles of Incorporation, Bylaws, Shareholder's Register, Annual Minutes, Annual Reports, Share Certificates, and any other minutes)
   - Your business tax returns (income tax, payroll tax, state-level franchise tax, sales and use tax, and unemployment insurance tax)
   - Equipment or vehicle purchase documents or lease documents
   - Long-term contracts (contracts that will continue for more than one year)
   - Loan or other credit documents (where repayment will take more than one year)
   - Insurance policies
   - General correspondence with federal or state agencies
4. Set up temporary record folders for such items as these:
   - Inventory purchase receipts
   - Sales (invoices, credit memos)
   - Other business-related purchase receipts, such as office supplies, packaging supplies, and so on
   - Business expense reports and copies of all expense receipts where you or another employee has been reimbursed for expenses you incurred on behalf of the business
   - Banking records, including deposit slips, cancelled checks, and monthly statements

5

Financial Statements Made Easy

L et's start off with a snap quiz. Quick—when you think of the words *financial statement*, which (if any) of the following comes to mind?

1. I know exactly what those words mean, what types of financial records are included, *and* how to read and interpret them.
2. I know what those words mean and I have a rough idea of the type of information that will be presented in them, but that's about it.
3. I've heard of that expression.
4. What's a financial statement?

If you answered either number 3 or number 4, then, believe it or not, you're probably in the majority. Financial statements, for the most part, are something that only CPAs fully understand. Not even all business owners truly understand their financial statements. Plenty of business owners out there rely on their financial advisors or in-house accounting staff to prepare the information and sign off on the finished product, hoping that everything is okay.

In this chapter, our goals are to make you a member of that select group of people who *do* understand what financial statements are all about, and to teach you how to read and analyze the information being presented. It's really not that difficult, and you'll be a better business owner for it.

Why People Don't Know How to Read Financial Statements

In all honesty, the reason that most people don't know how to read a financial statement properly is that they've never been taught. Our schools don't do a great job of teaching most of us financial literacy, apart from business or accounting majors. That's unfortunate, because every business owner, small or large, should have a rudimentary idea of what a financial statement is and how to prepare one. Otherwise, how can the businessperson know what money is available to spend and what needs to be reserved for expenses?

If you want your eBay business to be ultimately successful, you need to know how to read financial statements so that you can quickly determine its financial well-being.

Financial statements are made up of three main pieces:

- Balance sheet
- Income statement
- Cash flow statement

Each piece is like a snapshot that shows you part of a larger overall picture. You need all three to see the entire picture, and each one is equally important to the overall image.

The Balance Sheet

The balance sheet is probably the easiest and most well-known of the three financial statements. It shows you, at a glance, what your eBay business owns—and owes—as of the date the statement is prepared.

A balance sheet should show you three things: assets, liabilities, and owners' equity. *Assets* are things your business owns, *liabilities* represent money that your business owes, and *owner's equity* is the difference between the two and represents either your profit or loss. A healthy balance sheet should show a business with more assets than liabilities. A balance sheet going the other way could be a sign of a business in trouble.

> **Three Financial Statements That Paint Your Financial Future**
> - **Balance sheet:** What you are worth, at a glance
> - **Income statement:** How much money you've made over a specific time
> - **Cash flows statement:** Where the money went
>
> Together, they tell your financial story. What story do your numbers tell?

The Accounting Equation

You might not know exactly what these terms mean, but we're betting you've heard the phrase *accounting equation*. The accounting equation is the basic truth of any bookkeeping or financial statement and says this:

$$\text{Assets} = \text{Liabilities} + \text{Owner's Equity}$$

Balance is the goal here. If your assets total doesn't equal your liabilities and owner's equity totals, then your books are not balanced and something has been recorded improperly or is missing. If your books do balance, you should be able to rearrange these terms, just as you would do with algebraic equations. Instead of Assets = Liabilities + Owner's Equity, you could also have Owner's Equity = Assets − Liabilities. And for those of you who don't like algebra, this means that your equity is what you have left when you subtract your liabilities from your assets.

Now let's look at what each of these terms means and see how they fit together.

Assets

Assets are anything that your eBay business owns. On a balance sheet, these are usually broken down into two categories: current and fixed assets.

Current assets are cash and anything else that will be used up or can be converted into cash within one year. One example of a current asset is the inventory that you currently own and are selling. Another example is the money that other people owe you for sales you have made. This is money you haven't collected. In accountant's terms, it is called your *accounts receivable*.

Fixed assets are those with a longer lifespan and are usually tangible things such as equipment, vehicles, buildings and real estate, and machinery.

Liabilities

Liabilities are the debts that your eBay business owes. Like assets, liabilities are also broken down into current and long-term categories. A short-term liability would be something that will be repaid within a year. Some examples of short-term liabilities include taxes that you will have to pay, such as sales tax or income tax, and most accounts payable (money your business owes to vendors or other parties, such as the guy who just fixed your computer). Long-term liabilities are debts that are repaid over a longer period of time. Mortgages, car loans, and leases would all fit into this category.

Owner's Equity.   Owner's equity, or just equity, is the difference between your eBay business's assets and liabilities. If you were to add up all of your business's assets and then subtract all of its liabilities, the leftover amount would be your owner's equity, also called your business's *net worth*. It's not your business's equity, because after all, at the end of the day you own your business—it doesn't own itself.

If your business has fewer assets than liabilities, your owner's equity will be negative. That means that your eBay business has an overall negative net worth. But before you decide that's a bad thing, remember what we said about the overall picture, and that you need all three pieces to see it. Believe it or not, your eBay business may well have a negative net worth overall, even though it puts cash into your pocket each and every month.

Interesting, huh?

To show you what a completed balance sheet looks like, here's what Tia Olivia prepared for Jenny at the end of her business's first year of operations:

Jenny's Balance Sheet

Treasure Trove, Inc.
Balance Sheet
As of December 31, 2006

Current Assets		
Cash	$ 3,725	
Accounts Receivable	450	
Inventory	7,500	
Total Current Assets	$11,675	
Fixed Assets		
Furniture and Fixtures	490	
Less: Accumulated Depreciation	50	
	440	
Equipment	4,250	
Less: Accumulated Depreciation	650	
	3,600	
Total Fixed Assets	4,040	
TOTAL ASSETS		**$15,715**
Current Liabilities		
Accounts Payable	$ 1,410	
Sales Taxes Payable	130	
Short-Term Credit Card Payable	2,600	
Total Current Liabilities	$4,140	
Long-Term Liabilities		
Note Payable (owner loan for start-up expenses and inventory)	5,710	

Total Long-Term Liabilities	5,710	
TOTAL LIABILITIES		**$9,850**
Equity		
Capital Stock	1,000	
Owner's Equity	4,865	
Total Equity		5,865
TOTAL LIABILITIES & EQUITY		**$15,715**

The Income Statement

This piece of the picture shows your eBay business's income, expenses, and profit for the time period it represents. Another common name for this is the *profit and loss statement*.

One important difference between your balance sheet and income statement is that, while they might be prepared for the same period of time, you can't treat your income statement as a balance sheet, because the two statements display different things.

A balance sheet shows a snapshot of your business's overall financial status as of the date it is prepared. An income statement, on the other hand, shows you a summary of your business's income and expenses over a period of time. It doesn't show you how that income and those expenses relate to other aspects of your business. For example, if you had a large, one-time expense in July, your income statement for that month could show that your business had far more expenses than income, and therefore had lost money. If the income statement for that period was all you looked at, the overall picture of your business may be more negative than it really was. Likewise, if you made a significant sale, your business's income may be much higher than its expenses that month. Again, looking only at an income statement prepared for that period you may conclude that your business was much more profitable than it really was. That's why experienced financial analysts usually like to see comparative income statements—in other words, statements in which your currently monthly income and expenses are compared against your eBay business's year-to-date income and expenses.

> **Learning the Language of Financial Statements**
>
> Take a look at Jenny's balance sheet:
>
> - Are her current assets more than her current liabilities? (This is a good sign that the company has a little life left in it.)
> - Is enough cash available to pay all of the current bills? (If not, that could indicate a problem.)
>
> You can find the answers at www.taxloopholes.com/ebaysellers.

Income

Income is generally any money that your eBay business has already received or will receive during a specific time period. Income is classified into two sections: *sales* income and *service* income. Sales income is any money received from selling an actual product and is the income that your eBay business will generally be making. Service income is any money that a business receives from services that the business rendered, such as consulting, for example. Depending on how your eBay business grows and develops, it could very well make service income—especially if you become fabulously wealthy and launch a series of public lectures to teach others how to make their financial dreams come true using eBay.

> **Income Statement at a Glance**
>
> Income – Cost of Goods
> = Gross Profit
>
> Gross Profit – Expenses
> = Net Income

We separate the two types of income primarily because we want to be able to match up the right expenses to the right income. It wouldn't make sense to offset your service income from public speaking against your packaging and shipping costs from your sales items.

Expenses

Expenses are typically payments that your eBay business has made or will make during a specific time period. They're similar to your liabilities, although your liabilities actually represent a debt payable, whereas your expenses represent that debt after it has been paid. Your business's telephone bill, office supplies, packing and shipping supplies, Internet access, and payroll taxes are all examples of expenses.

> **Learning the Language of Financial Statements**
>
> Take a look at Jenny's income statement.
> - Is Jenny building or depleting inventory?
> - If this were your business, what would you do to make more money? (Sell more or decrease expenses?)
>
> You can find the answers at www.taxloopholes.com/ ebaysellers.

Profit. Your eBay business's *profit* is the difference between its income and expenses. The basic equation looks like this:

$$\text{Profit} = \text{Income} - \text{Expenses}$$

You can break this down even further. The *profit* from your eBay business's *service income* is that income minus the expenses associated with providing that service (travel costs to a speaking engagement, for example). The *profit* from your eBay business's *sales income*, on the other hand, is calculated by subtracting both the costs associated with selling that product (packaging materials and postage) and what it actually cost you to purchase that inventory item to begin with. That inventory purchase cost is also called your *cost of goods sold*.

Now that we've broken it down further, your expanded profit equation looks like this:

$$\text{Net Profit} = \text{Income} - \text{Cost of Goods Sold} - \text{Expenses}$$

Net profit is what you have left over, and this money flows back through the books to become a part of your owner's equity.

Jenny's Income Statement

Take a look at the following example that Tia Olivia prepared for Jenny at the end of her business's first year in operations. See if you can spot the similarities and differences in the information presented in the balance sheet:

Treasure Trove, Inc.
Income Statement
As of December 31, 2006

Revenue		
Gross Sales	$ 25,750	
Less: Sales returns & Allowances	200	
Net Sales		$25,550
Cost of Goods Sold		
Beginning Inventory Value	6,000	
Add: Purchases	7,075	
Add: Indirect Expenses	1,675	
Subtotal	14,750	
Less: Ending Inventory Value	7,500	
Cost of Goods Sold		7,250
GROSS PROFIT (OR LOSS)		**$18,300**
Expenses		
Advertising	$ 100	
Bank Charges	250	
Credit Card Fees	150	
Depreciation	700	
Shipping and Packaging	1,450	
Dues and Subscriptions	45	
Office Supplies and Expenses	2,090	
Operating Supplies	260	
Permits and Licenses	450	
Postage	1,850	

Telephone	465
Vehicle Expenses	460
Wages	4,225
Meals Expense	460
Internet Access	480
Total Expenses	13,435
TOTAL NET INCOME **(Gross Profit – Total Expenses)**	**$ 4,865**

The Statement of Cash Flows

The last of our three pictures is the *statement of cash flows*. The information presented here is quite a bit different from that presented in either the balance sheet or the income statement, but no less important.

A statement of cash flows begins with a business's net income and deducts items that impact cash, but not net income. Examples of that are increases or decreases in inventory or accounts receivable. An increase in inventory will not change your net income, but it certainly will impact your cash. The statement of cash flows also adds back items that impact your net income but don't cost you any cash. The best example of that is depreciation. In fact, we call it a phantom expense because it is an expense for income purposes, but never impacts your cash.

The statement of cash flows also breaks down other types of income, such as income from investments your business has made and income it receives from financing, and it deducts the direct costs from those other income sources as well. If you had a line of credit, for example, the statement of cash flows would show all deductions you made for repayments, interest, insurance, and any other costs to service that debt.

> **Understanding the Language of Financial Statements**
>
> Look at Jenny's statement of cash flows:
> - What is the major source of cash for Jenny's company?
> - Is this, or could it be, a problem?
>
> You can find the answers at www.taxloopholes.com/ ebaysellers.

Confused? You're not alone. The statement of cash flows is probably the most difficult of the three financial statements to understand, especially for small business owners who don't have a lot of business or financial education. We believe that's one of the reasons this statement isn't commonly prepared for small businesses. *But that is a real mistake.*

In Diane's opinion, the statement of cash flows is the best indicator of the strength of a business. As she tells it, a business could have plenty of income *and still fail.*

Success Almost Kills a Business

Odetta's eBay store business was growing at a phenomenal rate. Her customized aromatherapy business was a huge hit, and she was having trouble keeping up with the demand for her products. She decided to hire an assistant to help her out, even though she was concerned about the extra costs. Still, Odetta figured that two sets of hands could make twice as many aromatherapy potions, and even though she'd take a short-term hit while she trained Keisha, the money would come back even faster once Keisha was up to speed.

Odetta was also ordering more and more essential oils to broaden her inventory, and she was worried about this as well. But when she spoke to her CPA about her concerns, he assured Odetta that her business was making a lot of money and told her not to worry about it. Odetta didn't have time to study her financial statements but had a lot of confidence in her CPA. He kept showing her an income statement as proof of the buckets of money Odetta was making.

Things were going great until one day, when Odetta found she had no more cash to fund her business, and at the same time had a huge tax bill due on her profits. She didn't understand. If the business was so profitable, and she'd made so much money, where was it?

Odetta wondered if her CPA had done something wrong and took her accounting records to another CPA for a second opinion. The news she received shocked her. The huge inventory of oils she had purchased had eaten up her cash flow, but because inventory wasn't considered an expense or a deduction, she hadn't seen the downside coming. With no offsetting expenses, every time Odetta's CPA had shown her an income statement, she hadn't seen the whole picture and assumed that the huge profit was hers to spend as she saw fit. However, until she sold through her inventory and converted it into cash, she was asset rich, but cash poor.

Her new CPA showed Odetta a statement of cash flows while explaining what had happened. She told Odetta that, although this statement wasn't usually prepared for small businesses, it should be, because it formed a part of the whole financial picture. She added that if Odetta had seen a statement of cash flows six months ago, she may have made some different business decisions and might not be in the position she was in now.

Odetta agreed with her new CPA, but what was done was done, and she needed to focus on saving her business. She took out a second mortgage on her home to fund the business through its next year and moved her financial records to the care of her new CPA the next day. Fortunately, her product's popularity continued, and she was able to recover and stay in business.

The single biggest reason that new businesses fail is that they're undercapitalized (that is, they don't have enough cash flow). New businesses can chew up lots of cash while they're getting established, during slow times, or during times of rapid growth, and that cash has to come from somewhere.

Do you see now why it's so important for you to have a complete picture of your eBay business's finances, and what happens when you are missing a piece of the three-part picture? If you are using an outside CPA or another financial advisor to help with your eBay business recordkeeping, and that person doesn't prepare statements of cash flows for you regularly, ask him or her to do so. If your CPA or financial advisor tries to dissuade you, look for a new CPA or financial advisor.

Jenny's Statement of Cash Flows

Let's take a look at Jenny's statement of cash flows for her first year of operation.

Treasure Trove, Inc.
Statement of Cash Flows
As of December 31, 2006

Cash Provided by Operations

Net Income	$ 4,865	
Increase in Accounts Receivable	(450)[1]	
Increase in Inventory	(7,500)[2]	
Depreciation	700	
Increase in Accounts Payable	1,410	
Increase in Sales Tax	130	
Increase in Credit Card Payable	2,600	
Total Cash Provided by Operations		$ 1,755
Cash Used by Investments		
Investment in Furniture & Equipment	(4,740)	
Investment by Stockholder	1,000	
Total Cash Used by Investments		$ (3,740)
Cash Provided by Financing		
Increase in Note Payable	5,710	
Total Cash Provided by Financing		$ 5,710
Total Change in Cash Flows		$ 3,725
Beginning Cash	0	
Ending Cash	$ 3,725	

1. The reason the increase in Accounts Receivable is deducted is because people owe you money but haven't yet paid, so you have less cash than you would if they had paid you.
2. The reason the increase in Inventory is deducted is because you've spent money to increase your inventory, so you have less cash than you would have if you hadn't bought that inventory.

Analyzing Jenny's Debt-to-Income Ratio

Things were going well for Jenny's business. She and the boys were working their way quickly through all of the unused items around the house and were beginning to think about expanding their operations. Jenny did some research and found a product that she could buy at a price that would allow her to make a profit. She found a wholesale distributor of designer handbags and wanted to begin selling those on eBay as well. But the cost to buy inventory wasn't cheap. Some of these bags cost $1,000 or more at retail stores, and even though the wholesale prices were heavily discounted, she was still looking at an investment of almost $2,000.

Jenny decided now was the time to take out a small-business loan. She sat down with Tia Olivia one afternoon to evaluate her current and future business needs and determined that if she was going to sell designer bags successfully, she needed to upgrade some of her equipment. For example, she needed a better quality digital camera and a faster Internet connection to upload the larger, more detailed photographs she would be taking. She also wanted to upgrade her computer to handle the increased storage space. After running the numbers with Tia Olivia, Jenny decided to ask her bank for a $5000 loan.

The first thing that the bank asked from Jenny was her business's debt-to-income ratio. She learned that even if she took out the loan in the name of the business, she may still need to back it up with a personal guarantee, as her business was too new to have much of a credit rating and didn't have a lot of assets to put up as collateral. This was something Jenny had been expecting, so she didn't complain.

Jenny showed the bank the financial analysis she had prepared with Tia Olivia, which indicated that the business's debt-to-income ratio was 37 percent. They had arrived at this number by dividing the total liabilities (found on the balance sheet) by the business's net income (found on the income statement):

$$\$4,140 \div \$11,090 = 37.3 \text{ percent}$$

Treasure Trove, Inc.
Balance Sheet
As at December 31, 2006

Current Liabilities

Total Current Liabilities $4,140

Treasure Trove, Inc.
Income Statement
For the Year Ended December 31, 2006

Total Expenses 7,210

TOTAL NET INCOME
(Gross Profit – Total Expenses) $ 11,090

Her banker was comfortable with 37 percent and the bank agreed to grant Jenny the loan, as long as she backed it up with her personal guarantee.

The new debt-to-income ratio for her business was 82 percent, calculated as follows:

$$(\$4,140 \text{ (existing liability)} + \$5,000 \text{ (loan)} = \$9,140$$
$$\$9,140 \div \$11,090 = 82.4 \text{ percent}$$

This meant that for Jenny to obtain another loan for her business, she would first have to lower that percentage either by paying down the business's existing debts or increasing its income.

How to Analyze Your eBay Business's Financial Statements

Now that you have a more complete understanding of the types of information you'll find in financial statements, we'd like to show you how to analyze that information. By understanding and tracking the relationships among your eBay business's assets, liabilities, income, and expenses, you'll be able to identify successful trends and potential problems.

One of the easiest ways to analyze your business's financial status is by *ratio analysis*. If that sounds intimidating, it isn't. Why? Because we analyze ratios everyday—miles per hour, calories per day, and cooking measurements are all common ratio analyses that we make without much conscious thought. If someone asks you how fast you were driving, it is much clearer to say "I was driving 60 miles per hour" than to say "I drove 150 miles in 2½ hours."

Common Ratios

Several ratios are used to analyze the financial position of a business. Some commonly used ratios are listed in the table on page 91.

Working *in* Your Business—or Working *on* Your Business

Is your goal to work *in* your business or *on* your business? Be careful of your answer—the difference can be worth millions of dollars.

Early on in Diane's career as a CPA, she met two different contractors. They both made about the same amount of money—$50,000 per year. They both had the same type of bookkeeping system—a big cardboard box in which they threw every scrap of paper. At the end of their first year of business, the first contractor came to Diane and asked how much he owed

Ratio	Equation	Description
Current	Current Assets/ Current Debts	1:1 current ratio means the company has $1.00 in current assets to cover each $1.00 in current liabilities. Look for a current ratio above 1:1 and as close to 2:1 (or higher) as possible.
Debt	Debt/Net Worth	The higher the ratio, the greater the risk to a present or future creditor. Look for a debt-to-equity ratio in the range of 1:1 to 4:1. Most lenders have credit guidelines and limits for the debt-to-equity ratio. (2:1 is a commonly used limit for small business loans.)
Profit Margin	Profit/Sales	This ratio measures the ability of the business to make a profit.
Return on Sales	Net Profit/Gross Sales	Shows how much profit comes from every dollar of sales. Trends from year to year can show whether or not you are managing your operating and overhead costs.
Accounts Payable Turnover	COGS/Average Accounts Payable	The higher the turnover, the shorter the time between purchase and payment. A low turnover may indicate a shortage of cash to pay your bills or some other reason for a delay in payment.
Investment Turnover	Gross Sales/ Long-Term Assets	A volume indicator that can be used to measure efficiency of a business from year to year.
Return on Investment	Net Profit/Net Worth	Compare the return on equity to other investment alternatives, such as a savings accounts, stocks, or bonds.

in taxes. To answer him, her CPA practice had to compile all those scraps of paper and figure how much income he had really made. Of course, with that type of bookkeeping system, some expenses were missed. So, when it was all said and done, the first contractor got two big bills. One of the bills was to pay for all the back accounting services and tax preparation fees. He wasn't happy with that bill. The second bill was to pay for all his back taxes. He wasn't happy with that bill either. He went away blaming everyone for his bad luck.

The second contractor came in with his own big cardboard box. After all the work was done, he was also presented with two bills. The first was to pay for all of the back accounting services and tax preparation fees. He wasn't happy. The second bill was to pay for all his back taxes. That didn't improve his mood. But he asked a question that changed his financial future: "What do I have to do so that this never happens again?"

He set up regular meetings to review his financial statements with Diane and hired a bookkeeper to prepare accurate financial statements. He learned about assets and liabilities. He learned how to read the financial story that was hidden in the financial statements.

Ten years later, the first contractor was still making the same amount of money, about $50,000 per year. The second contractor made $1 million in his thriving business in his tenth year of business. What was the difference? The first contractor worked hard *in* his business. The second learned how to work hard *on* his business. The secret was learning how to read the financial statements and be accountable with his accounting.

Next Steps–Learning about Financial Statements

Financial statements are a window into your business, and show the truth of how your business is really performing. Learning what each element of a financial statement shows you and how to interpret what you see is a powerful tool that you can use to evaluate your business and that of your competitors, and it will also help you to tell the difference between good business opportunities and bad ones.

1. Prepare (or have prepared) financial statements for your business. If you don't yet have a business, prepare a financial statement for your personal financial situation. You can go to www.taxloopholes.com/ebaysellers for more examples of personal and business financial statements.
2. Review the ratios in this chapter. Pick at least three ratios from this chapter and calculate your personal ratios using the formulas here.
3. Compare your own debt ratio to Jenny's. Would Jenny's banker have given you a loan? If not, what can you do to fix that situation?

6

Step-by-Step Accounting Requirements Part 1— Getting Started

Here it is; the chapter you've all been waiting for! For the past five chapters, we've talked about *why* you need good bookkeeping and recordkeeping in your eBay business, but we haven't yet presented the *how to* section. That's what these next two chapters are going to do. In this chapter, we'll show you how to set up your books, and in the next chapter, we'll show you how to process your daily transactions. We've even provided a step-by-step walkthrough of the entire QuickBooks Pro EasyStep Interview that you can refer to when setting up your own file.

Before we begin, let's make one thing perfectly clear. The information in these two chapters isn't in any way meant to replace your bookkeeper or to give you the answer to every question you're going to have. What we hope to do is help you get started—you're still going to need more help along the way.

How to Keep Your eBay Business Records

You have two real choices about how to keep your business records: hire a bookkeeper to do it for you, and do-it-yourself. (A third option, don't do it at all, isn't a viable choice.)

Hire an Outside Bookkeeper

Hiring an outside bookkeeper may be one of the easiest solutions. Of course, as with anything easy, this comes with a price—you will pay bookkeeping fees. An outside bookkeeper is not an employee, so you won't have salary, medical, or payroll taxes to worry about. In fact, hiring an outside bookkeeper as an independent contractor is a great choice, because you can treat all of the costs associated with it as a tax-deductible business expense.

Depending on the volume of your business, you might find that the expense is well worth it. You won't have to worry about keeping your own records. If you are already working another full-time job, chances are good that your eBay business is going to take up a fair amount of your personal time, and adding bookkeeping on top of that may be more time than you are prepared to give up. Plus, passing the bookkeeping function to someone else means you get to concentrate on what you do best—making money on eBay.

You will need to find a good bookkeeper. That means you've got be able to tell the difference between a good one and a bad one. Sadly, some really bad bookkeepers are working out there, so you can't simply turn over the bookkeeping to someone and forget about it entirely. You've got to keep an eye on your books because you also need to be able to talk to your bookkeeper about what's happening financially in your business. If you think that accountants and lawyers seem to have their own language—they do, and you need to learn it!

Being completely ignorant of how bookkeeping works also brings in another set of problems. Plenty of business owners (and ex-business owners) have horror stories about leaving everything to a bookkeeper who was supposedly trustworthy, only to find out later that the bookkeeper had systematically stripped the company of all funds before disappearing.

We recommend you take a balanced approach. Use a bookkeeper as a resource to help you learn about keeping financial records, and allow that person to handle the bulk of your monthly transactions.

Your monthly cost for bookkeeping services can range from about $100 per month to $1,000 per month, depending on the volume of your business and the quality of the records you give to your bookkeeper. A shoebox full of receipts and bits of paper with cryptic notes on them will cost you more in bookkeeping fees than orderly expense sheets with receipts attached.

Find a Bookkeeper.   Look in your local business directory to find available bookkeepers close to home. Or, contact one of the national organizations such as the American Institute of Professional Bookkeepers (AIPB) and the American Institute of Certified Public Accountants (AICPA) to see if any members are listed in your area. Better yet, talk to your friends and other small-business owners. If someone uses a bookkeeper he or she trusts, you might contact that person. You can also find a list of bookkeeping service providers on the companion web site. These providers are all people we've personally found to be dependable, reliable, and helpful.

Supporting the costs of a full- or part-time bookkeeper can often be a difficult task for a starting business owner. That is why business owners should take a more hands-on approach at the beginning. We always recommend that business owners become familiar with all facets of their business—tracking and recording your business financial transactions is one of the most important facets of your business and requires more than just a general understanding of finances.

> Start your search for a bookkeeper and other qualified advisors at www.taxloopholes.com/ ebaysellers. We've compiled a list of people and businesses we personally trust and recommend.

Do-It-Yourself

Some people keep their books manually, using a paper ledger system and a pencil. Others use a spreadsheet program such as Microsoft Excel, which can also work well. The majority of business owners elect to purchase accounting software, such as Peachtree, Simply Accounting, or some form of QuickBooks.

> The quality of the questions you ask will determine the quality of the results you get. Go to the companion web site for a copy of the questionnaire we use to select advisors.

If you decide to do-it-yourself, and you don't have a bookkeeping background, we recommend that you use computer accounting software that is specifically designed for this purpose. Manual accounting methods can be very time-consuming and have the highest probability of something going wrong. Usually, what happens is that you forget to record one side or the other of a transaction—or, even worse, you transpose digits. Either way, your accounts don't balance at the end of the day, and you can spend hours of valuable time looking for the accounting equivalent of a needle in a haystack. With a spreadsheet, or preferably accounting software, that doesn't happen because it can't. The system comes with built-in checks and balances, meaning you can't enter a transaction if you don't have your debits and credits in order and for the same amounts.

Although several different software programs are on the market, our choice for operating an eBay business is QuickBooks Pro. It is simple to use and so widely used that the chances are your bookkeeper or CPA will be familiar with the software. This allows you tremendous freedom, as you can simply e-mail your business's file back and forth to your bookkeeper. In keeping with our ideal of shared recordkeeping, you can enter some transactions on your own, send the file to your bookkeeper along with any additional paper records, and your bookkeeper can easily check to make sure you have entered everything in the right place.

Which Version of QuickBooks Is Right for Your eBay Business?   Three versions of QuickBooks are suited to an inventory-based business: QuickBooks Basic, QuickBooks Pro, and QuickBooks Premier. For very large businesses, QuickBooks Enterprise Edition may also be suitable.

Of the three QuickBooks products, QuickBooks Pro is, in our view, the best of the three. It offers the widest range of services and the ability to grow and expand with your business. All three versions have a great Reports feature, which allows you to create all of the Financial Statements we talked about in the last chapter. In addition, all versions have a great Starting Interview procedure that helps you get your company's personalized files set up.

QuickBooks Pro and QuickBooks Premier have certain features that QuickBooks Basic doesn't, including the following:

- Allows vehicle mileage tracking
- Works with QuickBooks Point of Sale (allowing you to process credit cards—different from PayPal)
- Lets you create budgets automatically
- Lets you make cash flow projections
- Prints packing slips for FedEx and UPS shipments
- Integrates with Microsoft Word and Excel
- Works with more than 325 other popular financial and business software applications

QuickBooks Simple Start.   While writing this book, we took a look at one promising program—QuickBooks Simple Start. It was attractive for its price and ease of use. It was extremely easy to set up and use to record incoming and outgoing money, as well as to track sales and corresponding expenses. But we were disappointed to find out that Simple Start did not provide any method for tracking and recording inventory and does not work with eBay's Accounting Assistant. This limits its applicability for an eBay business, and for that reason we can't recommend it as a solution for your eBay business recordkeeping needs.

Microsoft Money.   Microsoft Money is another popular bookkeeping product, but it has many of the same limitations as QuickBooks Simple Start. Microsoft Money is primarily a personal financial tool. It's great for balancing your checkbook and preparing a personal budget, but it doesn't offer the range of features that you're going to need as an eBay business owner. For the "heavy lifting" of business accounting, we recommend that you use a program with business muscle.

Obtaining a Copy of QuickBooks.   You can purchase QuickBooks just about anywhere software is sold, or you can download it directly from its manufacturer at www.intuit.com or www.quickbooks.com. Intuit has a huge range of features, including online help and tutorials, and can even help you to choose the version that's right for you by walking you through an online quiz about your business.

> We recommend using Intuit's QuickBooks Pro for your inventory-based eBay business. The combination of inventory control features plus the likelihood that your bookkeeper and financial advisors will also be using this program all add up to fewer headaches for you.

Alternatively, eBay is an excellent source of software, and you can often find full, legal, licensed copies of all QuickBooks products at considerably less than retail. If you go this route (and there's no reason not to), make sure that you purchase a legal and licensable copy that has never been previously registered. We never advocate software piracy. Look at the feedback numbers and comments of software vendors closely. You'll find out quickly who is selling legitimate software and who isn't.

Final Thoughts on QuickBooks Selection.   If you purchase QuickBooks on eBay, don't be fooled by sellers who claim to be selling software that includes some of the add-on modules such as Payroll and are charging extra. Every version of QuickBooks Basic, Pro, and Premier includes these modules, but they are all subscription-based. You will need to register with Intuit and pay extra to activate them.

One other thing to bear in mind is that Intuit updates QuickBooks every year. While you might be able to purchase last year's edition at a great price, and it will work just fine, you may find that your bookkeeper is using a newer version that isn't compatible. Fortunately, the yearly upgrades cost less than purchasing a full version.

Educate Yourself

If you decide to do your own bookkeeping, then the very best thing you can do for yourself is to get some education. Take a class at your local community college or community center during the evening or on a weekend. You shouldn't have any problem in finding a class in your area at a time that suits you, as this is an extremely popular subject in most communities.

You can also go to the web site of your accounting software manufacturer to see what in-person and online courses they offer in how to use their products. Intuit, the maker of QuickBooks, is especially good at helping you learn how to keep your accounting records in good order.

QuickBooks Pro Interview Walkthrough

If you aren't familiar with accounting or bookkeeping terminology, you could end up with books that aren't properly set up, which could become a problem at tax time. One of the things we especially like about QuickBooks is its Easy Step Interview that helps you to learn basic book-keeping concepts and terminology, and helps you to set up your books.

The Easy Step Interview is the first thing you'll encounter after you've installed your software. This user-friendly interview was developed by the programmers at Intuit to help establish the right parameters for QuickBooks to operate within.

To show you how the Easy Step Interview process works, we'll walk you through Jenny Guerro's QuickBooks Pro interview for her company and explain a few things along the way.

Jenny Gets Started

Jenny sat in front of her computer as it installed her new version of QuickBooks. Tia Olivia had told Jenny that, while lots of great bookkeeping programs were out there, it would be easiest for her to use QuickBooks Pro, because that's what Tia Olivia used in her practice, and they could easily e-mail files back and forth without any conversion issues. Jenny had found an unregistered copy of an older version of QuickBooks for sale on eBay at a great price, and, after installing and registering it, had purchased the current update for less than it would have cost her to purchase a brand new copy.

As she waited, Jenny reviewed the materials that Olivia told her she would need: the software license number, her corporate documents with the company's legal name and date of incorporation, her company's tax ID number, and her inventory list.

After the software installation was complete, Jenny started up the program. The first thing she saw was the EasyStep Interview Welcome Page (Figure 6.1), which indicated that the interview would be broken down into four main sections: Welcome, Company Info, Preferences, and Start Date.

Jenny read through each screen in the Welcome section in turn. She wasn't asked to provide any information until she got to the Company Info section. The first screen asked her to provide her company's name and its legal name. This was a little confusing to Jenny; she had always thought of the two as being the same. A quick call to Olivia explained the difference: "If you were using a trade name with the public that was a little different from your registered business name, you would want to put that trade name first. That would allow you to keep doing business with the public in the name they already knew. So, if you wanted to, you could put your eBay user name in the first part and add your full legal name to the second line. It's up to you."

Jenny typed in her business's name and continued on (Figure 6.2). The next screen asked for her business's address and phone number, which she completed. When she clicked Next, a new screen asked for her business's tax ID number. Jenny looked through her corporate paperwork to find the number that Olivia had provided for her, and then typed it in. She was also asked for the first months of her income tax year and fiscal year. This was easy for Jenny; as an S Corporation she followed the same January–December calendar as W-2 employees. She typed in *January* for both answers and clicked Next to continue (Figure 6.3).

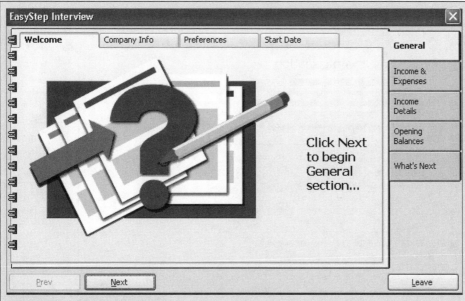

Figure 6.1 The welcome page.

EasyStep Interview

✓Welcome	**Company Info**	Preferences	Start Date

General

Income & Expenses

Income Details

Opening Balances

What's Next

Your company name

Enter your company name as you would like it to appear on invoices, statements, and reports. This is your "Doing Business As..." name:

Company Name

> Treasure Trove, Inc.

Enter your company name as you need to have it on legal documents:

Legal name

> Treasure Trove, Inc.

Tell Me More

What if I have more than one business? [More]

Prev | Next | Leave

Figure 6.2 Enter your business's name.

The next screen asked for the type of tax return her business would be filing. She clicked the arrow to see her choices and selected Form 11205 (S Corporation). Then she clicked Next (Figure 6.4).

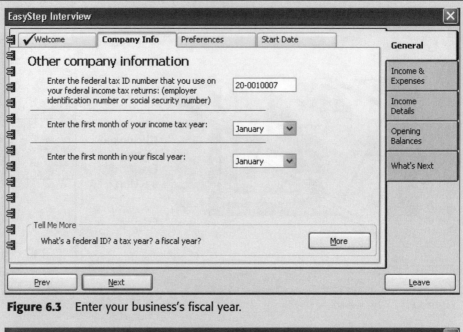

Figure 6.3   Enter your business's fiscal year.

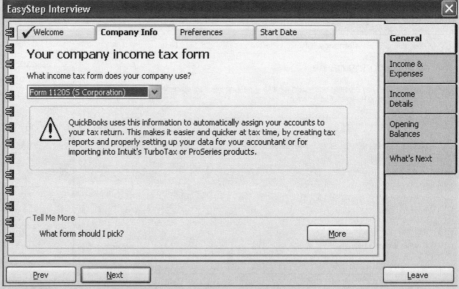

Figure 6.4   Select the right tax form for your business.

The next screen asked her for her business type. She knew from speaking to Olivia that this was an important question, because the IRS has classifications it has developed for businesses, and it expects to see certain types of income, expenses, and spending patterns for each classification. Picking the wrong type of classification could cause her business to present information that was outside of the IRS norms and could increase her business's audit risk. Jenny wasn't concerned about being audited, as she was intending to keep her records in proper order, but she certainly didn't want to invite trouble, either. She scrolled down through the choices and picked the Retail: General for her business, as that seemed the closest match (Figure 6.5).

After selecting her industry type, she went through a couple more informational screens before QuickBooks created her company file, naming it the same as her business name, Treasure Trove Inc.. It then moved on to the next screen, which showed her a chart of accounts and asked if she wanted to use that one or create one of her own. Jenny figured it would be easier to modify an existing chart than to create her own, and this way she wouldn't accidentally leave out anything important. She selected the Yes button and moved on (Figure 6.6).

The next screen asked how many other people would be accessing QuickBooks other than Jenny. She selected the default, 0, because she didn't want either of her sons, David or Roberto, to have access to the bookkeeping records, and Olivia would be working on Jenny's records from her own office. After she clicked Next, she was shown a screen that advised her that a single user, Admin, had been created and asked her to create a password. She did so, and clicked Next to move on to the following screen. She also made a note to e-mail Olivia her username and password when she e-mailed her completed QuickBooks file (Figure 6.7).

After she clicked Next, QuickBooks advised that she had completed the Company Info section and was moving into the Preferences section (Figure 6.8). She clicked through an information screen until she was presented with the next question screen, which asked her whether or not her business would be collecting sales tax. Jenny thought about this for a few minutes. She knew that if she sold to anyone

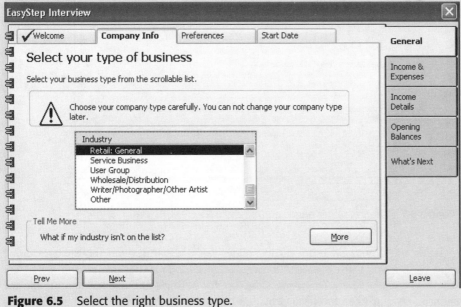

Figure 6.5 Select the right business type.

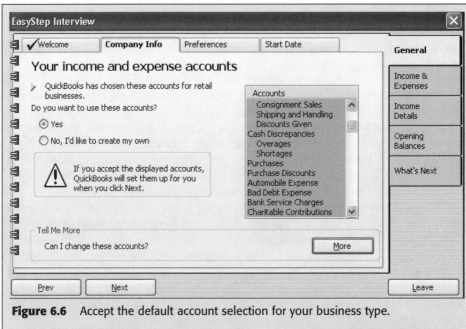

Figure 6.6 Accept the default account selection for your business type.

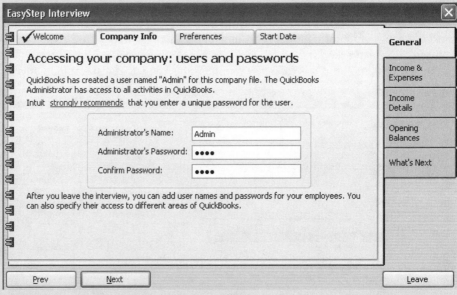

Figure 6.7 Create a user name and password.

in Texas she would be required to collect sales tax and, even though she didn't expect too many sales overall, she decided to click Yes. The next screen asked her whether she would be collecting sales tax for a single tax agency or multiple tax agencies. A quick call to Olivia provided her answer: "You will just be sending any

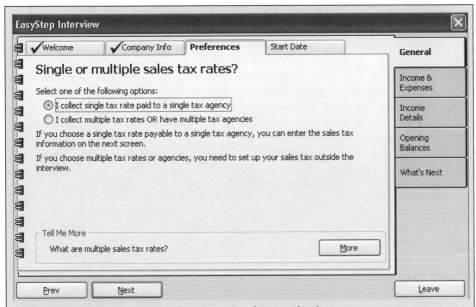

Figure 6.8 Select the right sales tax option for your business.

sales tax you collect to the Dallas branch of the Texas comptroller's office. If you had multiple locations across Texas, you may have different tax agencies and rates, but for your business, selecting the first option will be fine."

Olivia told Jenny to stay on the line while she clicked to the next screen, in case she had more questions. The next screen asked her the sales tax rate she would be collecting, and the name of the taxing agency (Figure 6.9). Olivia provided her with all of this information, and told her to visit the Texas Department of Revenue web site to review the procedures if she needed to (see Appendix 4 for a state-by-state listing of Department of Revenue Web sites).

Jenny clicked through to the next screen and selected an invoice type. She wasn't really worried about the format it took, as eBay produced its own invoices. The following screen asked her about payroll activities, and she clicked No. Olivia was going to help her with payroll and had told Jenny to select No in this instance, as they could set it up together in the future.

The next screen asked her about estimates, and the following screen asked her about tracking time for herself or employees. She didn't think either selection was relevant to her business and clicked No each time.

She then came to a screen that asked her about *classes*. The screen information told her that some businesses liked to track certain types of income against the expenses connected to that income. Jenny thought about this for a few minutes before deciding that it wasn't really going to be relevant to her business, at least at this point. She had only one type of income, after all (Figure 6.10).

After clicking No to the question of classes, she moved on to the next step, where she was asked about whether she wanted to enter her bill payments directly through

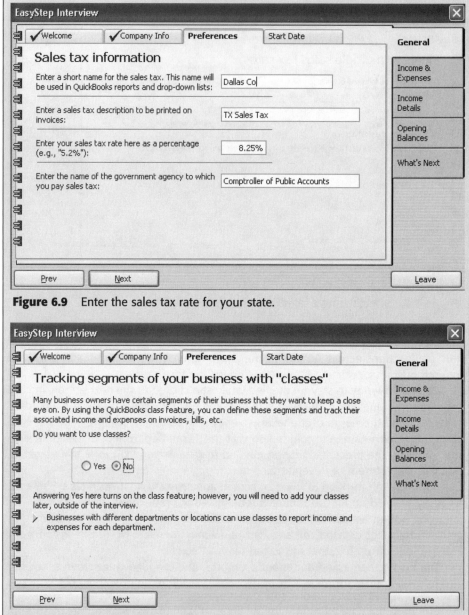

Figure 6.9   Enter the sales tax rate for your state.

Figure 6.10   Turn the "class" feature off for now.

the checkbook in a single step or whether she wanted to enter her bills first, and then enter her payments. It seemed to her that the single-step method would be much easier, as the less bookkeeping she had to do the better, and so she selected the first option (Figure 6.11).

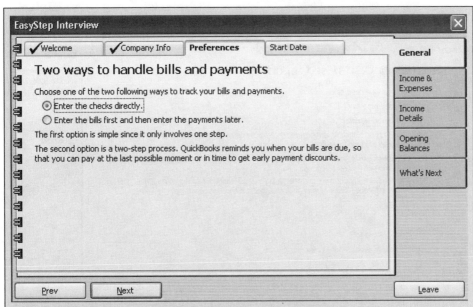

Figure 6.11 Select a method of tracking your bill payments.

The next screen asked Jenny to select when she wanted to view her Reminder list. She decided to keep the default option and moved on. Now, she was being asked to make a choice between *cash* or *accrual-based* accounting. This seemed to be a question for Olivia, so Jenny called her again. Olivia explained that with cash-based accounting, you reported income when you received money and an expense when you wrote a check or paid a bill. The cash basis form of accounting is often used by service providers such as doctors, lawyers, or Olivia's own accounting firm.

"The problem here, though," Olivia continued, "is that this isn't the most accurate method of tracking business expenses. It doesn't take into account money you will receive from sales, which we call accounts receivable, or the expenses you'll pay in the future, which we call accounts payable. The accrual basis of accounting takes both of these things into account."

Olivia explained that anyone who sells product has to be either an *accrual-based* taxpayer or a *hybrid-accounting* taxpayer. That's because the money that is spent buying inventory items is not immediately expensed. The inventory is actually an asset. In normal cash-basis, everything is expensed if you write a check for it (Figure 6.12).

Jenny decided to select the accrual-based method and moved on. She was now through the Preferences section, and moved into the Start Date section, where the first thing she was asked was the date when she wanted to begin entering transactions. She decided to select January 4, 2005, the date her company was formed (Figure 6.13).

After clicking Next, she was told that she was done with the General section and was moving on to the Income and Expenses section. She reviewed a couple of information screens and was then presented with a screen that showed her the income

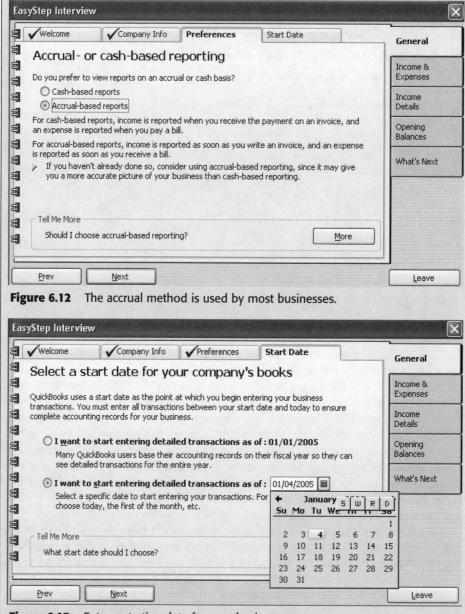

Figure 6.12 The accrual method is used by most businesses.

Figure 6.13 Enter a starting date for your business.

accounts that QuickBooks had selected and was asked whether or not she wanted to add any other income accounts. She noted that she had an income account for merchandise and figured that was all she needed at this point. She accepted the income accounts as presented and moved on (Figure 6.14).

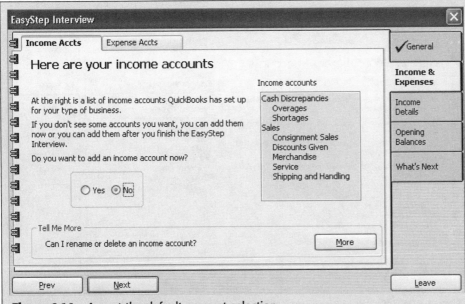

Figure 6.14 Accept the default account selection.

Jenny moved through information screens until she was shown an Expense account screen that was similar to the Income screen she had seen earlier. Again, she was presented with a list of expense accounts that QuickBooks had selected for her, and again she was asked if she wanted to add any more accounts. This time she clicked Yes, because she did want to add a couple of accounts to cover expenses she knew she was going to have: her eBay and PayPal fees (Figure 6.15).

Now she was shown a screen that asked her to select an Account Name and a Tax Line. She called this expense account eBay Listing Fees, and clicked the arrow on the Tax Line question to see her options. She was presented with a huge list of possibilities that included Income accounts, Cost of Goods Sold accounts, Deductions, Schedule K, and more.

The selection was long and confusing, so Jenny put in another call to Olivia. She apologized for asking so many questions, but Olivia assured her not to worry, and that it was more important that Jenny got things right. She asked Olivia about all of the different categories and said that she couldn't even read them all properly. Olivia told Jenny first to open up the drop-down menu by clicking the arrow next to the Tax Line, and then to grab the bottom right-hand corner of the drop-down menu, by clicking and holding it with her left mouse button, and then dragging it fully open by moving her mouse to the right. This expanded the window enough so that she could read each line fully.

"Now that you can see everything properly," continued Olivia, "scroll down to the Deductions section. You aren't operating a Schedule K business; in fact, if you read them, you'll see those entries all relate to real estate somehow. And because we're dealing with an expense here, it's not going to be associated with an Income

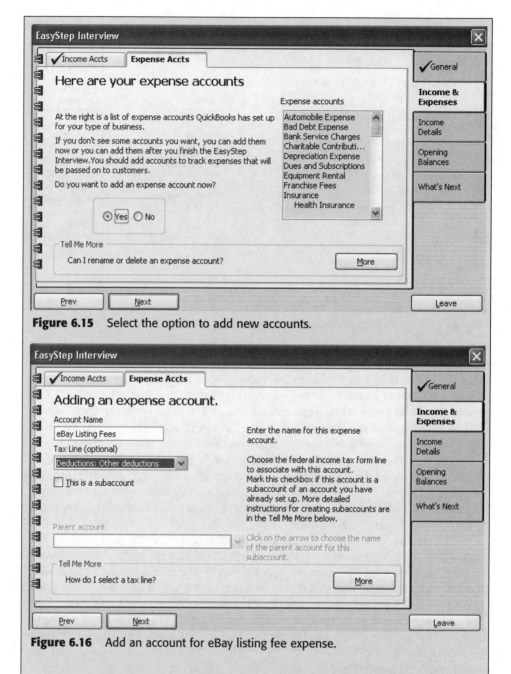

Figure 6.15   Select the option to add new accounts.

Figure 6.16   Add an account for eBay listing fee expense.

or a Balance Sheet item. So, what you need to do is select the most appropriate item from the Deductions options (Figure 6.16). If you can't find one that matches, don't worry about it. Just select the Deductions: Other Deductions category; that'll be fine."

Jenny finished creating her eBay Listing Fees Expense account and then followed the same steps to create her PayPal Fees Expense account. She then told QuickBooks that she was finished creating Expense accounts, and worked through the next few screens until she reached the next section, which asked her about Income Details. The first question here was whether or not Jenny received payment in full when she sold an item, and she clicked Always. She certainly wasn't planning on shipping any eBay items until she had been paid (Figure 6.17).

She moved through the next few information screens until she was asked about whether or not she wanted to set up an account for Service Items. As she was selling only merchandise and not services, she clicked No and moved to the next screen, which asked her about Non-Inventory Parts.

This was another confusing question! Jenny thought about it carefully. She didn't think that she had any non-inventory parts, but what about the things that she purchased to help improve her existing inventory, such as new cables or power cords? Would they count here?

Another call to Olivia set her straight. The improvements she made to her inventory items would become a part of her inventory and could be expensed out as a part of her Cost of Goods Sold. She selected No and moved on. The power cord she bought to fix her office printer would be considered a non-inventory part. It was necessary for her to do business, not to improve the inventory items she sold (Figure 18).

Now she was asked whether or not she wanted to set up an "Other Charges" item. Jenny saw that QuickBooks mentioned shipping that was charged to customers as a typical Other Charges item, and decided to set up a shipping and handling item, clicking Yes (Figure 6.19).

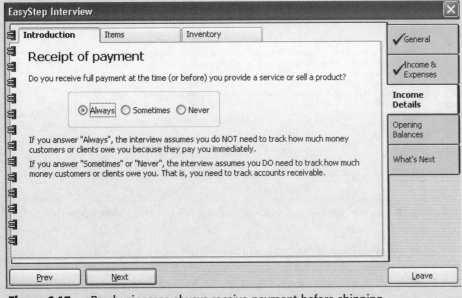

Figure 6.17 eBay businesses always receive payment before shipping.

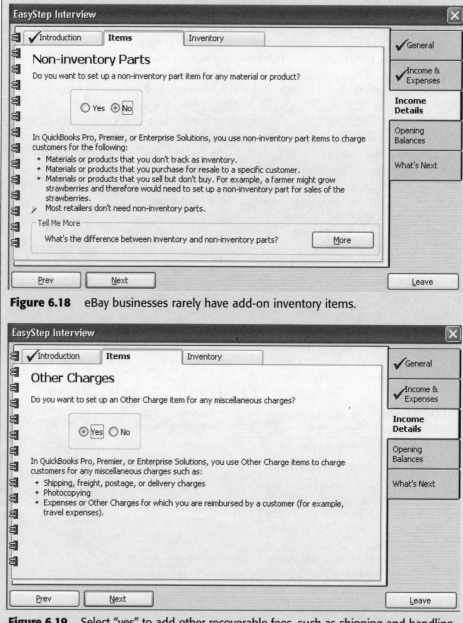

Figure 6.18   eBay businesses rarely have add-on inventory items.

Figure 6.19   Select "yes" to add other recoverable fees, such as shipping and handling.

She named the item "Shipping and Handling," and left the sale price blank, as this would change with each item she sold (Figure 6.20).

Clicking Next, she was then asked for an Income account to associate with her Shipping and Handling item. When she clicked the drop-down arrow, she

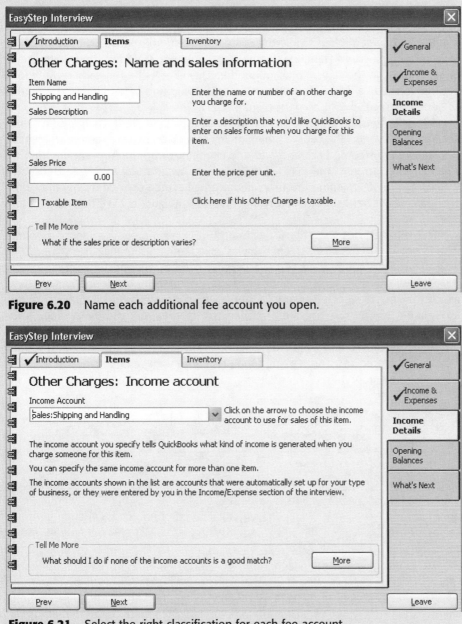

Figure 6.20   Name each additional fee account you open.

Figure 6.21   Select the right classification for each fee account.

saw an Income account called "Sales: Shipping and Handling" and selected it (Figure 6.21).

The next screen asked if this was an item for which she was reimbursed. When she clicked Yes, she was taken to a screen that asked her for some corresponding purchase information. She entered "Shipping and Handling" again, and left the cost blank, as again, this would differ with each sale she made.

The next screen asked Jenny to provide an offsetting Expense account that went with her Shipping and Handling charge. This time, she used the drop-down menu to scroll through the Expense accounts that QuickBooks had already created. She decided to create a new Expense account, called Shipping & Handling, and used that as her offsetting Expense account (Figure 6.22).

After she finished creating her Shipping & Handling Other Charge item, Jenny decided to move on. She couldn't think of any more Other Charge items, and figured she could always come back and add one later, if it came up. After clicking through a couple more screens, she reached the Inventory section. She told QuickBooks that she wanted to set up some Inventory items, and a screen opened for her first item.

She got out her list of inventory and started in (Figure 6.23). The first item was *Used CDs*.

She left the Sales Price blank because the CDs would sell for varying amounts. When she went to the next screen, she was asked to associate the sales of Used CDs with an Income account. She selected Sales:Merchandise, and moved on (Figure 6.24).

She left the next screen, about Purchase Information, blank and clicked Next, which took her to a screen asking for her opening quantity and value. She typed in the number of CDs she and the boys had collected to sell, and the average value they had assigned for their CDs of $5.00 each, or $450.00 in total (Figure 6.25).

After she clicked Next, she was asked if she wanted to enter another Inventory item. Jenny clicked Yes, and repeated the procedure until she had typed in all of the beginning inventory items. When she was finished, she clicked No to indicate she

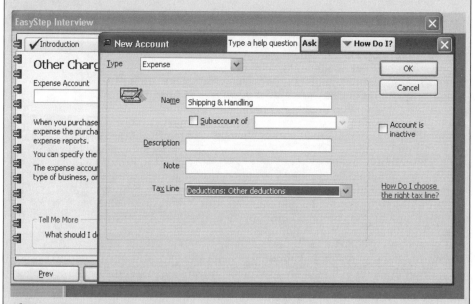

Figure 6.22   Create an offsetting expense account for each recoverable fee account.

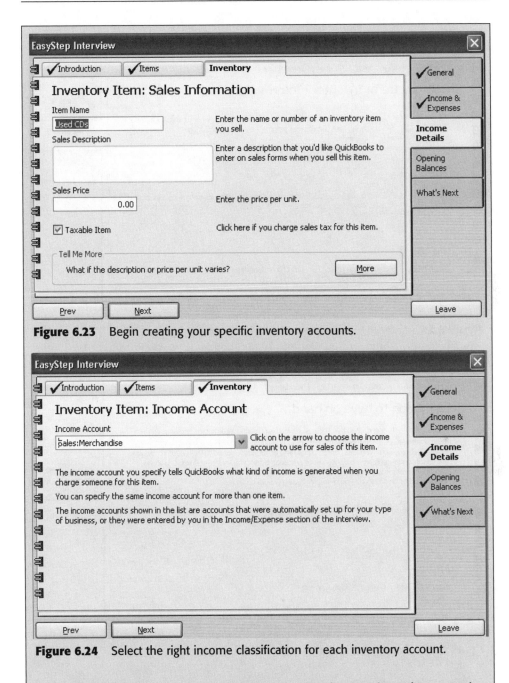

Figure 6.23   Begin creating your specific inventory accounts.

Figure 6.24   Select the right income classification for each inventory account.

would not be entering other Inventory items. She saw the Opening Balances section. She reviewed some information screens until she reached a screen telling her about information she needed to have handy before continuing. She stopped briefly to double-check her paperwork before moving on (Figure 6.26).

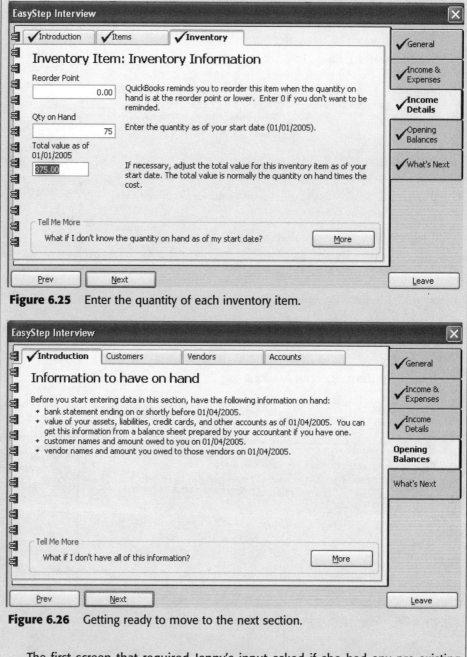

Figure 6.25   Enter the quantity of each inventory item.

Figure 6.26   Getting ready to move to the next section.

The first screen that required Jenny's input asked if she had any pre-existing customers who owed her money. As all of her eBay purchases had been paid already, she selected No. Then she got curious, and selected Yes instead. A new screen asked for the customer's name and the amount owing. Curiosity satisfied, she clicked Prev until she got back to the Enter Customers screen and reselected No (Figure 6.27).

Now a screen told her she didn't need to enter Vendors, the people or businesses her company would owe money to, because she had earlier elected to record her bills when she wrote out her checks, and she could set up her Vendors later (Figure 6.28).

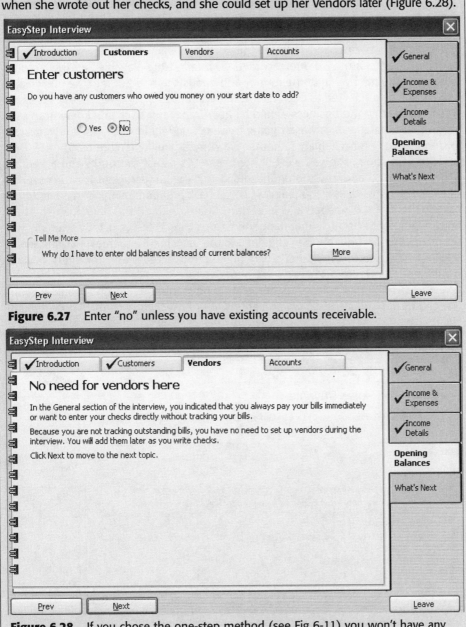

Figure 6.27   Enter "no" unless you have existing accounts receivable.

Figure 6.28   If you chose the one-step method (see Fig 6-11) you won't have any vendors.

The next screen asked if she had any business credit card accounts to set up. As she didn't, she clicked No here and moved to the next screen, which asked her whether her business had any lines of credit that needed to be recorded. Again, as she didn't, she chose No and clicked Next. Now, she was asked if she had any Notes or Loans Payable, and this time she clicked Yes, as she needed to record the money she had put into the business so far for its startup expenses, and for the value of the inventory she had transferred to the business (Figure 6.29).

The next screen asked Jenny to name the Liability account and provide the opening balance amount. She recorded "Owner's Note Payable" as the account name, and the total value of the money and goods she had put into the business of $3,570. She also selected to characterize the account as a Long-Term Liability, as she wasn't sure when the business would be able to pay her back and knew from talking to Olivia that if a debt wasn't going to be repaid within one year, it was characterized as a long-term liability rather than a current liability (Figure 6.30).

The next screen showed a list of her business's liability accounts and asked her if she wanted to add any more. She didn't think so, and clicked No to move on. Again, she reasoned, she could always come back and add anything that she forgot or didn't realize she needed at a later date. She didn't add the bank loan she took out (in Chapter 5) because that happened much later in the year, long after she had set up her original books. When she did add the bank loan, later that year, she would create a new account from her Chart of Accounts screen, and the entry process would look like Figure 6.31.

Now QuickBooks asked whether or not she wanted to set up a bank account. She clicked Yes and chose to set up her business's checking account. As soon as she

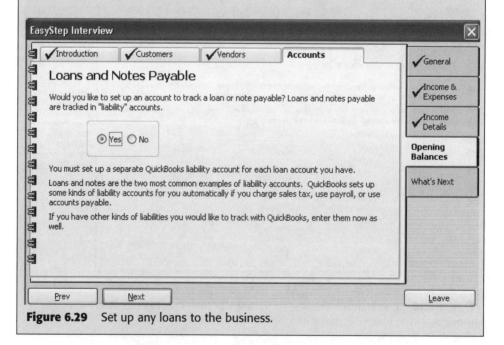

Figure 6.29   Set up any loans to the business.

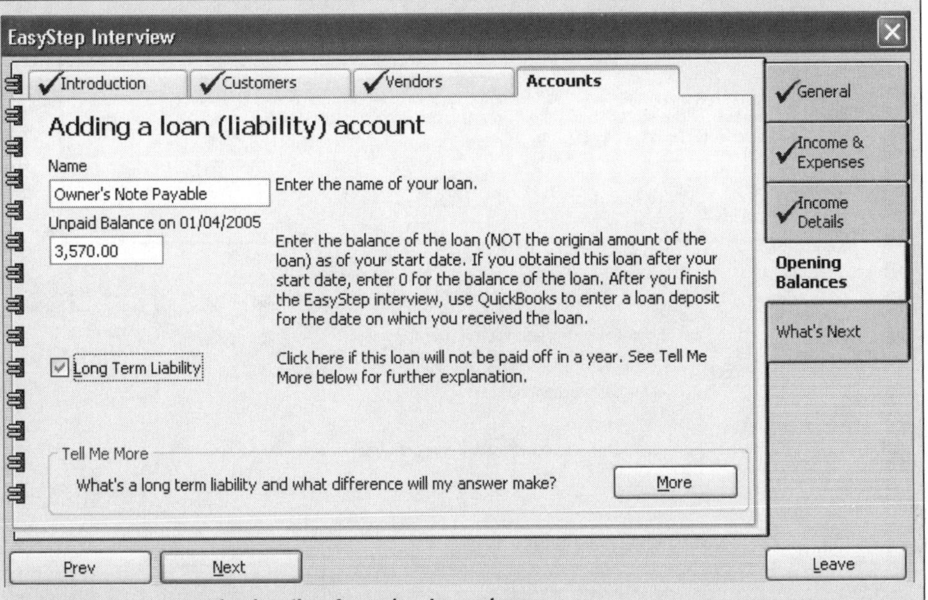

Figure 6.30 Provide details of any business loans.

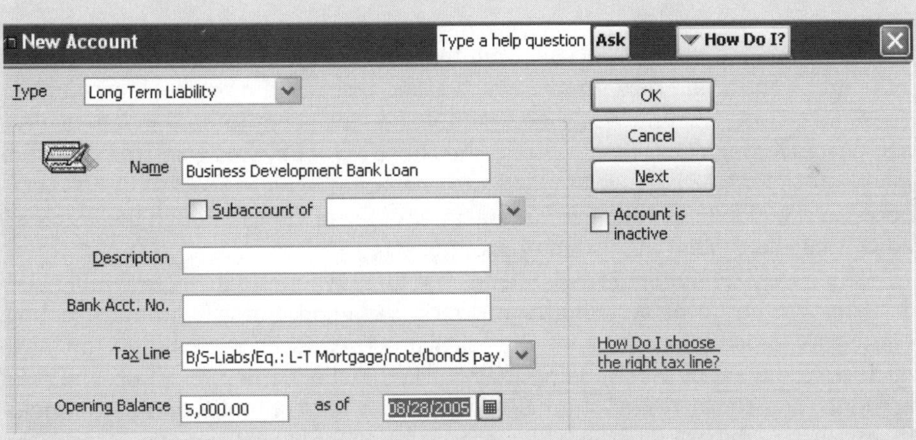

Figure 6.31 Classify any business loans and starting dates.

had typed the name of her bank and clicked Next, a screen asked her about the opening balance for this account, which could be found on the bank statement issued before the business start date.

This was really confusing. She hadn't opened her bank account until after her business had been incorporated. Then she noticed a statement that said exactly this: What if the account wasn't opened until after the start date? She clicked More, and a pop-up window appeared with the answer to how to complete that screen (Figure 6.32).

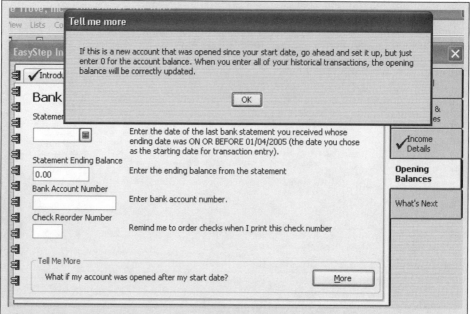

Figure 6.32   Set up your business's bank accounts.

Jenny entered her bank account number, left the Statement Ending Balance at 0.00, and went to the next screen, which asked if she had more bank accounts to open. She chose No, and was then asked if she was going to be printing invoices and checks through QuickBooks. Again she chose No—eBay was going to be her primary source for creating invoices, and she was going to write checks from a checkbook, so she didn't see the need to run either of these things through the automated QuickBooks system at this time (Figure 6.33).

Jenny was beginning to get tired and wondered when this interview would end! It seemed to her to be very thorough, which was good, but very time-consuming. Clicking Next to move on from the deposit slip question, she went through an introductory screen about assets, before being asked if she wanted to set up any asset accounts. She chose Yes, as she needed to record her computer and office equipment, along with her other bits and pieces, such as the digital camera. Because the items she was entering all qualified as *fixed* assets (in other words, assets that wouldn't be used up within one year), she clicked the drop-down box and selected Fixed Asset (Figure 6.34).

The next screen asked if she tracked depreciation. Olivia had told her to choose Yes, so she did so and moved to the next screen. Now, she was being asked for the original cost of the item plus the amount of appreciation to be credited to that account as of the starting date for her business. This prompted one more call to Olivia, as Jenny wasn't sure whether the original amount meant what she had paid for her computer, or what it was worth when she sold it to her business. Olivia told her that in this instance she needed to record the cost the business paid for the com-

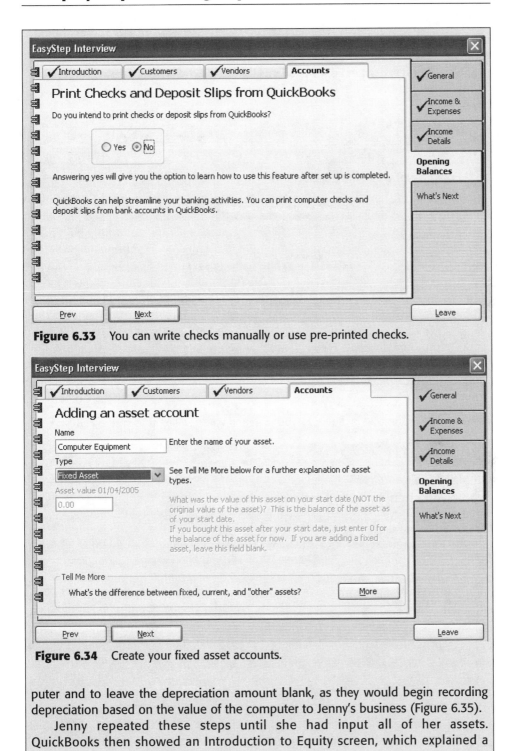

Figure 6.33   You can write checks manually or use pre-printed checks.

Figure 6.34   Create your fixed asset accounts.

puter and to leave the depreciation amount blank, as they would begin recording depreciation based on the value of the computer to Jenny's business (Figure 6.35).

Jenny repeated these steps until she had input all of her assets. QuickBooks then showed an Introduction to Equity screen, which explained a little bit about what the Equity accounts were and how they worked (Figure 6.36).

She then saw a list of Equity accounts that QuickBooks had assigned to her business (Figure 6.37).

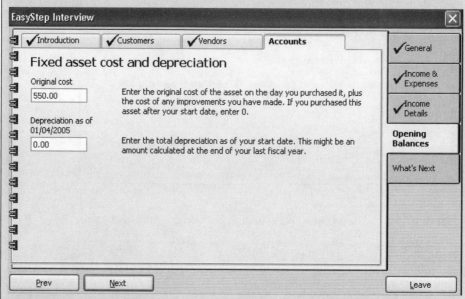

Figure 6.35   The cost is the value you assigned when selling it to your business.

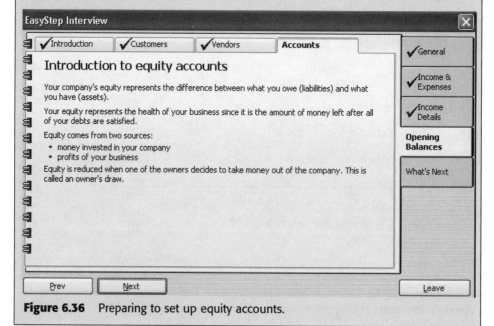

Figure 6.36   Preparing to set up equity accounts.

When she clicked Next, she saw a welcome surprise! QuickBooks told her that she was finished with the immediate setup and set out a list of recommended tasks for her to do before her books would be considered complete. Each bullet point was dealt with separately on the next few screens that followed (Figure 6.38).

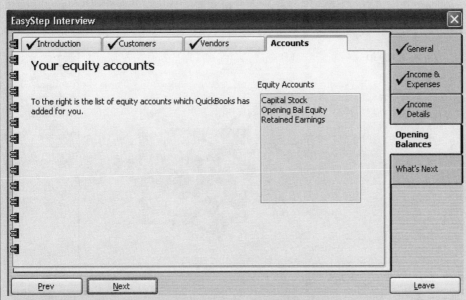

Figure 6.37 Standard equity accounts for an S Corporation.

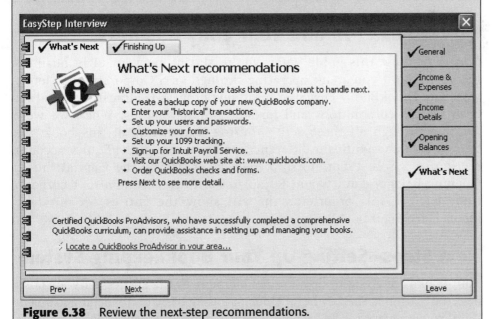

Figure 6.38 Review the next-step recommendations.

Jenny clicked through each screen in turn. It seemed to her that the first thing she needed to do was to get all of her historical data transactions entered—but not just yet. It had been a very long computer session. When she reached the final screen, she clicked Leave and shut down QuickBooks for the time being (Figure 6.39).

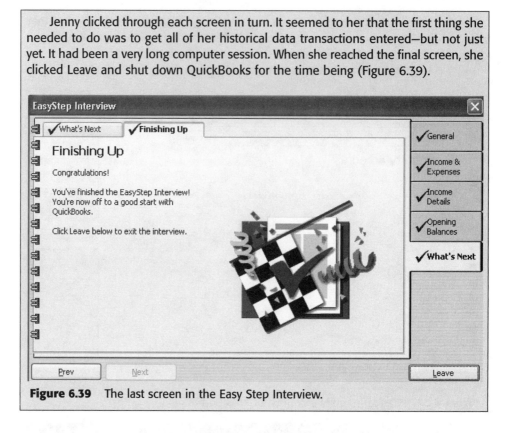

Figure 6.39   The last screen in the Easy Step Interview.

QuickBooks Pro and Your eBay Business

You can follow this guide when you're setting up your eBay business records, even if you aren't operating through an S Corporation, as Jenny was. The QuickBooks EasyStep Interview process is almost identical for both regular corporations and for sole proprietorships. When we were running through all three setups during the writing of this book, we found only one significant difference, and that was in the Equity account section of a Sole Proprietorship. Instead of having the Capital Stock, Opening Balance Equity, and Retained Earnings accounts that corporations have, a sole proprietorship will show the entries set out here instead (see Figure 6.40).

Next Steps—Setting Up Your Bookkeeping System

Your books are going to be a crucial element to the success of your business. Education is the key here! Understanding basic bookkeeping is essential if you are planning to keep your own accounting records. Even if you're

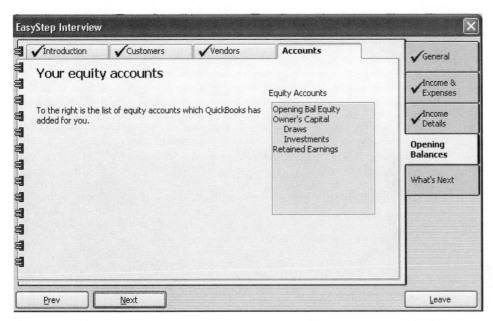

Figure 6.40   Standard equity accounts for a sole proprietorship.

planning on getting outside help, understanding basic bookkeeping will help you to protect yourself by keeping an eye on your business's finances and not being completely dependent on an outside bookkeeper.

1. If bookkeeping is new to you, consider taking a night or weekend class to learn some bookkeeping fundamentals and how to record different types of transactions.
2. Review accounting software needs. If you have decided to have an outside bookkeeper perform all functions, you may still want to consider using the software for your personal financial statements.
3. If you, like the majority of experienced eBay users, decide to use QuickBooks Pro, review the tutorial that accompanies the package.
4. Begin setup. As you go through the Easy Step Interview, these are some of the items you'll need to know:
   - Company name
   - Address
   - EIN (tax ID number)
   - Beginning month of year-end
   - Inventory list
   - Asset list

7

Step-by-Step Accounting Requirements, Part 2—Basic Bookkeeping Techniques

Now that you've got your books ready to go, it's time to input daily transactions, pay bills, record eBay sales, account for your PayPal fees, balance your business checkbook, and do all those other bookkeeping tasks.

If you've had bookkeeping experience, keeping records of your eBay business probably isn't going to be difficult. But if you're a bookkeeping newbie, and you plan to do the books for your eBay business, our first suggestion is to take a night class in bookkeeping. In fact, even if you have decided to turn your records over to a professional bookkeeper, it's still a good idea to understand the basics of how books are kept. Knowing what's what means less risk for you, since you aren't as vulnerable to fraud and can avoid bad bookkeeping practices.

First, let's go through a bit of terminology and the double-entry bookkeeping concept to make sure we're all clear on the basics.

An Accounting Primer

You've already learned about the accounting equation (Assets = Liabilities + Owner's Equity). You keep that equation balanced by making sure that every entry you make to one account is offset by an entry (or entries) to another account. That's called *double-entry bookkeeping* because two or more entries are made for every transaction.

Each entry should include both a positive entry (called a *debit*) and a corresponding negative entry (*credit*). When we say *positive* and *negative*, we're referring to math terms only. Although assets are generally positive (they increase a business's value), one of the things that offsets them is owner's equity (your ownership share), which is on the other side of the equation. But your share certainly isn't negative, right? In fact, it's a pretty darned positive thing!

Debits make accounts on the left side of the equation go up. Adding cash to your bank account from a sale makes it go up and would show as a debit entry in your cash account. Spending money, on the other hand, would make your bank balance go down. That entry would be represented as a credit to your cash account.

Figure 7.1 shows a *T-account*. We call it a T-Account because the lines we use to divide the debit side from the credit side are shaped like the letter "T." Figure 7.1 demonstrates how money flows in and out of a business's checking account.

Credits make accounts on the right side of the equation go up, while debits make them go down. Increasing your debt by taking out a car loan, for example, would increase your liabilities, and would be represented by a credit entry in your car loan account. Making a payment on your car loan would decrease your liabilities and would be represented by a debit entry. If you increased your loan for any reason, that increase would be represented by an additional credit entry.

Figure 7.2 shows the T-account for a car loan.

To keep your accounting equation balanced, you need to make sure that each entry you've made in your cash and car loan accounts has a corresponding entry somewhere else. If you look at Figures 7.1 and 7.2, you can see that the $494.00 loan payment shows up as a credit to your cash account and has its corresponding debit in your car loan account.

Sometimes, your debit and credit will be made on the same side of the equation. For example, the $25.00 you earned from selling an item on eBay

Cash Account		
Debit	Credit	
2,000.00		Opening Balance
	494.00	Money you spend is shown as a credit
25.00		Money you earn from selling items is shown as a debit
1,531.00		Balance after debits are added and credits are deducted

Figure 7.1 T-Account demonstrating cash moving in and out of business bank account.

Car Loan Account		
Debit	Credit	
	30,000.00	Opening Balance
494.00		A payment on the loan is shown as a credit
	10,000.00	An increase to the loan is shown as a debit
	39,506.00	Balance after credits are added and debits are deducted

Figure 7.2 T-Account demonstrating how car loan payments are recorded.

would also have a corresponding credit to your inventory account, as it has just been reduced by that item. Both of these items are asset items, so they would completely offset each other and your overall equation would not change. In this case, you wouldn't need to make an entry to the liabilities or owner's equity side of the accounting equation because the overall asset balance hasn't changed—it's just been redistributed between asset accounts. Figure 7.3 illustrates this.

That's really all bookkeeping is—just making sure that two entries are made for every transaction and that at the end of the day, the Assets = Liabilities + Owner's Equity equation is kept in balance. The rest of the job is simply knowing what account to debit and what account to credit for each transaction you record.

> You can download a customized chart of accounts for eBay businesses at the companion web site, www.taxloopholes.com/ebaysellers.

Chart of Accounts

Establishing your eBay business's chart of accounts is the first step you will take. Much of this will be taken care of during the Setup Interview QuickBooks takes you through when you first install the program.

The chart of accounts is your eBay business's roadmap and will contain every account you will be using. It will include some basic categories: income, expenses, assets, and liabilities, as well as equity accounts.

Income Accounts

Income accounts track the income your eBay business earns, and they appear on its income statement or profit and loss statement. Your business will probably earn most of its income from eBay sales, but income can come from other sources as well. For example, if you are working as a trading assistant you will be earning commission income. The number of income accounts you use will depend on how far you want to break down your income. We've provided a few examples in Table 7.1

Sample Balance Sheet

Assets:		Liabilities:	
Cash	$ 7,250.00	Car Loan	$ 8,333.00
Inventory	4,350.00	Accounts Payable	795.00
Total Assets:	**$11,600.00**	**Total Liabilities:**	**$ 9,128.00**
		Owner's Equity	$ 2,472.00
		Total Liabilities and Owner's Equity	**$11,600.00**

After recording the $25.00 sale, the Balance Sheet would look like this:

Sample Balance Sheet

Assets:		Liabilities:	
Cash	$ 7,275.00	Car Loan	$ 8,333.00
Inventory	4,325.00	Accounts Payable	795.00
Total Assets:	**$11,600.00**	**Total Liabilities:**	**$ 9,128.00**
		Owner's Equity	$ 2,472.00
		Total Liabilities and Owner's Equity	**$11,600.00**

Increasing Cash by $25.00 and decreasing Inventory by $25.00 does not change the Total Assets amount.

Figure 7.3 Sample balance sheet demonstrating change within assets.

Table 7.1 QuickBooks Chart of Accounts for Income Accounts

Number	Account Name	Description
101	Income from sales	Income received from goods sold on eBay
102	Income from commissions	Income received from trading assistant sales
103	Income from sales discounts	Income received from bulk product discounts
104	Miscellaneous income	Income received from miscellaneous sources

Expense Accounts

Expense accounts track the expenses that your eBay business incurs and also appear on its income statement or profit and loss statement. This is going to be one of your largest categories, especially if you are taking advantage of all of the business deductions available to eBay business owners. That makes these accounts particularly important at tax time, and, in fact, we recommend that you categorize these accounts with taxes in mind.

The following table shows a list of some common expense categories that you might use. We have broken down all of the potential eBay expense accounts that you could use, but you could also choose to combine several of these items into a single "eBay Listing Fees" account, or add an "eBay Enhanced Listing Fees" account to cover some of the other items, such as paying extra for featured listing status, and so on.

Table 7.2 QuickBooks Chart of Accounts for Business Expenses

Number	Account Name	Description
201	Advertising Expenses	Money spent on advertisements
202	Accumulated Depreciation	You can break this out into separate accounts to detail your businesss ho me office depreciation, vehicle depreciation, and personal property depreciation, which all accrue at different rates
203	Auto Expenses	Gas, repairs, insurance, and so on
204	Bad Debts	Accounts payable that won't be collected
205	Bank Fees	Service charges
206	Books and Professional Publications	Educational materials (such as this book)
207	Bookkeeping and Accounting Expenses	Payments for bookkeeping, CPA services, and tax preparation
208	Charitable Contributions	Organizational charity donations
209	Computer Supplies	Computer accessories and supplies
210	Dues and Publications	Business association memberships, subscriptions to business-related magazines or newsletters, and so on
211	eBay Bold Lettering Fees	Display fees
212	eBay Border Fees	Display fees
213	eBay Featured Plus Fees	Exposure costs
214	eBay Final Value Fees	Fees for additional detail
215	eBay Gallery Featured Fees	Display fees

Table 7.2   continued

Number	Account Name	Description
216	eBay Highlight Fees	Display fees
217	eBay Homepage Featured Fees	Exposure costs
218	eBay Listing Designer Fees	Display fees
219	eBay Listing Fees	Fees incurred from listing on eBay
220	eBay Opinions, Authentication, Grading	Grading fees
221	eBay Picture Pack Fees	Fees for additional picture services
222	eBay Picture Show Fees	Fees to display multiple pictures
223	eBay Reserve Fees	Fees to insure minimum price
224	eBay Schedule Start Time Fees	Fees to date your sales
225	eBay Show as Gift Fees	Display fees
226	eBay Store Fees	Rent for your eBay Store
227	eBay Subtitle Fees	Fees to provide additional detail
228	eBay Super Size Picture Fees	Fees to make larger pictures
229	Education Expenses	Seminars, workshops, eBay University classes, and so on
230	Insurance Expenses	Insurance premiums
231	Interest Expenses	Interest that you pay on any loans your business has
232	Internet Fees	Internet service provider fees
233	Legal Expenses	Attorney fees
234	Meals and Lodging	Must have a business purpose
235	Office Supplies	Pencils, staplers, paper, and so on
236	PayPal Mass Payment Fees	Fees per payments
237	Paypal Money Back Guarantee Fees	For buyers only
238	PayPal Transaction Fees	Fees per transactions
239	Payroll Expenses	Business payroll expenses such as workers compensation and unemployment insurance
240	Payroll Taxes Expense	Business payroll taxes (half of the total Social Security and Medicare payments that the business makes)

Table 7.2   continued

Number	Account Name	Description
241	Payroll Taxes—Employee Contributions	Records the other half of payroll taxes that are deducted and withheld from salary checks
242	Postage	Shipping and postage expenses, including additional fees such as insurance, delivery confirmation, and so on
243	Sales Tax Expenses	After you have paid the sales tax you've collected from sales it becomes an expense on your books
244	Shipping Expenses	Packaging supplies such as boxes, packing peanuts or bubble wrap, labels, tape, and so on
245	Telephone	Telephone usage for business (including cell phones)
246	Trading Assistant Expenses	Expenses such as postage, shipping supplies, and mileage associated with your trading assistant activities
247	Utility Expenses	Energy costs (heat, light, water, electricity, gas), garbage collection
248	Wages and Commissions	Payments to others (for example, you, your kids, or any independent contractors you use)

Asset Accounts

Asset accounts are made up of your eBay business's current assets and fixed assets and appear on its balance sheet. Some of these accounts will be broken down even further in QuickBooks. For example, accounts receivable would be broken down into individual accounts, so that you can see either a total figure or a detailed per-customer view.

Following is a list of typical asset accounts that your eBay business might use:

Table 7.3   QuickBooks Chart of Accounts for Business Assets

Number	Account Name	Type
301	Accounts Receivable	Current
302	Bank Checking Account	Current
303	Bank Savings Account	Current

Table 7.3   continued

Number	Account Name	Type
304	Computer Equipment	Fixed
305	Digital Camera Equipment	Fixed
306	Inventory	Current
307	Office Furniture	Fixed
308	Office Equipment	Fixed (photocopiers, postage machine, postage weigh scale, printers, scanners, network equipment, cables)
309	Vehicles	Fixed

Liability Accounts

Liability accounts comprise current and long-term liabilities and offset the assets on your eBay business's balance sheet. Like the asset accounts, some of these will also be broken down further in QuickBooks. Accounts payable would be broken down into individual accounts, as would loans payable or notes payable if you had more than one.

Following are some typical liability accounts you might see in an eBay business:

Table 7.4   QuickBooks Chart of Accounts for Business Liabilities

Number	Account Name	Description
401	Accounts Payable	Money that your business owes others
402	Loans Payable	Loans that your business owes for vehicles, equipment, and so on
403	Notes Payable	Loans that your business owes to you for start-up money, equipment, inventory, and other personal property that you transferred into the business, or to others who contributed other money to help finance your business
404	Sales Tax Payable	Money that you have accrued to pay sales taxes but haven't submitted to the taxation agency yet
405	Interest Payable	Interest that has accrued against a loan or note each month (or other period) before you make the payment; when you pay it, the liability is removed and transformed into Interest Expense

Table 7.4 continued

Number	Account Name	Description
406	Payroll Taxes Payable	Payroll taxes that have been deducted from employee checks and for the employer's portion, but which haven't been paid to the government yet; once paid, this liability is removed and transformed into Payroll Expense

Did you notice how some of these liabilities turn into expenses after they're paid? That's a part of the recordkeeping process!

Equity Accounts

Equity accounts show the portion of the company that belongs to you. Typically, it is made up of two parts—*capital stock*, which is the stock you own in your business, and *retained earnings*, which is the profit your eBay business made at the end of the day. Following is an equity chart of accounts:

Table 7.5 QuickBooks Chart of Accounts for Equity Accounts

Number	Account Name	Description
501	Capital Stock	Money that you paid into the business in return for ownership shares
502	Retained Earnings	Net profit that will flow through to the shareholder-owners if the business is an S corporation or that can be distributed to the shareholder-owners if the business is a C corporation

In the beginning, it's easier to set up fewer accounts. You can always add and delete accounts as you go. The chart of accounts we've made available at www.taxloopholes.com/ebaysellers is a simple version, created especially for those of you who don't have a lot (or any) bookkeeping experience. As you get more comfortable with your eBay business's books and bookkeeping procedures, you can branch out and get more detailed.

Jenny's Books

For the rest of this chapter, we'd like to show you how Jenny Guerro set up her books and what some of her typical entries look like. Let's start by taking a look at Figure 7.4, which is the QuickBooks Chart of Accounts for

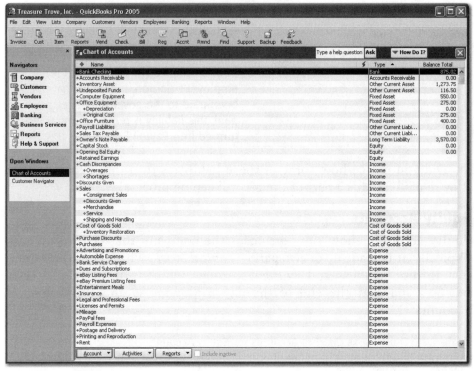

Figure 7.4   Treasure Trove, Inc., chart of accounts showing opening balances.

Jenny's business. It shows you Jenny's opening balances, and how she transferred her personal property into her eBay business.

If you look at the entries Jenny made, you can see how she has transferred her personal property into the business and assigned it to various categories. She has also lent her business $1,000 for its bank account, so that it can pay its own expenses right away.

Jenny is treating the money and personal property she has transferred into the business as a loan. She has created an Owner's Notes Payable account and has credited that account with a total of $3,570, being the value of all of the money and property she has transferred in. By setting this up as a Owner's Notes Payable entry, she can have the business pay her back over time. This will help Jenny to lower her business's taxes, as the payments will be a liability to the business, reducing its income. It will also help Jenny because the money the business pays her is not earned income, so isn't subject to any tax.

Jenny's Opening Inventory

The Inventory Asset balance of $1,345 that you can see in Jenny's Chart of Accounts was created from the list of items that Jenny and the boys collected to sell, and from the average selling price values they found through their research. When she set up her inventory in QuickBooks, it prompted her to create different categories for each type of item she will be selling, and an overall value. Figure 7.5 shows you the breakdown of Jenny's

> You can find the corporate papers that Jenny prepared to document her loan to the business at our web site, www.taxloopholes.com/ebaysellers.

Inventory Account. (You can open any account displayed in a QuickBooks Chart of Accounts simply by double-clicking the account balance.)

Recording Jenny's Sales

Recording sales in QuickBooks for an eBay business is also easy. Because most eBay sales will be paid immediately, she is using the Sales Receipts feature and indicating that the payment method used is PayPal. If the customer pays with a check or money order, she can make that distinction as well.

If you look closely at Figure 7.6, you will see that Jenny has set out $10 for shipping. This will be recorded as another type of income. Later, when Jenny goes to the post office and mails this item, she will make an expense

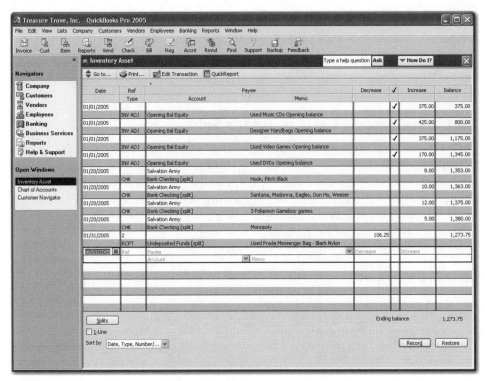

Figure 7.5　Inventory account breakdown for Treasure Trove, Inc.

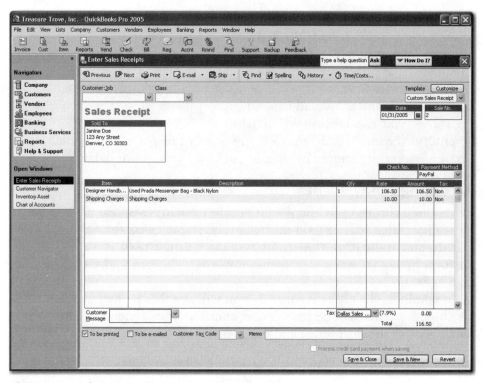

Figure 7.6 Sales receipt for Treasure Trove, Inc.

entry, where she debits her Shipping Expense account and credits her Bank Checking account.

Recording Jenny's Costs of Goods Sold

Because Jenny's business sells goods, she needs to track her inventory and her purchase costs. If she has to do anything to an item to make it saleable, such as paying to have something professionally cleaned or adding connector cables to a video game system, for example, she also needs to be able to track these costs. That's because all of these items go into creating her eBay business's Costs of Goods Sold.

The Costs of Goods Sold (COGS) equation:

Beginning inventory

+   Additional inventory purchases

+   Costs to make items saleable

−   Ending inventory value
_____

=   Cost of Goods Sold

Figure 7.7 shows how Jenny recorded the costs to have her leather handbags cleaned before putting them up for sale on eBay.

Jenny can track her Costs of Goods Sold through QuickBooks simply by double-clicking the Costs of Goods Sold account in her Chart of Accounts. Figure 7.8 illustrates the Cost of Goods Sold account after Jenny's first recorded sale.

Recording Jenny's Inventory Purchases

As you buy new goods for resale through your eBay business, you will also need to record your purchases. QuickBooks makes this really easy. You record your purchase in the Check Register, and by listing each inventory item you purchased at the bottom of the screen, QuickBooks is able to calculate the Cost of Goods Sold. If you look closely, you can see that you have two account choices: Expenses and Items. Inventory purchases must be made under the Items tab, to make sure you are adding inventory to the proper accounts.

Figure 7.9 shows an example of a typical purchase made by Jenny to add to her inventory.

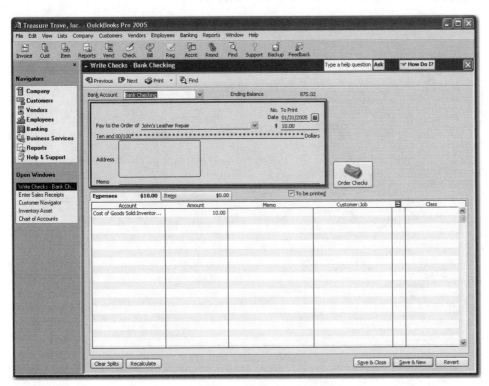

Figure 7.7   Cost of goods sold entry to recapture cleaning costs.

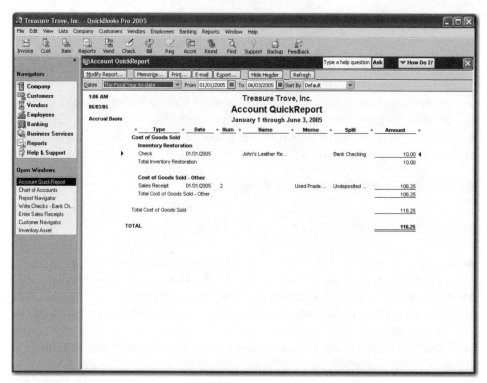

Figure 7.8 Detailed view of cost of goods sold account.

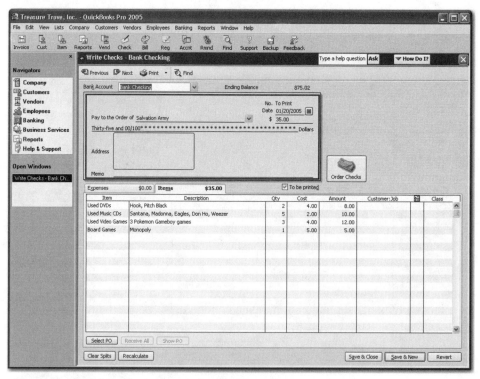

Figure 7.9 QuickBooks entry recording purchase of inventory.

Recording Jenny's Expenses

It's easiest to record expenses as you go. This is another really straightforward entry that you can make through the QuickBooks check register. Each time you make a payment, either online or by writing a check, you can immediately assign an expense account and let QuickBooks take care of the rest.

Jenny shows you how it's done in Figure 7.10.

How Frequently Should You Update Your Books?

> **More at Our Web Site**
>
> You can find lots of other QuickBook entries on our web site that show you how Jenny recorded all sorts of business-related transactions, including how she charged her eBay business rent for her home office, how Jenny repaid some of the notes payable, and how Jenny was reimbursed for expenses she paid on behalf of her business. All these and more can be found at www.taxloopholes.com/ebaysellers.

If you're working with an outside bookkeeper, he or she will probably ask you to provide your receipts, invoices, deposit slips, and other bookkeep-

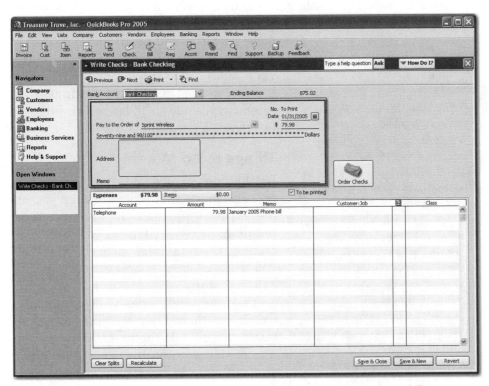

Figure 7.10   QuickBooks entry to record payment of January 2005 phone bill.

ing documentation. If you're doing it on your own, you should create a schedule and stick to it! Yes, bookkeeping can be tedious and time-consuming, and it can take you away from more interesting and profitable pursuits. But once your books get out of date, things have a way of snowballing, and before you know it, you're missing deadlines to remit taxes or other payments. If you wind up turning the whole mess over to a bookkeeper to sort out, you can guarantee that you'll spend more than you would otherwise, because your materials are going to be disorganized and incomplete.

Following are our thoughts on when you should perform certain bookkeeping tasks.

Things to Do Daily or Weekly

The majority of small business bookkeeping involves tracking your expenses. Remember to take full advantage of all possible business deductions; you're going to be recording hundreds of transactions over the course of a year. To keep this manageable, and to ensure you don't forget any transactions, we suggest that you try to record each transaction within 24 hours of when it occurs.

eBay has policies regarding invoicing and recommends that a buyer be provided with an invoice and payment instructions within three business days after the end of an auction. It is a good idea to get into the habit of checking your auctions at least once a day and invoicing any completed listings that same day. Besides, the faster you bill, the faster you'll get paid.

Some transactions that should be done daily or weekly:

- Input your business expenses at least weekly.
- Input the mileage you have recorded weekly.
- Send out invoices for all eBay sales made each day on a daily basis.
- Input all transfers from PayPal to your business checking account at least weekly.
- Input all PayPal and eBay fees at least weekly.
- Input all checks you have written or payments you have made with a check-cashing card at least weekly.
- Input all purchases you have made at least weekly.

Things to Do Monthly

At the end of each month, you can run certain reports that will help keep you on top of your finances. If any upcoming problems exist, such as a cash-flow crunch when a large debt comes due, you'll be in great shape to plan for the coming storm. A lot of people learn quickly to keep a weekly, or even daily, watch on their cash account. But they might not ever do the monthly reporting. The benefit of monthly reporting is that you can start to see trends in your business. It's the old case of not being able to see the forest for the trees—if you're dealing with too many trees each day, you might miss the forest each month.

If you have set up your sales and use tax accounts and your payroll accounts properly, the calculation can be done through QuickBooks, meaning that all you have to do is click a button and write a check. All of the other reports listed here can be prepared with a few simple mouse clicks.

Things to Do Quarterly

If you aren't operating as either an S or a C corporation, you'll need to prepare an income statement at the end of each quarter (March, June, September, and December), so that you can determine your estimated income, payroll, and self-employment taxes.

If you are operating through an S corporation or a C corporation, you will probably be preparing a Form 941 and paying withheld income tax, Social Security, and Medicare taxes. You will be able to get these amounts right from your QuickBooks accounts, and, if you are a QuickBooks payroll subscriber, you can prepare your Form 941 as well.

Activities and reports that you should do or prepare monthly
• Calculate and remit sales and/or use tax to local authorities.
• Calculate and remit payroll taxes to the IRS (unless you are paying quarterly).
• Prepare a bank reconciliation for your business checking account (and any other cash accounts that you have).
• Prepare an income statement (called a profit/loss report in QuickBooks).
• Prepare a statement of cash flows.
• Prepare a balance sheet.

Quarterly checklist:
• Prepare IRS Form 941.
• Prepare state payroll and sales tax reports, if required.

Things to Do Yearly

Don't forget why you're doing this—to save taxes! If you have been keeping your books up to date, then all you'll need is a few minutes and a few QuickBook reports to hand over to your accountant. QuickBooks makes it really easy, too. A menu item walks you through the entire year-end procedure and prepares everything for your CPA or tax preparer. No shoeboxes, no piles of paperwork, no stress, and no midnight run to the post office on the tax-filing deadline.

NOTE: Corporate tax returns are due 2½ months after its fiscal year-end. For calendar-year businesses, this means your S corporation's return is due March 15, and not April 15, when your personal

Annual checklist:
• Hold annual meeting.
• Prepare annual minutes.
• File annual report with state.
• Renew resident agent contract for the upcoming year.
• Prepare state and federal annual tax returns or franchise tax returns.

return is due. You can extend this filing deadline for another six months if you apply to the IRS *before your corporate tax return is due.*

Final Thoughts on Step-by-Step Accounting Requirements

We've given you a lot of information in this chapter and, as we said in the very beginning, it is *not* a complete picture by any stretch. In fact, one of the best things you can do for yourself and your business is to take an evening course or weekend course in basic bookkeeping, preferably one that uses QuickBooks. You can use the course to ask questions, learn about the program, and hopefully work through your own books, all at the same time.

Oh, and did we mention that the course would be a deductible business expense? If you think about it, that's like being paid to keep your own books!

Next Steps—Beginning and Basic Bookkeeping Entries

Bookkeeping is an ongoing process and definitely not something that you want to let get too far behind. Reserve a time each week to sit down and review your business's transactions and to record them in your accounting records, or to prepare them to go to your bookkeeper. You may want to write notes on any transactions that are a little outside the usual, so your bookkeeper doesn't have to guess at what happened.

1. Determine how you will keep your accounting records—with a manual system or with QuickBooks.
2. If you are going to hire a bookkeeper, begin interviewing. We recommend that you always interview advisors using the DKA Advisor checklist, a completed sample of which is provided in the appendix. You can also download a blank copy for your own use from the companion web site.
3. If you are doing the bookkeeping yourself, arrange to take a beginning bookkeeping class, so that you can become comfortable with basic bookkeeping tasks and QuickBooks in general.
4. Compile a list of beginning expenses for the bookkeeper or yourself. Don't forget items such as the cost of items you have contributed, such as your cell phone, computer, desk, chair, and the like. Also, don't forget fees for legal consultation and bookkeepers and even the cost of this book. That's all deductible as soon as you have your business in place.
5. Follow our four "Things To Do" headings to keep your books up to date and accurate.

Part 3

Lowering Your Taxes through Loopholes, Deductions, and Income Recharacterization

8

Finding Your Hidden Business Deductions

I n Chapters 6 and 7, we talked about setting up expense accounts in QuickBooks so that you can track your expenses and take as many business deductions as possible. But to do that, you'll need to know what a business deduction is. In this chapter we cover various business deductions—those that are obvious and straightforward, and those that are less obvious, but no less powerful.

Reducing Your Taxes

Before we have some fun finding your hidden business deductions, let's go back to taxes for a couple of minutes. For most of you, about the only time you think about taxes is each year between January 1 and April 15, when you're filling in information on your tax return and either writing a check or planning how to spend your refund. But if you want to reduce your taxes for next year, now is the time to begin planning for that.

You can reduce your taxes in three main ways: decrease your taxable income, increase your tax deductions, and decrease your tax rate. If you can do all three, so much the better.

Let's start by learning about ways you can decrease your taxable income. First, you need to understand what taxable income actually is.

To pay less tax:

- Reduce taxable income
- Increase deductible expenses
- Reduce tax rate

Three Types of Income

As far as the IRS is concerned, three types of income are of interest: earned, portfolio, and passive. Each of these income types is taxed at different rates, with earned income being taxed at the highest rate and passive income taxed at the lowest (or not at all, in some cases). If you want to reduce your taxes, take a look at changing your income type.

Earned Income.   *Earned income* is income that you or your business earns through the provision of services or goods. It's also subject to the highest levels of tax—at the federal level, this can be as high as 35 percent, or more if you fall into the dreaded AMT (Alternative Minimum Tax) category.

The AMT category was created to make sure that even the wealthiest people and businesses paid some taxes. An AMT taxpayer has fewer deductions available than other taxpayers and must calculate tax payable at both the regular rate and the AMT rate (at whatever extra cost that involves), and then pay the higher of the two. With inflation and bracket creep, more and more Americans and small businesses with moderate to high incomes are being caught in the AMT trap and are being hit with extra taxes.

Worried about falling into the AMT trap? Visit the companion web site at www.taxloopholes.com/ ebaysellers to learn more and take a quick test to see if AMT is a problem for you—and what you can do about it.

The group with the highest earned income rate is the ordinary, working taxpayer who isn't self-employed and works for someone else. In addition to being taxed at the highest rates, working taxpayers also have the fewest hidden deductions available—a double-edged sword if there ever was one.

So what's an ordinary working taxpayer to do? Along with starting a business to take advantage of the deductions available to businesses, you have another powerful option—change the type of income you earn, by increasing your portfolio and passive income, while decreasing your earned income (more on that in Chapter 12).

Portfolio Income.   Portfolio income is income you receive when your money is working for you. Portfolio income includes interest, dividends, and capital gains. Capital gains occur when you hold an asset for more than a year and then sell the asset at a profit.

The majority of portfolio income comes from dividends and capital gains. Those types of income have a maximum tax of 15 percent—20 percent lower than the maximum tax rate for earned income. So, if you are an employee looking to reduce your tax burden, one step could be to establish and build a stock portfolio. That way, as your portfolio begins to return income, you may be able to use that income to replace a portion of your current earned income, which will lower your overall tax burden (because your tax rate will be lowered as your earned income amount goes down). You can even fund your portfolio from your eBay business earnings, which will give you twice the advantages—because this money has already been tax-leveraged once when you offset all of your hidden business deductions against it.

Here is a quick primer on the most popular portfolio options:

Roth IRA Account. A great way to hold a stock portfolio is through a Roth IRA account. That's because, unlike a regular 401(k) (discussed next), all the money that goes into a Roth IRA comes out tax-free. In a regular 401(k), the money comes out as earned income. Regular 401(k)–type plans allow you to take a tax break up front, whereas a Roth IRA gives you the tax savings on the other side. As you've spent years contributing to either one with the expectation that it will grow and be larger on the other side, wouldn't it make more sense to get the tax advantages on that side as well? Instead of saving the tax on every dollar going in, we'd much prefer to save the tax on every dollar that comes out, especially since more dollars come out.

Roth IRA accounts are open to all U.S. residents, with some limitations. You can invest a maximum of $4,000 per year, but this will increase to $5,000 per year in January 2008. After that, beginning in 2009, your contribution rate will increase by $500 each year. As your income increases, your ability to contribute to a Roth IRA decreases. If your income reaches $110,000 gross per year (or $160,000 for married couples who file a joint return), you can no longer make Roth IRA contributions.

> If you knew you had a choice between paying taxes on your retirement income and not paying taxes on that income, which would you choose?

401(k). Most people are familiar with the 401(k) pension plan. A 401(k) works by deferring the taxes that you pay. Every dollar that you put into your 401(k) is before-tax money, meaning that you deduct it from your income before you calculate how much tax you owe. That money is then invested into mutual funds and other stocks, where hopefully it will appreciate over time. Eventually, you hope that it will appreciate into a substantial fund for your retirement. However, unlike Roth IRAs, when you withdraw money from your 401(k) pension plan, that money is considered regular earned income, meaning that you're going to be paying the highest tax rate on those withdrawals.

401(k) plans are usually set up by employers and are most often found in larger companies, although there is nothing to stop you from setting one up through your eBay business. The maximum contribution amount is higher than that of a Roth IRA—in 2005 you could contribute up to $14,000, and if you are 50 or older, this amount was even higher, to $18,000. In larger companies, employers often choose to match employee contributions, and nothing stops you from using some of your eBay business's profits to do that for your own plan. The employer contributions don't count toward your personal contribution limit, so theoretically you could contribute between $28,000 and $36,000 per year through your eBay business.

Bear this in mind, however: Making a 401(k) your primary retirement planning tool works only if you are planning to be in a lower tax bracket when you retire. That often means you have a lower income, too, which we don't think is such a good idea. With so many retirement planning options available, you can do better and hopefully retire making as much or more income than you make now. And another thing to think about is this: You should start contributing to a retirement plan in your early career stages, when your income and tax rate is lower. But when you start taking that money out, you are likely to be at a much higher tax rate. So, you'd be paying more taxes to take that money out than you would have paid years ago when you put it in.

Have a 401(k) by all means, but keep your other options open as well. Don't put all of your investment eggs in the same basket.

The Roth 401(k).   January 2006 marks the debut of another type of 401(k), called a Roth 401(k), This new type of 401(k) has all of the benefits of a regular 401(k) with the exception of the up-front tax break. But like a Roth IRA, a Roth 401(k) will grow tax-free, and you won't pay any tax down the road on money you take out. There's also a way for your employer to contribute to your Roth 401(k), although you will have to pay tax on your employer's contributions when you withdraw that income later. But, having your eBay business make matching contributions to your personal Roth 401(k) is a great way to both reduce your business's taxable income and grow your retirement savings.

Traditional IRA.   The traditional IRA is a blend of a Roth IRA and a 401(k). Like a Roth IRA, you put the money in using after-tax dollars, and the contribution limits are the same. However, unlike a Roth IRA, in some circumstances, you may be entitled to take a tax deduction on those contributions. Your ability to deduct your traditional IRA contributions is going to depend on several factors, including your tax filing status and whether or not you or your spouse already participate in an employer-sponsored retirement plan such as a 401(k). The best way to find out if you qualify for a deduction on your traditional IRA contributions is to talk to your tax advisor.

Unlike a Roth IRA, your withdrawals from a traditional IRA are taxed as regular earned income, so it has the same tax disadvantage as a 401(k).

Note: These are just a few retirement planning options. To get a complete picture of what's available and what might work best with your situation and your eBay business, talk to your own retirement planning advisor.

You have three possible plans for your retirement.
You can
- Plan to be poor
- Plan to be middle class
- Plan to be rich

Which path have you chosen?

Passive Income. Your final option is *passive income*, which we like best. That's because passive income usually isn't subject to taxes at all.

Passive income is typically income you receive through real estate investments. Consider this: Use your eBay earnings to buy a rental property, and rent it out. While the rents you receive from your tenants is earned income to you, if

As an employee:	
You	EARN
You pay	TAX
You get to	SPEND
	Whatever's left
As a business owner:	
You	EARN
You	SPEND
You pay	TAX

you set up your real estate investments correctly, there should be enough offsetting expenses and depreciation deductions to eliminate the taxes payable on that earned income—even though you still make money each and every month.

What Is a Business Deduction?

Simply put, the IRS defines a *business deduction* as "all the ordinary and necessary expenses paid or incurred during the taxable year in carrying on any trade or business." The IRS has gone further to define ordinary and necessary expenses as follows:

- **Ordinary**—Expenses that are normal, common, and accepted under the circumstances by the business community.
- **Necessary**—Expenses that are appropriate and helpful.

That's a pretty wide door, don't you think? In fact, in the right circumstances, and with properly documented receipts and paperwork, just about anything can be considered an ordinary or necessary expense for operating your eBay business.

What Is a Hidden Business Deduction?

We define *hidden* business deductions as those things for which you're already spending money that you could *redefine* as a business deduction. By redefining these items, you shift the money to pay for them from after-tax dollars to pre-tax dollars. And every pre-tax dollar you spend on business expenses reduces your taxable income, and thus your tax payable.

As you can probably imagine, this category can be (and often has been) spectacularly abused by hustlers and charlatans

> **Challenge Yourself!**
> What are your plans for the money you hope to make in your eBay business? Are you planning to use it to help make ends meet—or to make something more? Can you see a way to use your eBay earnings to help your financial future, as well as your financial present?

who set up a nonexistent business as a way to write off personal deductions. The IRS is wise to all of these tricks—that's why you need to make sure your eBay business is established and set up properly. If you use these deductions, and you have the receipts and documentation to back up your expenses, the IRS is more likely to allow the deductions than deny them.

On the other hand, taking every single possible deduction allowed under the law is not only moral and ethical, it's also been approved. Here's what Justice Learned Hand had to say on the subject, in *Helvering v. Gregory*, 69 F. 2d 809, 810 (2nd Cir, 1934), aff'd 293 U.S. 465 (1935), a famous case that is widely considered to be the beginning of modern tax planning:

> *Anyone may arrange his affairs so that his taxes shall be as low as possible; he is not bound to choose that pattern which best pays the treasury. There is not even a patriotic duty to increase one's taxes. Over and over again the Courts have said that there is nothing sinister in so arranging affairs as to keep taxes as low as possible. Everyone does it, rich and poor alike and all do right, for nobody owes any public duty to pay more than the law demands.*

You might be reading your first deductible business expense, *Tax Loopholes for eBay Sellers*. Did you save the sales receipt?

Finding Hidden Business Expenses.   When looking for hidden business expenses (that turn into deductions), first concentrate on the activities that you're going to be doing in your eBay business and the expenses that could be associated with those activities.

Learning Activities.   Learning activities are the first things you need to do. Learning how eBay operates, how a business operates, basic bookkeeping and recordkeeping—all of these are going to be necessary to help you get your business up and running. And the expenses associated with learning are also deductible. That means money you spend on seminars and educational products as well as the courses you attend at eBay University are deductible. You also get to deduct the money you spend on financial advisors, attorneys, CPAs, bookkeepers, and the like. Do you remember Jenny taking her aunt out for lunch back in Chapter 1? That was a business expense that would fall in this category. Think about it. As soon as you have a business, the government will subsidize your education by letting your take a deduction for just about anything that makes you smarter.

Start-Up Activities.   If learning is the equivalent of dipping your toes into the business swimming pool, then actually getting started in business is the equivalent of being up to your shoulders in the pool and about to start swimming.

The money you spend on startup activities and items is one of the most overlooked expense categories, because you're typically spending your own money, and your business hasn't been formed yet. Most people don't realize that this doesn't matter—those expenses are still business-related and perfectly deductible.

Getting started expenses include the following:

- **Incorporation costs**—Costs such as filing fees and other costs such as lawyer's fees, resident agent fees, and incorporator fees
- **Licensing costs**—State and local business licenses, seller license, and similar costs
- **Bookkeeping and recordkeeping setup costs**—Purchasing accounting software, hiring a bookkeeper to set up your books and similar costs
- **Computer equipment costs**—Computers, printers, cables, network switches and routers, Internet costs, and similar costs
- **Software costs**—QuickBooks or other accounting programs, eBay software costs such as Accounting Assistant, Selling Manager, Selling Manager Pro, and other costs
- **Office equipment costs**—Desks, office chairs, bookshelves, filing cabinets, fax machine—even the art you hang on your office wall
- **Business-specific equipment costs**—Cell-phones for you and each employee, digital cameras to take pictures of items, a postage-scale capable of weighing larger items, and other costs
- **Inventory purchase costs**—Once you've cleaned out your garage or attic and valued the items you will be selling, transfer those to your corporation and record the cost to your business of purchasing those items
- **Inventory storage costs**—Shelving or other storage-related costs for your inventory
- **Other inventory-related costs**—Cleaning supplies if you need to clean or recondition items before sale, batteries or power cords if necessary to test or sell with items, any replacement parts required before items are in saleable condition, and similar costs
- **Office supplies**—Paper, pens, ink, and shipping supplies such as boxes, packing peanuts, packing tape, tape dispensers, and other costs

Business Activities.   These day-to-day activities include driving to the office supply store, post office, and around town looking for merchandise; the time you spend cataloging and listing items on eBay while sitting at an Internet Café; the lunch you grab on the run because you're looking for merchandise; the weekend trip you make to a neighboring town or state looking for merchandise; the eBay University seminar you attended to learn more about how to maximize your eBay business; and the trip you made across town to the bookstore to buy books to help you in your business. All of your costs associated with these activities are deductible, including the mileage you're putting on your vehicle making all of these short and long trips.

Bad Debts.   Here's another business expense you might not have considered—bad debts! From time to time, most eBay business owners have experienced a crooked buyer who gets the better of them. The expenses you incur in connection with those rogue transactions, including the cost of the item itself, are all deductible as bad debt expenses.

To claim a bad debts write-off, though, you must make sure that you have recorded all of the income you thought you had made on the transaction—so that the IRS can see that you paid tax on money that you didn't wind up collecting. This is something that many people forget to do, and it can cost them the write-off.

Automobile Expenses.   This is another area that is all-too-often overlooked. The IRS allows you to take a deduction for automobile operating expenses when a vehicle is being used for business purposes. These deductions are available for new vehicles or existing vehicles, whether they are owned by you personally or by your eBay business. Regardless of whether you own your vehicle or you decide to run the ownership through your eBay business, you must carefully document these expenses.

You can deduct auto expenses in two ways: via actual expenses or via a mileage allowance. With actual expenses, you need to track expenses such as these:

- Gas and oil
- Tires
- Repairs
- License and registration fees
- Loan payments (or lease payments)
- Garage costs (if you rent space to store your vehicle)
- Insurance fees
- Depreciation

You may take a pro-rata portion of these expenses based on the time the vehicle was used for business purposes. So if you use your vehicle 50 percent of the time on business, 50 percent of each of these items would become deductible.

The second alternative is to track your business-related mileage and take a straight deduction of that amount. For 2005, the IRS set a mileage rate of 48.5 cents per mile. Each year, the cents per mile amount will change.

Leasing a Vehicle.   Many times, leasing a vehicle can give you a higher overall tax deduction than if you buy one. That's because you can often write off a large portion of the lease payments, along with the taxes your business pays on those lease payments. Because your eBay business's lease payments remain constant every year, in the long run you will get a higher deduction than you would get by using the regular depreciation method. For example, a $350 per month lease payment would give your eBay business a $4,200 deduction each year, but a comparable depreciation deduction would exist only in the first year you owned the vehicle. After that, the depreciation deduction amount would drop quickly. It's best to review the numbers with your own tax advisor to see which is the best alternative for your own circumstances.

Note that if you decide to lease a car in the name of your eBay business, watch the value of your vehicle. If you buy a luxury automobile, defined as anything worth more than roughly $15,500, a small amount of your lease expenses will not be deductible.

> Keep a small notebook in your vehicle so you can easily track your mileage when beginning and ending your trips.

Three Special Vehicle Loopholes.   Here are three loophole opportunities that relate specifically to automobiles:

SUV Tax Loophole.   The *SUV tax loophole*, also called the *heavy vehicle deduction*, was originally intended to benefit businesses that transport or deliver goods, but it is available to anyone with a business.

If you buy a vehicle that is more than 6,000 lbs. GVW (Gross Vehicle Weight), the luxury automobile limitation does not apply. In this case, your business can depreciate the vehicle as though it were any other piece of capital equipment. That includes taking a special depreciation deduction (called a Section 179 deduction).

The Section 179 deduction says that you can take a one-time deduction of up to $25,000 for a vehicle purchased and placed into service in the same year. And that vehicle doesn't need to be brand new, either. The Section 179 deduction applies to both new and used vehicles.

To use the Section 179 deduction, you must have a legitimate business. Employees (people who receive a W-2) who are not also operating a legitimate home or other business are not entitled to take this deduction. What a *huge* loophole for eBay business owners!

Clean-Fuel Vehicles Tax Loophole.   What about going green? If you don't want to purchase a large, heavy vehicle but still want a great loophole, we have one for you. The government has established a $2,000 tax deduction for people and businesses that purchase certain hybrid vehicles before December 31, 2005. If you purchased one of the approved vehicles a couple of years ago and didn't take the deduction, don't worry—you can file an amended return for that year and claim the deduction. If you purchase a qualified hybrid vehicle after December 31, 2005 you won't be able to take the $2,000 credit, but you will be eligible for a new, sliding-scale tax credit the government has just introduced.

The IRS updates the list of approved vehicles every year. The current qualified vehicles are:

- Ford Escape—2005 model
- Toyota Prius—2001–2005 models
- Honda Insight—2000–2005 models
- Honda Accord Hybrid—2005 model
- Honda Civic Hybrid—2003–2005 models
- Lexus RX 400h—2006 model
- Toyota Highlander—2006 model

Stay tuned to the TaxLoopholes web site (www.taxloopholes.com) for information on how the new tax credit will be calculated

> Tax law is constantly changing. Make sure you and your advisors have the most current information so you pay the least amount of tax legally possible.

Year-End Tax Loophole.   Here's one more loopholes tip for you. If you are thinking about trying to grab a great end-of-year deal on a new or used vehicle, shop around for a low-down offer. Why? Because even though you may have only put out $1,000 or so toward your vehicle, you can still take the entire Section 179 deduction on the overall vehicle purchase for that entire year.

> **Auto Deductions at a Glance**
> - Low cost, high mileage—consider cents per mile method
> - Luxury auto—consider leasing
> - SUV weighing more than 6,000 GVW—check out Section 179 deduction for purchase
>
> In all cases, keep good records to prove the business use.

Meals and Travel Expenses Loopholes.   An old saying goes something along these lines: "Never mix business with pleasure." But as far as we're concerned, that's (a) old, and (b) just a saying. There are plenty of ways for you as an eBay business owner to deduct many of your travel and vacation costs—as long as you know and follow the rules.

Meals Expense Loophole.   If you have a meal with another person, and business is discussed during the meal, you can deduct 50 percent of the costs of that meal. Good notes on the meeting (who, what, when, where, and so on) should be kept with the receipt to prove that business did actually occur during the meal. So, for example, if you are out with your kids or other family members looking for eBay merchandise and you grab a meal, keep the receipt. The same goes if you are having a meal with one of your advisors—your bookkeeper, CPA, or attorney, for example.

Don't get greedy with this one, however. You can't eat out with your kids five times a week and claim each meal as a legitimate business expense without raising a few eyebrows at the IRS. On the other hand, if you are on a merchandise-buying trip that takes you out of town, you can deduct 50 percent of your total meal expenses for the duration of the trip.

In a couple of instances, you can claim 100 percent of your meal expenses. For example, if you bring a meal into the workplace for the convenience of your business (for example, in Jenny's case, where she and the boys had spent all day rearranging the apartment to create their home office and inventory storage space), then you can deduct the entire cost. Or, if you are attending a seminar or other event where meals are included, you can also deduct the entire cost of your meals.

Travel Expenses Loophole.   Here are the rules for deducting your eBay business travel expenses:

1. If you travel within the United States, your travel expenses are fully deductible, as long as you do business on the first and the last days of your trip. Those expenses could include airfare, gas, taxi and train fares, travel insurance, hotel accommodation, and more. Your meals would be deducted as outlined earlier. The business you conduct needs to be more than a single telephone call each day, and it is best to try and document that you conducted business every day of your trip, even if you also spend part of each day doing personal things. That documentation might include keeping a log of stores or other places that you have visited look-ing for merchandise, and any other business-related activities that you conduct—which could include stopping at an Internet café to check your eBay auctions and sales status.

2. If you are traveling outside the United States, you can deduct a percent-age of your overall expenses that are equivalent to the number of days of your trip you spent on business. For example, if you headed to Mexico for seven days and spent three of them browsing for merchandise in Mexican artisan markets to resell on eBay, you could deduct about 42 percent of your travel expenses. Meals, again, would be treated in the same fashion as mentioned earlier.

3. If you are combining your business trip with some personal time, the things that you do on your own time are considered your own expense. For example, you can't stop in a thrift shop to check for merchandise on your way to Disneyland, and then claim the cost of entry into Disneyland as an expense.

4. Sometimes, you can claim items such as dry cleaning or the cost of a hair-cut as a legitimate business travel expense—but you must prove that you had a valid business intention for that day, and that the costs you incurred were relevant to your business purpose. Clothing itself is usual-ly a nondeductible item, unless you can prove that the clothing was nec-essary for your business purpose. So, if you were being interviewed on TV about the secret behind your great eBay business success and decided to purchase a new suit or outfit for the taping, those costs (along with the costs for hair cutting or styling, make-up, and jewelry) could be considered legitimate business deductions.

> **Alert!**
> Most beginning business owners forget to give themselves credit for the items they contribute to the business. Don't make this common beginner's mistake.

Remember to Repay Yourself

Repaying yourself for the value of all of the items you are transferring into your eBay business, and for all of the costs you've already incurred, is another big area that new business owners often overlook. Typical items you'll want to transfer into your corporation are computer and office equipment and furniture. To get a realistic value for these things, take a look on eBay or in your local classifieds to see what items similar to yours are currently worth. You can't charge what you initially paid for them, unless the items were purchased within the last three to six months and you've still got the original receipts. That's because these items depreciate over time, and it will be difficult to prove to the IRS that your three-year old computer is really still worth the $2,000 you paid for it three years ago.

You'll also want to do the same thing with your eBay business's opening inventory. That's where your beginning inventory list will come in handy (see Jenny Guerro's story back in Chapter 1), because one of the things you did when you created it was to assign a current value by researching similar sales on eBay.

While you'll obviously want to begin paying your business's costs from your corporation's account as soon as possible, realistically you'll be footing the bill personally in the early days. Remember to document all of those costs, because your corporation will need to reimburse you for all of those expenses. You may also want to provide your corporation with some seed money in its business account, so you can pay bills directly from its account. (You saw Jenny do that in Chapter 7.)

After you've finished calculating these three areas of costs, document the debt your corporation owes you. You can do this in several ways, but one of the easiest and most tax-advantaged ways is to enter into a promissory note between yourself and your corporation. If, for example, the total amount of goods, equipment, and startup costs you've put into your eBay business is worth $5,000, then you can set up that amount as a debt owed by your corporation to yourself. This way, as you pay yourself back from your corporation's profits, the money you'll be receiving won't be considered taxable income—it will be the repayment of a loan. (This is how Jenny dealt with her startup costs. You can download the paperwork that she used from the companion web site.)

Dealing with Recurring Monthly Expenses

A few expenses are probably in your name personally and won't wind up transferring over to the corporation's name—at least not in the beginning. Two examples would be your monthly Internet service bill and cell-phone bill. That's okay—you can either pay these bills personally and submit an expense account to your business each month for repayment, or you can submit your bills to the corporation and have it pay these expenses directly. Whatever method you decide to use, just make sure you document it each month, so that you can substantiate what these payments were for and why they were made. As your business grows, and contracts come up for renewal, you may want to transfer them over to your business.

Catching Up with Jenny

Jenny looked around her former den-turned-home office and nodded her head in satisfaction. Since her lunch with Tia Olivia, she and the boys had been very busy. First, they'd taken a look at their apartment and decided how they were going to create some home office space. Jenny had been using the smallest bedroom as a den, with the idea of giving it to one of the boys for his own bedroom at some point. She and the boys had talked about space and decided that one of their goals with the eBay business would be to find larger living quarters. Until that point, the boys had agreed to continue sharing a bedroom so that the den could become the family eBay business headquarters, and Jenny had agreed to give the boys the large master bedroom, so they would have more room.

As everyone had worked together to move things around the apartment, they discovered that they had more room that they thought, once all of the inventory items had been moved into the closet of their new home office. Two desks were in the office—one for Jenny to use and one for the boys to use when they were researching items—and Jenny had set up a wireless network system so that everyone could easily access the Internet to check on their auctions.

Jenny had measured out the square footage of the office and of their entire apartment. She knew now that their home office took up 25 percent of their entire square footage, and that she could now begin to invoice the business for 25 percent of the rent, light, electricity, and heating costs she was currently paying. She had picked up shelving for the business closet, along with a desk and some other office furniture. She had also prepared an inventory list of all of the personal equipment she was transferring into the business and the approximate value of those items. Between that list and the list of eBay items she and the boys had prepared, she was a bit surprised at the total, which was around $4,000.

Jenny was also amassing a pile of receipts for items she had bought, or expenses she had incurred—including her lunch with Tia Olivia—and had started noting her mileage in a small notebook she had attached to the dashboard of her car. It was difficult to remember everything, especially the mileage, because she wasn't used to tracking herself so closely. But she was persevering, and it was getting a bit easier. Thinking about the money she was going to save on taxes that year also helped to motivate her.

The phone rang as Jenny was standing in the office doorway. It was Tia Olivia, who was ready for Jenny to pick up her paperwork. "I've made you extra copies of your articles and bylaws for the bank," Olivia told her, "because you'll need those to open a bank account. Make sure you give them your Tax ID number as well, or you won't be able to get your account opened. Will you have time to go through some basic accounting procedures when you come down?" continued Olivia. "Now that you've set up your QuickBooks records I want to show you how you can record some of your transactions and make sure you're on track with your bookkeeping. I'll help you with payroll when you're ready, but we don't need to do that right away."

As Jenny prepared to drive to Olivia's, she told the boys that she'd be back in a couple of hours and would bring pizza, as they had all been working hard and it would be too late to start a meal from scratch. It occurred to Jenny as she was driving that the pizza may qualify as an ordinary and necessary business expense, given that they'd been working so hard, and she made a mental note to ask Tia Olivia about it when she arrived.

Helpful Resources

Keeping track of all these expenses, mileage, and other items might seem like a burden in the early days of your business, but if you need a little motivation, think about the money you're going to save.

You'll find a set of documents in this book's appendixes to help you, including an expense sheet that you can use to track your startup and recurring expenses. Take the quiz to help you determine where your money goes every month, so that you can begin to determine where your own hidden business deductions lie. And check out our list of more than 300 possible business deductions in Appendix G for more helpful information.

> The quality of your questions will determine the quality of the answers you get.
> **Weak question:** "Can I write this off?" (The easy answer is "no.")
> **Powerful question:** "How can I write this off?"

Next Steps—Finding Your Hidden Business Deductions

Starting your own business opens up a door to a new and powerful set of tax deductions you can use to reduce your taxes and increase your income. Investing that money in yourself, by creating passive and portfolio streams of income, and you'll see rewards—fast.

1. Go to www.taxloopholes.com/ebaysellers to take the "Where Does Your Money Go?" quiz.
2. Review the 300-plus possible business deductions in Appendix G.

3. Make a list of items for which you currently pay with personal income that could actually be business deductions. Are they ordinary and necessary to the production of income?

4. As needed, review these expenses with your advisor. What will you need to do to prove that they are legitimate business deductions?

5. Create a list of expenses that you paid for with personal money so that your corporation can reimburse you. (Expense for the company, tax free for you).

5. Track the expenses in your accounting system.

6. Re-read the sections on portfolio and passive income. If you haven't yet made arrangements, talk to a financial advisor about how you can use some of your eBay profits to grow your future retirement fund and save on your current taxes.

9

Business Loopholes for Homeowners

Whoat is the largest expense you have each and every month? If you're like most people, it's the rent or mortgage payments and other expenses required for your home. For many people, a home is their largest asset as well. But is it really an asset that puts money in your pocket? Or is it more like a huge debt that you have to struggle to pay each month? Using loopholes, you can turn much of those big payments into legal business deductions.

Homeowners who also operate a home-based business have even more advantages than other business owners when they take advantage of home loopholes. In this chapter, we explore the benefits of using your home for business, including special benefits that are available *only* to homeowners. Who knows—these savings alone might be enough to get you into business!

The Benefits of a Phantom Loss

Before getting into the home office loopholes available to homeowners, let's talk for a minute about *phantom losses* and what they can mean for your overall tax-saving strategy. A phantom loss is a loss that occurs on paper but doesn't actually involve any money being paid out of pocket. Depreciation is a great example of this type of loophole—we will explain it in more detail a little later in the chapter.

Q: When can a loss be a good thing?
A: When it's a phantom loss. That's a legal tax write-off that doesn't cost you any money.

Usually, a phantom loss doesn't mean that your business didn't make any money. You might have a positive cash flow every month, yet on paper, at least, your business has lost money. By taking all of your available business expenses, combined with some of the great home office loopholes available to homeowners, you can create an overall paper loss for your eBay business. And that paper loss, a phantom loss, can be used to offset your W-2 income, which in turn will lower your tax bracket, even though your eBay business is making money every month.

Your Home Office Can Be Your Biggest Deduction

In Chapter 8, you learned that business deductions are hiding everywhere if you know where to look—including inside your own home or apartment. In fact, as Jenny found out, you don't even have to own your home to save on taxes by having a home office. Jenny is now able to deduct 25 percent of her rent and utilities in connection with her home office.

But if you own your home, some extra loopholes are available that can really help to save you money. Let's explore some of the loopholes available for the small business owner who also owns a home.

Remodeling Tax Loophole

We talked about the ability to charge your eBay business rent for your home office. So, for example, if your home office takes up 25 percent of your overall living space, you can write off 25 percent of your mortgage interest, heat, lights, power, gas, garbage, water, taxes, insurance, and other expenses. But did you know that if you remodel the room you use for your home office, those costs are deductible as well? Some common examples are converting a closet into storage, repainting, or adding new built-in cabinets. In fact, any expense you incur by improving the room in which you office resides is deductible.

Home Office Depreciation Tax Loophole

Depreciation is one of our all-time favorite tax loopholes. Even though land appreciates in value, and we buy and sell real estate on the assumption that it will gain in value over time, as far as the IRS is concerned, buildings depreciate. That means in the eyes of the IRS, every year your real estate investments are worth a little bit less.

This is an amazingly powerful deduction for a couple of reasons. First, you can apply the depreciation deduction to your home office the same way you apply the percentage of square footage to your mortgage interest and utilities. So, if your house has a depreciable basis of, say, $160,000, and you're using 20 percent of your total square footage for your eBay business, you will have a depreciation basis of $32,000 (calculated as $160,000 × 20 percent) for your home office. Now you can deduct a portion of that $32,000 each year against your business income and hopefully create a paper loss that you can use to offset your other income. Remember that paper losses equal less tax.

When you sell your property, you do not have to attribute any part of the gain to the business you've created by using a home office. But you will have to recapture the home office–related depreciation that you have taken and pay taxes on it. That's okay, because the tax rate for capital gains is only 15 percent, and you will have had the use of all that money you weren't using to pay taxes. Besides (and this is important), the IRS has the right to assume that you've been taking that depreciation all along and will tax you on it in any event, so you really owe it to yourself to take this deduction.

Home Office Rules

1. Space for your home office must be used exclusively and regularly for business purposes.
2. Inventory space must be used to store inventory.
3. Calculate the available deduction by dividing the square footage of business use by the total square footage of the house. (For example, 300 square feet of business divided by 1,200 total square feet for the house is 25 percent.)
4. Apply this business use percentage to all home-related costs—rent, mortgage interest, property tax, insurance, utilities, homeowner dues, and the like.

You've now turned a personal expense into a business deduction.

Section 179 Deduction Tax Loophole

We talked about the Section 179 deduction in Chapter 8, as it relates to vehicles. You can also use Section 179 in connection with your eBay home office to save money on taxes. The amount of the deduction limit increases, though. Instead of the $25,000 limit on vehicles, you now have a potential $102,000 deduction per year.

Keep in mind the following when using the Section 179 deduction for your home office:

- The deduction can be taken only once per tax return per year.
- You can't use a Section 179 deduction to create a loss.

Let's go over those two rules again. If you and your spouse both start independent businesses as S corporations, the business income and expenses end up flowing to your personal return. Remember, the S corporation is a "flow-through" business entity, so that income and expenses end up getting reported on your personal return. Now let's assume that you and your spouse each end up spending $100,000 in capital improvements that qualify as Section 179 deductions. Together, that's $200,000. But because your companies both end up getting reported on your joint return, you're limited to $102,000 in deductions. Complicated? A little. Talk to your accountant to clarify if you're going to have a lot of expenses.

The second rule tells us that, unfortunately, you can't use Section 179 to create one of those paper losses we love to apply to other income. So, for example, if your company has income of $50,000, the Section 179 expense of $75,000 is useful this year only to bring your income down to zero. The rest of the Section 179 expense will roll over into the next year.

Extra Inventory Tax Loophole

If you find that your eBay inventory is exceeding your home office storage capacity, don't worry. Inventory doesn't need to be stored in your home office for you to use the percentage of storage space it is taking up as a deduction. While your home office does need to be in a space used exclusively for business purposes, your inventory can be stored elsewhere in your home. In fact, you might be better served to store your inventory in another part of the home, as this will increase the percentage of your home that you are allocating to your business.

> **What can your home do for you?**
> - Home office deduction
> - Remodeling write-off
> - Home office depreciation
> - Section 179 deduction
> - Inventory storage write-off
> - Tax-free gain when you sell

What you need to remember with inventory storage, though, is that you can take only the percentage of space that your inventory is physically taking up—not the square footage of the entire room, as you can with your home office. Of course, the cost of a storage unit or warehouse space is also deductible. Even better, you can take a deduction for both the storage unit and the home space used for storage.

The Homeowner Loophole

This is, hands-down, one of the best loopholes available to anyone who owns his or her own home. In fact, we think it's the best tax gift that Congress has ever given us. Once you have lived in a home for two out of the previous five years, you become entitled to take a portion of the gain (profit) you realize on the sale, completely *tax-free*. The amounts would surprise you, too. As of the 1997 tax year, singles can exempt up to $250,000 of the sale proceeds from taxes, whereas a married couple filing jointly can exempt up to $500,000 earned from the sale from taxes.

Now, on the face of it, this loophole has absolutely *nothing* to do with your eBay business, but it is important enough that every single homeowner in America should know about it. Housing costs are rapidly increasing, and in some parts of the country appreciation is occurring at double-digit rates. Being able to access the equity in your home can be one of the fastest and best ways to build wealth, especially if you use that equity to purchase residential or commercial rental properties. The combination of tax savings that you can receive as both a small business owner *and* a real estate investor can reduce your taxes to the point where you pay little, if anything at all, in taxes.

Besides, there *is* a way to tie this loophole in to your eBay business.

We said that this loophole kicks in once you've lived in your home for two of the last five years. But what if you haven't lived there that long? If the IRS considers you to have purchased the home with the intent to quickly turn it over for a profit (typically a purchase and sale within a year), they may consider you to be in the business of real estate, and will consider the profit you make to be earned income, and subject to regular tax rates. Alternatively, if the IRS doesn't consider the sale as a business transaction, you'll need to declare the income you make on the sale of your house and pay taxes on it at the capital gains rate (currently around 15 percent)—*unless* you can qualify under one of the IRS's "unforeseen circumstance" exemptions to this rule. Those exemptions are as follows:

- Change in employment
- Becoming self-employed
- Changing self-employment type
- Death or disability
- Multiple births from the same pregnancy (who'd have thought twins could be a tax break?)

Notice the second and third bullet points: becoming self-employed or a change in self-employment type. Starting your eBay business could certainly qualify. And, if you can qualify under an unforeseen circumstance exemption, you can move in less than two years and take a pro-rata portion of the gain you make on your home sale tax free. In other words, if you have lived in your house for only one year but qualify under an unforeseen circumstances exemption, you can take the gain you make on a sale tax-free up to 50 percent of the previous limit. For example, if you had lived in the home for one year, you could exempt $125,000 of the sale proceeds for a single taxpayer or $250,000 if married, filing jointly, from being subject to capital gains tax.

So, how does this apply to you as an eBay seller with a home-based business? Read what happened to Joe to see how he turned things to his advantage.

Joe Catches a Break

Joe had reached a fork in the road of his business path. The problem was, he could take two possible directions, and he didn't have a map showing which was the better route to take.

In the time since Joe had branched out onto eBay, his business volume had significantly increased. He was moving a lot of equipment and making money. In fact, his eBay earnings were far outstripping the sales he was making from his shop directly. His lease was just about up, and he had to decide within the next 48 hours whether he was going to pick up the option on his lease or shut down his store. He was concerned that shutting down his store would be financially unwise—not so much from the fact that it was a profit center, but because it was a great source of business deductions. He was worried that if he took the store out of the equation, he'd actually wind up in a worse situation from a tax perspective, because he'd have more income and fewer expenses. Although it sounded strange, Joe thought he might *need* the store to continue his business success.

But before he did that, Joe thought he'd take the idea to his CPA, Marty Cheung, and see what Marty had to say. Later, Joe was heard to tell anyone who'd listen that this was the best idea he'd ever had. That's because Marty helped Joe to save even more than he'd imagined.

The first thing Marty asked Joe was how long he had owned his home and what its square footage was. Joe gave Marty an odd look and asked what that had to do with anything—to which Marty replied, "Everything.

"Joe, depending on how much extra room you have in your home, you've got an awesome built-in deduction right there. If you can take the inventory you're storing at your shop and store it at home instead, you can take a business deduction equal to the amount of square footage it's taking up. In other words, if your inventory is going to take up 30 percent of your home's square footage, you can deduct 30 percent of all of your housing costs—mortgage, interest, utilities, insurance, and so on. You can charge your business rent to store the inventory at your house. Although you'll declare the rental income on your personal return, the write-off from your business will more than make up for it, so you'll be better off than before.

"The other thing you want to be thinking about is if you have one spare room that you can convert into a home office. This would be treated separately from your inventory storage, but the same idea would apply. It has to be an exclusive-use deal, though—nothing but work going on in that space. And, if you need to do some remodeling to make the space work as an office, that's all deductible, too.

"Oh, and don't forget about depreciation. I'll have to check your back tax returns to see what your depreciable basis on the house is, but then I'll be able to allocate a portion of the basis to your business operations. The business portion becomes a depreciable asset. And that depreciation works to bring your corporation's taxable income down even further. How long have you owned your home, anyway?"

Joe told Marty that he'd had the house for 11 months. He couldn't resist adding that in that 11-month period, the house had seen appreciation of more than $55,000, based on comparable sales in his neighborhood.

Marty was impressed, and continued: "If the only reason you're hanging on to your store is for the deductions, then my professional advice to you would be to drop it. As a homeowner and a business owner, you've can realize some great tax advantages by moving your operation to your house. All of your current deductions for rent, light, heating, property taxes, Internet access, telephone, advertising, and so on can be transferred to your home office, and you'll lose the monthly leasing costs. The changes you've made to your business mean you really don't need to maintain a storefront—if you need to work on someone's machine you can either make a housecall or have them bring it to you. Any mileage you put on your car for work is deductible by your business, *and* you don't have to declare the money the business pays back to you for mileage. Besides, with the amount of time you spend on the road at auctions and liquidation sales, you are spending more time out of your store than in it, so why waste money on leasing a space that you just don't need? Joe, you've already made the switch to an Internet business—your financial records prove this is where your money is being made—so finish what you've started and take your business virtual."

Joe had to agree with Marty—he really wasn't running a traditional brick-and-mortar store anymore, and if he could still take the tax savings (and more, it sounded like), there really wasn't much reason to hang onto the storefront. He figured that he could use part of his garage to store the bulk of his inventory, and now that his eldest kid was going to college, Joe could use that room for his home office.

Things were continuing to look up for Joe. When he got home that evening he excitedly told his wife about the options Marty had laid out for him. He told Marie that he was planning to bring home all of the store inventory and store it in the garage and was going to remodel the spare bedroom for his home office. When Marie asked him how he was planning to pay for the remodeling costs, he told her that he thought they might be able to take out a second mortgage on the home and loan that money to his business.

But Marie didn't respond as Joe had thought she would. "Joe, you're talking about taking *our* equity in this house and putting it into *your* business. I know your business is doing better, but if the business doesn't make enough money to pay us back, or if it doesn't work out and you have to shut it down altogether, then we will be out the money, not the bank. Our garage is not that big, and it's going to be difficult to get our cars in if you've got stuff everywhere. You're talking about taking a third of our living space away, and I'm not sure that's such a good idea. This house isn't that big to begin with. Joe, I love you and I want to support you in the business, but not by risking our future. If you are serious about doing this, let's find a compromise that we can both agree on."

Joe felt deflated, but he wasn't ready to give up entirely. He decided to talk to Marty again and tell him about Marie's concerns. Perhaps Marty would be able to say the right thing that would make his wife feel better and allow him to proceed with his plans.

When Joe laid out the conversation for Marty the next day, Marty asked Joe if he could meet with him and Marie together. "I've got an idea that might solve everything, but it's better if the three of us meet to talk it over. Why don't we get together around 3 this afternoon? I can meet you at your house."

When Marty arrived, he asked Marie to lay out her concerns again, just to make sure that he clearly understood what was troubling her. Then he nodded and laid out his new idea.

"So the situation here, as I understand it, is that Joe needs room to run a home-based business, and, Marie, you aren't sure that your house is big enough to do that, nor are you sure that you should pull equity from the home to remodel. So why don't you move to a bigger house? If your house has appreciated by $55,000 already, then you have the extra equity you need to trade up to something that can handle Joe's business needs, while not jeopardizing your equity."

"But we have only been here for 11 months," protested Marie. "And I read somewhere that if we sold before two years was up, we'd have some tax consequences?"

"That's normally true, Marie," Marty replied. He then explained the "unforeseen circumstance" exemptions. "While the IRS will let you and Marie take up to a $500,000 profit on your house before taxes, that is contingent upon the two of you living in the house for two years. But, the IRS also allows people in certain circumstances to sell their homes before that two-year period is up and still take a percentage of the tax-free gain. One of those circumstances is a change in employment or self-employment. As Joe will be closing down his brick and mortar business and operating exclusively on the Internet, that should qualify you to take just over $125,000 in profit out of a house sale tax-free. If you make a smaller profit it's obviously all going to be tax free, and if you were to make more than $125,000 on the sale, you'd pay tax on the difference, but only at the capital gain rate of 15 percent."

"If you'd lived in the house for less than one year, and you didn't qualify under the 'unforeseen circumstances' rule," he continued, "things could be a bit different. In that case you might be looking at paying personal income tax on any profit you made on the house. The IRS may consider you as real estate flippers and would insist that you pay ordinary income tax on the sale profits instead of the capital gains rate. Your tax rate is currently in the 25 percent bracket, so in that case you'd pay a 25 percent tax on your after-sale profit.

"But, as you have a strong argument that you qualify under the 'unforeseen circumstances' rule, again, why don't you look at moving to a house that can support Joe's business without infringing on your personal living space. Between the appreciation this house has seen, plus your original equity when you bought the house, you should have more than enough to trade up a notch."

Joe held is breath as he waited for Marie to speak first. Finally, she smiled and nodded her head. "That is definitely a solution I can live with. Joe, why don't we sit down and figure out how much space you think you're going to need, and then contact our real estate agent to see what's available."

Next Steps—Finding Your Home Office Loopholes

A home office can be a significant source of tax deductions for you, regardless of whether you buy or rent your home. Make sure you are taking full advantage of the loopholes and tax savings opportunities we've discussed in this chapter by following the Next Steps set out below.

1. Identify your own home office, using the home office rules.
2. Measure the square footage of your home office.
3. Identify the square footage used for inventory storage.
4. Measure the inventory square footage.
5. Measure the total square footage of your home.
6. Determine the business use percentage (business use divided by total square footage).
7. Begin compiling home-related costs to give to your tax preparer at year-end.

10

Tax Benefits for the Family eBay Business

Your entire family can benefit from your eBay business—and that benefit isn't just from "trickling down" more dollars in the house. Your family can benefit directly by becoming involved in your eBay business. In this chapter, you'll be surprised at some of the ways you can help your family and build your business at the same time.

How does having extra income, medical and dental plan coverage, retirement savings benefits, family vacations, college tuition, helping elders with their expenses, and offsetting your kids' cell phone bills sound? Every one of these things is possible through a successful home-based business.

If you support one or more children or older relatives financially, you can get them involved in the business, so you can begin to shift the after-tax money you would be spending anyway to pre-tax dollars. You can even continue employing your children while they're away at college. After all, when it comes to knowing what's hot and selling, who's a better barometer of current pop culture trends than your kids?

Employing Your Kids and Other Dependents

There is nothing illegal or immoral about employing your kids in your business. In fact, you can teach them valuable life lessons about business, selling, finances, responsibility, and commitment by involving them in your business. And you can save taxes doing so.

You need to take note of three requirements for employing your children or other dependents in your business. First, you need to develop a job description for everyone working for you, including your kids or other family members. It's a great idea to put it in writing, just in case the IRS asks to see it. The tasks that your children perform should be linked to their abilities. Your 8-year-old is completely unqualified to be the chief financial officer, but she may be perfectly capable of taping up boxes or wrapping sheets of bubble wrap around items in preparation for shipping. Older children may be capable of much more—if your son or daughter is a business or accounting major in college, for example, you may have just found your new bookkeeper!

Your children can also help you collect and value items you are planning to sell. Face it, in many instances, the items you're going to be selling belong to your kids, anyway—so who better to tell you about any flaws, problems, defects, or even some neat features of a toy or game that you were completely unaware of?

> Three requirements to employing dependents:
> 1. Written job description
> 2. Written record of hours worked
> 3. Pay a reasonable wage

You can get your kids involved in researching and valuing items, as Jenny did with her teenage boys. And, if your research leads you to particular toys or games that command a high price on eBay, consider sending your kids out to various second-hand shops and thrift stores around town on buying trips. If you are also working fulltime outside the home, this division of labor will help to keep a steady supply of merchandise coming in, as well as keeping your kids engaged in the business (and out of trouble). College-aged children can also continue these activities when they're away from home—giving you a fresh and potentially lucrative additional source of merchandise.

The second requirement is to make sure that your dependents are tracking their hours. If the IRS ever asks, you need to prove that they were keeping track of the time and were paid for work they legitimately did.

Finally, make sure you pay them a reasonable wage for work done. You can't pay your 8-year-old son $100 an hour in order to move income to his tax bracket, no matter how creatively he takes out the trash.

These same ideas can also be applied to other dependents. Again, the work they perform must be within their capabilities, and the wage paid must be a fair-market wage. With more and more research showing the benefits of elders keeping motivated and engaged with society through work and activities, it seems a slam-dunk to get some help from your elderly relatives, and you can take the tax break in return.

Paying Your Kids and Other Dependents

Make sure that you set up each child or elder in your books as an employee in your business and in your payroll system if you are using one. They may be fulltime or part-time employees, but bear in mind that if one of your goals is to provide healthcare insurance through your eBay business, they will need to be fulltime employees if they are too old to qualify under your dependent coverage.

Of course, using your kids and other dependents as employees also means that you may wind up with some additional costs. You'll have increased payroll, unemployment, and workers compensation expenses. But consider this: Paying your kids a salary may mean that they have to pay taxes (likely at the lowest rate); or, if you pay them less than $4,800 per year, they pay no taxes at all. The money they make working for your business is considered *earned* income. On the other hand, *unearned* income has a hidden tax issue.

Kiddie Tax

The *kiddie tax* happened after the IRS noticed that some high-income earners were making their young children part owners in the family business and distributing profits to those children as a way to lower the business's overall tax burden. This income would be considered unearned revenue because the profit was distributed due to ownership in the company, not because any work had been done. If work had been done, it would be considered earned income.

> When should you start paying your kids?
> - **Earned revenue:** As soon as is reasonable
> - **Unearned revenue:** Age 14 and up

Being wise to the ways of these clever taxpayers, the IRS came up with the kiddie tax, which isn't actually a tax, but a cap on the amount of unearned income kids under the age of 14 may receive. Kids may receive a small portion of unearned income tax-free, but once they exceed that amount their earnings begin to be taxed—at mom and dad's rate. Once a child turns 14, he or she is then treated as an adult for tax purposes and would be required to declare his or her earned income and investment income separately and file a separate tax return.

You can avoid the entire kiddie tax issue by paying your kids a reasonable salary—plus, you can give them all sorts of great additional tax-free benefits as well.

Income Tax and Your Kids and Other Dependents

You can pay each of your children up to $4850 per year in salary and other payments before he or she is required to declare and pay tax on that income. Even if you pay your children more than that amount, they are still likely to have a significantly lower tax rate than yours. Up to about $10,700, their earned income tax rate is 10 percent.

It's a little trickier for elders. You'll have to be aware of their maximum earning amount before their Social Security payment becomes affected. This amount will differ from senior to senior, depending on his or her age at retirement and when he or she first began earning income. It's simply easier to talk to an expert or check out the relevant IRS information when trying to determine a salary in this instance. You can find a link to the IRS table at our companion web site, www.taxloopholes.com/ebaysellers.

Tax Reduction Strategy for High-Income Earners

Here's a great tax loophole strategy for those of you who have a high-income job and are already in one of the highest tax brackets. In this case, your goal isn't more income—it's more deductions. Your eBay business may well lose money (on paper) through a combination of expenses and deductions, including the salaries you are paying to your kids and other dependents. This paper loss can be used to offset and reduce your net income, thus reducing your taxes. A large enough loss may even drop your income into a lower tax bracket, saving you even more. All of this would happen even though your business may be cash-flow positive and earn money for you each and every month.

Expenses and Your Kids and Other Dependents

As employees of your eBay business, your children and other dependents will be entitled to take advantage of the same tax deductions and write-offs that you do. If your kids are out looking for merchandise for the business, it's a reasonable assumption that they'll need a cell phone to keep in touch with other business employees. Likewise, your mother is just as entitled to take a mileage deduction for her trips to the post office or office supply store as you are when you're out and about on your business-related activities.

The key to claiming all of these deductions is that they are properly documented. Busfare or cabfare can be a write-off if your child or elder has made notes of where he or she was going (in addition to keeping receipts for any merchandise he or she purchased). So consider lumping errands together—a doctor or dentist's visit in conjunction with a scouting or merchandise buying trip, for example. A little discretion will be called for on your part with some of these items. When it comes to cell phones, you may not want to claim your child's entire amount each month—especially if he or she has spent 95 percent of the time on the phone with friends.

You can find an expense sheet in Appendix G that's handy for both you and your eBay business's other employees. We've also provided a downloadable version of this form at the companion web site.

Medical Coverage and Your eBay Business

This is where the C corporation shines. Both C and S corporations can purchase healthcare coverage for their employees and their dependents and have the costs be a write-off for the business. Even better, C corporation employees aren't required to declare the value of those benefits on their tax returns, because the benefits are not considered taxable by the IRS. That means you have a tax write-off for your eBay business with no corresponding impact to you as an individual taxpayer.

S corporation employee-owners aren't quite so lucky. While the corporation can take the deduction for healthcare expenses, every employee-owner who owns more than 2 percent of the S corporation must declare the healthcare benefit he or she receives as taxable income. Still, half a strategy is better than no strategy at all, and you can always adjust the income you receive from your S corporation to provide for this scenario.

> **Caution:**
>
> If you elect to set up a health-care insurance plan, the same rules apply to you that would apply to any nonfamily business—namely, that all employees must be offered the same type of coverage.

One thing we really love about this tax loophole is that it can come in especially handy when your children are older and going off to college. By keeping them on your eBay business's payroll as employees, they will remain covered, even after your kids are older than 25 and no longer eligible for dependent coverage. And, although most colleges do offer some medical coverage to their students, with your own coverage in place, you can be assured that your kids' healthcare needs are protected.

It is much easier for a corporation to obtain healthcare coverage than it is for private individuals. Even though your eBay business may be your sole source of income and you the only employee, operating through a corporation may be your best way to get around a healthcare insurance provider's reluctance to insure individuals. Establishing a group benefit plan for your business may also be your way of getting a family member covered who would otherwise be considered uninsurable by healthcare insurance providers—a growing problem in this country.

Medical Reimbursement Plans

If a company-paid medical insurance plan is not feasible or economical for your eBay business, consider implementing a medical reimbursement plan instead. Your eBay business can reimburse family medical costs directly, bypassing the entire health insurance industry. You can set up a medical reimbursement plan to be as open or as restrictive as you like. For example, you can set a per-year cap on individual expenses or elect to reimburse only certain procedures. Because it is a plan between your eBay business and its employees, it can be structured in whatever way best fits your and your family's needs.

To show you how easy it is to set up a medical reimbursement plan, we've prepared some additional information and forms that you can use as a base to draft the medical reimbursement plan options that are right for you. You can find this information on the companion web site.

Vacations and Your eBay Business

In addition to the obvious personal benefits of vacations, they are a great way to hold an annual meeting for your business. If you have a C or S corporation, you are required by law to hold an annual meeting and produce annual minutes. You're also entitled to take a deduction for the expenses incurred to hold that annual meeting. So, while on your vacation, reserve space on one day to hold your company's annual meeting and make that portion of your vacation deductible as a business expense.

If you are vacationing within the United States, you can deduct your airfare as well, as long as you do business on the first and last days of your vacation. If you're out of the country, you can take a percentage of your airfare, the same way you are already doing with your hotels and meals for the days that you are working. So, a five-day vacation with annual meeting still nets your eBay business 20 percent of your vacation costs as a deduction.

This is a wonderful way to combine business with pleasure and for everyone to share in the benefits of your family eBay business!

Retirement Planning and Your eBay Business

Are you sitting down? Good. This next part surprised even us.

If part of your overall eBay business plan is creating a better financial future for you and your family, consider this: A child who begins investing at an earlier age can contribute less and earn more at retirement than an adult who begins investing later in life.

> **Choices in Saving for Retirement**
> • Save 6 years at $2,500 per year
> Or
> • Save 40 years at $29,703 per year
> The end result is the same.
> The difference is when you start.

We talked about why we love Roth IRAs earlier in the book. Here's another reason to love them. The reason we like Roth IRAs so much is because the income you make is tax free, which means *tax never*. A regular plan is tax deferred, which means later. Tax never is always better than tax later. The plan that follows works equally well for regular pension plans.

Say you are paying your 12-year-old daughter the maximum tax-free earnings before tax amount of $4,580, and of that amount you put $2,500 per year into a Roth IRA (she's got to have *some* spending money). Do this every year for your daughter between the ages of 12 and 18. Then allow the Roth IRA to grow. When your daughter is ready to retire at age 65, that little Roth IRA will have grown—a lot. In fact, according to our data (run through an amortization program called "T-Values 5") your child's little Roth IRA nest egg would be worth a whopping $1,871,367.85, assuming a 10 percent growth rate!

Contrast that to an adult starting to save for retirement at age 45. Even though the 45-year-old will have 20 years to save for retirement at age 65, he will still need to put $29,703.08 away each and every year to catch up to your daughter's little Roth IRA.

But you don't have to limit your retirement planning to young children. All of us are going to need to be increasingly responsible for looking after our own financial futures. If eBay can help you to look after yours, then why not get started tonight? Here are the numbers for a 40-year-old person who clears $5,000 from an eBay business and invests the current maximum of $4,000 per year into a Roth IRA for the next 10 years:

Earn 5 percent on your money	$200,454
Earn 10 percent on your money	$432,727
Earn 20 percent on your money	$2,265,509

And remember that in both of these instances, your current tax burden has been reduced, while at the same time you've been moving a percentage of your after-tax expenses to pre-tax dollars, so you haven't been living like a miser, either.

Do you see how owning an eBay business and operating it in a tax-advantaged manner might benefit you and your family?

Jenny's New Plan

Jenny sipped her piña colada and watched the boys play in the surf from her chaise lounge under a large umbrella. They were enjoying the sunshine in Cancun, Mexico, after a year of hard work.

When Tia Olivia had finished the books and the tax return was filed, Jenny's corporation had put about $7,000 in cash into her pocket. The paper losses it had sustained had also helped to drop her from her previous low end of the 25 percent tax bracket into the high end of the 15 percent tax bracket, saving Jenny another 10 percent of her existing salary in taxes. All in all, that little eBay idea had come up as a big winner. Jenny had decided to make sure that everyone shared in their wealth, so she booked a week in Cancun for herself and the boys. A quick chat with Tia

Olivia had also yielded Jenny some more good news—holding her company's annual meeting one of the mornings they were in Cancun would save her about $1,200, as that portion of their trip now became a write-off that Jenny could expense back to the company. She and the boys had held their meeting earlier that day to talk about what their eBay business had done for them so far and where they wanted it to go.

One of the things they had learned during the year was that Roberto was a great merchandise hunter. He had done a lot of research into which video games were commanding a good price on eBay, and two days a week, Roberto went out after school on a scouting expedition to the local second-hand and thrift shops. David was a little less patient than his brother and didn't like combing through "all that junk," as he called it. His contribution to the family business was in packing items, labeling packages, and keeping track of what had sold and what hadn't.

Both boys enjoyed their new cell phones—Roberto used his extensively when he was out product hunting. He'd take a picture of an item and send it to David, who manned the computer and was able to tell him instantly what the item was worth and whether or not it was worth buying. They both also enjoyed the fact that they could have fancy family vacations in exotic places like Cancun.

But the boys didn't enjoy sharing a bedroom, even if it was the biggest bedroom in the apartment. So, one of the things Jenny and the boys had discussed was what to do with their profits. Jenny had taken some investment and business education classes and had recently begun reading books on real estate and real estate investing. It seemed to her that if the family could keep its eBay business's profits consistent, or even grow them over the next year or two, that owning their own home—with at *least* three bedrooms—wasn't out of the question. Jenny explained it this way: "We can move to a larger apartment, and pay more in rent, and probably still have enough left over to go to Cancun every couple of years. But that won't solve our long-term problems. At the end of 10 years, we'll still be living in someone else's property. Or, we can save for our own home and pay more for our mortgage than we do for rent now. We might not get to Cancun as often, but at the end of 10 years we'll have the equity we've earned and the appreciation our property has accumulated—which might be enough to let us rent the house out to someone else as an investment property, take out some of our home equity, and *move* to Cancun. What sounds better to you?"

The minutes had recorded a resounding "aye!" to that particular vote, and the annual meeting had concluded with high-fives around the table and a sense of excitement among the company owners about the possibilities and their new corporate goal.

Next Steps—Finding Benefits for Your Whole Family

The benefits to running an eBay business can go further than you think, and allow you to provide for children and other dependents using pre-tax dollars. If you have children or support other people, raising your awareness of these tax benefits could lower the taxes you'll pay. Determine who you want to help support (or are likely to in the near future). Include children, parents, nieces, nephews, or anyone else that you know you'll be helping to support. Then, employ them in your eBay business.

1. Identify jobs for them within your company.
2. Write up job descriptions.
3. Have dependents keep time sheets.
4. Pay reasonable wages.
5. If you're employing a child, determine an investment plan.
6. Consider implementing a health-care plan or a medical reimbursement plan to cover your dependents and shift medical expenses to pre-tax dollars.

Part 4

For Advanced eBay Sellers

11

What Happens When You've Sold Everything in Your Garage?

Until now we've been discussing your eBay business as a fairly small-scale operation. Let's expand your horizons a bit and see what else you can do with eBay. After all, the stuff you have in your garage isn't going to last forever—and you'll need to think about what happens to your business when it's gone.

Find a Passion (and Sell It!)

Most of us love to do some particular thing. We have a passion. The trick is to find a way to combine your passion with your business. For example, handcrafted items such as knit afghans, wood carvings, and quilts all have a market on eBay. How about restoring old wooden furniture or art deco table lamps? Once you start looking, you'll see plenty of room for creativity and art on eBay.

How about food items? If you are a barbeque sauce maker, or you love to make jam for your neighbors, consider expanding your market. These items are both saleable on eBay—you just need to make sure that you're in compliance with any local licensing or food production requirements.

When Diane lived in Reno, Nevada, she would occasionally go to the main post office on Saturdays. Without fail, every Saturday a man would come in just before the post office closed with 50 to 60 packages. Through shameless eavesdropping and asking the postal clerks for information,

Diane learned that the man's wife had a business on eBay selling appliquéd wall clocks. She would take a plain, white plastic wall clock and decorate it in a variety of patterns, selling the completed product on eBay. Given the volume of packages (as evidenced by the weary sighs of the postal clerks each time this man came running in minutes before the post office was supposed to close), business was good.

Note: A couple of caveats: You can't sell lottery tickets, guns, tobacco, alcohol, body parts, sexual acts, or humans. You also can't sell copyrighted items, except in a few instances (for example, you can sell used books but you can't photocopy and sell copies of used books). To learn more about items that are completely prohibited or prohibited except in certain circumstances, visit eBay's web site at http://pages.ebay.com/help/sell/questions/prohibited-items.html.

Wholesaler and Drop Shipper Lists

You can develop new product lines and grow or continue your eBay business by purchasing goods through a wholesaler or using a drop shipper. You can purchase a specified lot of items from a wholesaler that you can then resell through your eBay business. If you work with a drop shipper, you act as a portal. Buyers buy the item from you at whatever price you negotiate or offer, and then you in turn purchase the item from the drop shipper, who ships the item directly to the purchaser.

Designer items such as handbags and shoes are hot-selling items on eBay. Judging by the number of sellers (many with feedback numbering into the thousands) who are operating in these areas, a lot of people have purchased one or more wholesaler lists and are taking advantage of these contacts to start and build their eBay businesses. DVDs, computer equipment, and handheld electronics are other popular sale categories.

Caution: Be careful when you are looking to find a wholesaler or a drop shipper list. Many of the lists you see offered for sale are not what they advertise themselves to be, and some are downright fraudulent. eBay recommends World Wide Brands, a certified wholesaler; this should be your first stop when researching new product lines. You can find them on the web at www.worldwidebrands.com. Another trusted site to source wholesale goods is What Do I Sell, which you can find at www.whatdoisell.com.

> Are you knowledgeable about and confident enough to sell a particular line of products? Then again, with the advent of researching on Google, you don't necessarily have to know anything about what you are selling—only how to sell it!

Become a Trading Assistant

A consignment shop is a retail establishment where people can take merchandise to be sold through the shop. The merchandise owner and the shop owner agree ahead of time on a price range. The shop owner looks after displaying, marketing, and selling the item in return for a portion of the sales price. After the sale has been completed, the shop owner sends the merchandise owner his or her share of the profit.

The same idea applies to eBay Trading Assistants; they are virtual shop owners, and a *trading post* is their consignment shop (although not every trading assistant operates a trading post). People wishing to sell merchandise can search the eBay Trading Assistant listings for someone in their area and arrange to drop off their merchandise for listing and sale. They can take advantage of the trading assistant's selling and marketing expertise to get their items sold on the most favorable terms possible. Each trading assistant runs his or her own independent business—trading assistants don't work for eBay as employees or independent contractors.

Trading assistants make consignment sales easy by handling all aspects of the auction, from listing and selling the item, to all communication and shipping issues. Trading assistants are also responsible for payment of all eBay and PayPal fees on the sale.

Generally speaking, trading assistants take a commission of between 20 and 40 percent of an item's final selling price.

It's easy (and free!) to become a trading assistant by setting up a profile in eBay. Just make sure you meet these four requirements before you create your profile:

- You've sold at least four items in the past 30 days.
- You have a feedback score of 50 or higher.
- At least 97 percent of that feedback is positive.
- Your eBay account is in good standing.

You can find out more by going to http://pages.ebay.com/tahub/index.html, where you will find information on legal contracts, how to price your services properly, and how to use eBay marketing tools, including business cards.

When setting up your profile, the more information you can provide the better. eBay does not certify or guarantee any of its trading assistants, and most potential clients want as much information as they can get from you before they even pick up the phone. By answering the most critical questions in your trading assistant profile, potential clients may be more willing to contact you, instead of another local trading assistant who is vague on the important details (such as fee and payment terms).

Here are some of the basic questions for which you'll want to provide answers in your listing:

- What kinds of items do you accept? Do they need to be of a certain minimum value?

- Do you pick up merchandise or are you a drop-off business? If you pick up, do you charge extra for that service?
- What, if any, input do clients have in the item's description or listing price?
- Do you charge a fee, and if so, how much? Do your fees vary depending on item size, item type, and final sale price? Does your fee include the eBay listing fees?
- How long after a sale do you pay the client, and in what fashion? Check, PayPal, money order?
- What happens if a client's item doesn't sell? Do you return the item, request that the client pick it up, or drop it off at a local charity or thrift store? If you dispose of an item for a client, do you levy any additional charge for that service?

eBay has some excellent resources to help you explore becoming a trading assistant. Try the Trading Assistant Toolkit, which you can find at http://contact.ebay.com/ws/eBayISAPI.dll?TradingAssistant&page=toolkit, or the Trading Assistants Discussion Board at http://forums.ebay.com/db1/forum.jspa?forumID=106, for some great information and feedback from other eBay trading assistants.

Open a Trading Post

If you're operating a large and successful eBay business, you might want to think about opening an eBay Trading Post. The requirements here are much tougher than becoming a trading assistant—to start with, you need to have a sales volume on eBay of at least $25,000 every month. You also need a feedback score of at least 500, with a positive rating of 98 percent or more, and a staffed drop-off location with regular business hours that clients can visit without calling ahead. These are certainly advanced requirements, but those eBay sellers who qualify may receive preferential listing treatment.

Whatever You Do, Do Something!

If you've gone to all of the work of creating an eBay business and have begun to enjoy the fruits of your hard work, don't let it go to waste. The value and tax savings that your eBay business can provide really do make it worth continuing—even after the garage is empty!

Catching Up with Joe

When we last visited Joe, he and his wife were thinking about moving to a bigger house so that Joe would have room for his eBay business. Joe had learned, through discussions with Marty, his CPA, that between saving money on rent and the excellent business deductions they would get through operating a home office, closing his shop and opening a home office made sense.

Six months later, Joe and Marie had moved, and Joe's eBay business was doing well. Even so, Joe was now looking at his expansion possibilities. He had noticed that at the auctions he was visiting, a large volume of office furniture and equipment were also up for sale. Joe figured there was a market for this stuff, too, if he could figure out the logistics. The storage and shipping puzzled him—even though he had more room for his inventory in his new house, he didn't have enough room to begin storing desks, conference tables, and filing cabinets, yet the used furniture market on eBay sure seemed brisk.

Joe decided to do a little more research. He began by looking at the types of items for sale on eBay, looking carefully at the sellers and how they operated. What he discovered was that in many instances, the buyer was responsible for making shipping arrangements and picking up the merchandise. That seemed fairly safe to Joe, because it meant he wasn't responsible for ensuring delivery to the buyer, so he wouldn't be scammed by some unscrupulous buyer claiming nonreceipt of an item. Buyers could make whatever shipping and pickup arrangements they wanted, and as long as Joe had a signature that an item had left the building, he would be safe.

In terms of space, Joe wondered if he could sell items directly from a client's office or other location. He knew that plenty of offices around town had old furniture or desks kicking around in storage and would appreciate someone getting rid of the stuff for them. If he really needed to, Joe thought he could probably rent a storage locker from a local facility and keep any merchandise there until it sold.

As he was researching office furniture resales on eBay, Joe noticed that many of the items were being sold by people and companies advertising themselves as eBay Trading Assistants. He researched further and learned that trading assistants sold items on a consignment basis. This seemed like a great idea to Joe, as it meant that his out-of-pocket costs would be very low, since he wasn't buying the item for resale. He could negotiate a selling price range with a client and list the item for them. The item could stay at the client's location in most instances until the sale, when it would be picked up by the purchaser. He could also negotiate a guaranteed fee if the client took matters into his or her own hands and sold the item out from under Joe. But ideally the client wouldn't have to do anything, which Joe thought would be an attractive incentive—and he wouldn't have to do much either, other than take a few pictures and run an auction.

Joe liked the idea, so he went to the Trading Assistant section on eBay and designed his profile. He noted his success and positive feedback rating in his description, and set out his selling and consignment terms. He decided to keep his fees and commission fairly small, as he wouldn't have any significant costs or overhead with this new project. Besides, he reasoned, he could always raise prices later, depending on whether or not the concept took off.

Joe decided that the best way to promote his new service was to advertise locally. He arranged for a one-page flyer insert describing his services to go into a local newspaper with a large circulation among businesses in the area. The results were slow but steady, and Joe was soon doing a thriving business as a trading assistant in addition to his regular used computer equipment eBay business.

Next Steps—Taking the Steps toward a Larger Business

Once you're comfortable with your business operations you might want to start thinking about how you can expand and grow your eBay business. Many people start small, but get so much satisfaction from operating their own businesses they look for ways to turn things around and make that part-time business a full-time occupation.

1. Now is your chance to dream big. What is next step you'll need to take your eBay business to the next level?
2. Where do you see your business in one year? In three years? In five years?
3. What action step can you can take in the next week to make that more of a reality?

12

Advanced Tax Loopholes and Business Strategies

I n Chapter 11, we began discussing ways to expand and continue your eBay business. In this chapter, we show you some techniques you can use to continue saving taxes and increasing revenues as your business income increases. We also introduce some solutions for the question we hope you'll ask: "What should I do with all this money I've made?"

Create Intellectual Property

Intellectual property consists of tangible things like a visual style, logos, trademarks, and patents. But it can also consist of systems and methods you've developed to do certain things. Colonel Sanders' "secret blend of 11 herbs and spices" is a perfect example of a method. Microsoft's source code for software applications is another example. The design and layout of a fast food restaurant franchise is an example of a visual style that serves as intellectual property. The method that restaurant franchise uses to prepare its food is an example of a system.

Do you have a logo to go along with your business name? Do you use a tagline in connection with your business name or logo? Do you manufacture and sell a unique product? These are all great examples of intellectual property.

Intellectual property also includes things like a specialized color-coded filing system used in a doctor's office, or a chiropractor's office setup that moves patients through the office in a time-efficient manner. It could also be the way that you carry out certain business-related tasks: how you code your inventory to know what items are for sale, sold, pending payment, and ready to be shipped; how you deal and negotiate with wholesale suppliers; or how you deal with clients as a trading assistant. The way you do things is actually a *system*. If it's effective, properly documented, and written up, it is also an asset. And that means it has value.

Why is this important? Because you now have an asset that you can protect by having it trademarked or patented. You can also earn money with this asset by licensing it to other people or businesses to use. If the license agreement is set up properly, you may receive the license fees or royalty income as *passive* income for tax purposes, rather than *earned* income. And, as you learned back in earlier chapters, passive income is taxed at a lower rate than earned income. This intellectual property asset has now created a whole new source of income for you.

Trademarks, Copyrights, and Patents

If you have developed a business logo or a tagline that you want to associate with just your company, you can apply to have it trademarked. A trademark essentially claims ownership of its subject, meaning nobody else can legally use that logo or tag line without acknowledging your ownership and/or compensating you for it in some way. That's the simplified version—obtaining a trademark is somewhat more complicated. For example, you can choose to trademark your logo or tagline in an individual state or states, in the United States as a whole, in Canada, in Europe, or elsewhere in the world.

You've also got to think about categories. Trademarks may be classified into hundreds of different categories. When you file your trademark application, you choose the categories you want to cover, however, bear in mind that the more categories you select, the higher your costs will be. It also doesn't guarantee blanket protection. If someone came along at a later date with a logo or tagline that is similar or even identical to yours, but was using it in a different category that you had not selected, you would have no right to object.

Then there's enforcement. To protect any sort of intellectual property, you need to be ready, willing, and able to take action against anyone who would try to copy or use your trademarked property. Under intellectual property law, you can't pick and choose when you fight an infringement battle—you must stand up every time.

Of course, all of these things are expensive. This isn't to say that you should forget trying to protect your intellectual property at all, but you will need to weigh the costs of obtaining and defending a trademark against the overall value that trademark brings to your business.

The best place to learn more about trademarks is at the U.S. Patent and Trademark Office's web site, www.uspto.gov. You can usually find information about state-level trademarks on each state's secretary of state web site.

Copyrights are much cheaper and easier to file than either trademarks or patents (which are the most expensive of all).

> You can usually find information about state-level trademarks on each state's secretary of state web site. Links to all 50 web sites are found at www.taxloopholes.com/ebay_sellers.

Copyright protection is usually granted to any written or otherwise personally created works. Books, music, plays, software programs, speeches, and paintings are all examples of typical copyrighted items. Filing a copyright can be as simple as completing a form, attaching it to a copy of the thing you want to copyright, and sending your application in to the Library of Congress, where all of the copyrights are recorded and stored. The fee to file a copyright usually runs around $30. Visit www.copyright.gov to learn more about this program.

Patents are the "big daddy" of the intellectual property world. A patent is usually placed on a unique product or a system or method of doing things. A common example of a patented product is a prescription drug formula—all of the major drug companies spend millions of dollars patenting and protecting their drug formulas. Although a patent is the strongest form of intellectual property protection, it's also the most difficult protection to get—and the most expensive. Getting a patent can be an exhaustive and lengthy procedure, as your patent advisors try to make sure they have accounted for and protected all possible variations and permutations of your product. But depending on the value of your intellectual property, it may be worth the cost and effort.

Here's a famous example of a lost patent: The person who invented the paperclip filed a patent over his creation, which was granted. But because he didn't specify that a paperclip could be made of anything other than smooth metal, he left the door open for competitors to come to market with the crimped style of paperclip, as well as paperclips that are covered in multicolored plastic, triangular-shaped paperclips, and more. Because the original inventor had not filed a patent that protected his design from such variations, he didn't have a claim for patent infringement, he couldn't stop these other paperclip designs from entering the market, and he wasn't entitled to receive any license fees or royalties from their sale.

You can find information about the patenting process at the U.S. Patent and Trademark Office's web site, www.uspto.gov (the same place that trademarks are filed).

Caution: Intellectual property is a huge and complex subject that's far beyond the scope of this book. You need good legal and business advice and assistance if you're going to pursue intellectual property protection. If you have something unique, and you're serious about protecting it, don't be the paperclip guy. Get an expert to help you make sure your intellectual property is fully protected.

Ways to Save Taxes with Business Structures

Let's say your business is really taking off. You have more money than you know what to do with. That's when the fun starts! The first tax-saving strategy has to do with using *business structures.*

Most small businesses will start as an S corporation or a limited liability company (LLC). Now might be the time to take a second look at the type of business structure you're using. If you decided to use a standard LLC (taxed as a sole proprietorship or a partnership) to begin your eBay business, but are now ready to do a little extra work and pay a lot less tax, you can elect a different taxing structure (an S corporation or a C corporation) for your LLC.

On the other hand, if you began your eBay business as an S corporation, it might be time to re-examine becoming a C corporation. A C corporation has two main benefits over an S corporation: First, the C corporation allows you to take more tax-free benefits, such as 100-percent deducted medical insurance and a medical reimbursement plan. Second, the C corporation is a separately taxed structure. The first $50,000 of taxable income within a C corporation is taxed at 15 percent. Let's assume that you have a high income and are currently being taxed at the highest personal rate of 35 percent. If you can move $50,000 of that business income to a C corporation from an S corporation, you'll move 35-percent taxed money into 15-percent taxed money. The tax savings in this case is a whopping $10,000!

You can accomplish this move in a couple of ways. First, you can "flunk" the S corporation test, so that your corporation automatically becomes a C corporation. Or, you can file a form with the IRS requesting the change from S to C corporate status. Be sure of your decision before you proceed. The IRS will only let you change a corporation's tax status once.

If you want to keep the S corporation intact, you could open a separate corporation and form it as a C corporation. You could then move over part of your eBay business or charge a fee from your S corporation to the C corporation. The fee charged would reduce the S corporation income and increase the C corporation income. In effect, you upstream your income from one entity to another.

Using Real Estate as a Wealth-Building, Tax-Saving Strategy

One of our absolute favorite tax-savings strategies is to use the profits from a business to buy a piece of commercial property, such as a warehouse or office building. Your eBay business can then rent space from the entity holding the building, and you can earn money by renting out space in that building to other tenants.

Ideally, you should buy a building that has multiple tenants and not just your eBay business. You don't want the IRS to get the idea that you are playing a shell game with your income; that's the stuff that breeds audits and isn't healthy for your business operations. Plus, your eBay business will write a rent check (deduction) and pay the rent to a protected entity. For holding property, nothing beats an LLC or a limited partnership (LP). The rent received is income, but, with real estate loopholes, you will be able to write off that income as well. The bottom line is that you have created a deduction with no resulting taxable income. At the same time, you have acquired an asset that should increase in value.

You can apply the same idea to other types of assets (equipment, furniture, computers, and so on) as well. Any type of asset can be purchased by a tax-advantaged LLC or LP and licensed to your C or S corporation eBay business.

Holding Assets in an LLC or LP

For holding assets that you expect to appreciate over time, nothing beats an LLC or LP. Each of these business structures is ideally set up to protect your assets from creditors, while flowing the profits back to you in the most tax-advantaged way possible. These structures also have the best tax treatment when you sell appreciated assets.

Here are some of the advantages that LLCs and LPs offer:

- They allow for flow-through, single-level taxation (that is, the profits and losses flow through to the personal tax returns of the LLC's or LP's owners).
- They act as a shield to protect the assets held inside from creditors of the owners.
- They act as a shield to protect your family home without losing the valuable IRS homeowner mortgage interest tax deduction.
- If set up properly, they allow for estate planning and succession to your children on a tax-free basis through gifting.

In some states, LPs are the best choice, because sometimes LLCs are taxed at a higher rate than LPs.

These are just general, introductory concepts. You can find out all you ever wanted to know, and more, about LLCs and LPs at www.taxloopholes.com.

Why LLCs and LPs Protect Your Assets Better than Corporations Do

In Chapter 2, we mentioned that LLCs and LPs were better entities to hold appreciating assets, and that we'd tell you more about it in Chapter 12. Here's the scoop.

In most states, a creditor's right to seize and sell assets that belong to an LLC or LP are severely restricted, except in certain circumstances. For example, if you were sued personally, all of the assets that you held through an LLC or LP would be safe from a judgment creditor (the person or company who wins a lawsuit against you), because most state laws don't consider those assets to be your personal property. In addition, most state laws won't allow a judgment creditor to seize your interests in an LLC or an LP. This is *not* the case for your shares in a C or S corporation. Where corporations are concerned, a judgment creditor can apply to the court to be granted ownership of your shares. Once a judgment creditor has taken ownership of your C or S corporation shares, that creditor can sell off the assets of the business to pay the judgment.

If someone was suing your LLC or LP directly, the situation would be different. In this case, a judgment creditor could reach the assets of the LLC or LP, because the judgment is directly against the entity. So, the idea is to keep the entity that does business with the public and has the most risk of being sued separate from the asset-holding business structure. If your LLC or LP is operating quietly in the background, holding title to the building out of which your eBay business corporation is operating, it will be much more difficult for an angry individual to claim that your LLC or LP was somehow involved in whatever actions led to the lawsuit. That individual will be stuck with a claim against the C or S corporation only, as that was the structure with which he or she did business.

Asset Protection: A corporation protects *your* assets against acts of the business. An LP or an LLC protects *business assets* against acts committed by you.

On the chance that someone threatens to name you personally in a lawsuit, remember that as long as you haven't done anything illegal and have been acting in the best interests of the company, you should be protected by corporate law, which says that officers, directors, and owners can't be personally sued along with a corporation.

Segregation of assets is one of the best legal methods available to protect yourself. And make no mistake—as your eBay business expands and you come in contact with an increasing number of other people and businesses, your risk will grow proportionately. Some think tanks estimate that one in ten Americans will become the subject of a lawsuit at least once in their lives. Operating through a proper business structure and using other business structures to segregate and hold your appreciating assets may be the best business move you make—and the one that saves you from losing everything you've worked so hard to build.

One more special side note about LLCs. We discussed how having an LLC can protect your assets better than a corporation. But, as you learned earlier, a corporation (either S or C) is generally the best structure to use for your business for tax purposes. You might want to consider combining both. An LLC can actually elect how it wants to be taxed, and that means you can elect to be taxed as either an S corporation or as a C corporation. This election is made on Form 8832, which you file with the IRS.

Create Wealth through Your eBay Business

Diane offers a program through her company, TaxLoopholes, LLC, called *Jump Start Your Wealth*. You can use this seven-step program to create massive amounts of wealth for yourself and your family. And that little eBay business that you started back in Chapter 1 can be the catalyst.

> To learn more about Diane Kennedy's *Jump Start Your Wealth* program, along with other tax-saving and real estate investing strategies, visit her web site at www.taxloopholes.com.

Jump Start works for clients from all walks of life. It consists of seven essential steps for people who want to change their lives by taking control and changing their wealth. These seven steps are the same for everyone, no matter what your current financial situation. That's because the critical element to Jump Start isn't *how much* money you make; it's *how you make* your money.

Here are the seven Jump Start steps:

- **Step 1**—Create a business and maximize your business income with tax loopholes.
- **Step 2**—Maximize your tax-free benefits with tax loopholes by discovering your "hidden" business deductions.
- **Step 3**—Once you have minimized your taxes from your business, pay your taxes.
- **Step 4**—Invest in real estate and maximize your real estate investments with real estate loopholes.
- **Step 5**—Maximize your cash flow with real estate loopholes.
- **Step 6**—Buy a house and maximize your home investment with home loopholes.
- **Step 7**—Get money out of your house! Maximize your cash flow with home loopholes.

Create a Business and Maximize Your Business Income with Tax Loopholes

Creating a business is step one of Diane's seven-step Jump Start Program. You must decide what type of business you will have, and from there, design your loophole strategy. This is where your wealth-building process really begins.

Businesses get the best tax breaks—and that shouldn't come as a surprise. After all, businesses use supplies, produce products, and most importantly hire employees and advisors. People who work pay taxes and buy products. It's called *circular economics*—the more people who are working, the stronger our economy.

The majority of tax loopholes are in areas that the government would like us to be more active—for example, in starting and operating your own businesses and investing in real estate. In fact, when it comes to having a home office, the IRS is downright aggressive in its promotion efforts.

Maximize Your Tax-Free Benefits with Tax Loopholes by Discovering Your "Hidden" Business Deductions

In step two, you discover your "hidden" business deductions. These are expenses that you currently pay for with after-tax money. Now, with a legitimate business (don't forget step one!), you can look at these expenses with new eyes. In this step, we review the theory behind what is deductible, look at more than 300 items that could be expensed, and then work through an exercise to review every single personal expense that you have.

Remember, though, that you must have a legitimate business and a legitimate business purpose for the expenses you deduct. The IRS takes a very dim view of the periodic hustlers who sell people on the idea that they can set up a nonexistent business just to write off personal expenses. You must have a business purpose, and you must have a real business.

Once You Have Minimized Your Taxes from Your Business, Pay Your Taxes

Step three is to pay your taxes. Diane's CPA firm, D. Kennedy & Associates (www.dkacpa.com), works hard to find innovative methods for legally reducing taxes.

Steps one and two helped you reduce the amount of taxes you will pay through legal means. In step three of Jump Start, we look at the way you are currently paying taxes and show you different ways to pay your taxes that can benefit you. Even if you are a W-2 employee, you can use certain strategies to maximize the return from your tax money. But if you are a business owner, even more strategies are available to you.

Invest in Real Estate and Maximize Your Real Estate Investments with Real Estate Loopholes

The first three Jump Start steps dealt with starting a business and taking advantage of all of the deductions and loopholes available to business owners. Steps four through seven all relate to real estate. Why? Because real estate grows wealth quickly, especially when you take advantage of the Jump Start leverage and velocity wealth-building strategies.

In step four, you get started buying real estate. We show you how to look for good, solid real estate investments that will return positive cash flow to you. The goal is to invest as much as possible from your business income into real estate. In fact, your ultimate goal will be to receive mainly passive income. In step three, you learned about the types of taxable income and their tax rates. Passive income has the lowest rate of taxable income, so you can use the money from your business to build a basis of real estate for yourself.

Maximize Your Cash Flow with Real Estate Loopholes

As your property appreciates in value, what you do with that money becomes important. That's where step five comes in. We show you how to leverage the equity in your properties to build your portfolio quickly and with minimum risk.

Buy a House and Maximize Your Home Investment with Home Loopholes

In step six, it's time to buy your home. And while creating a business first and buying a home second may seem backward, if you think about it for a few minutes it makes sense. By creating a business first and investing the profits into real estate investments, you have created sources of income for yourself that can help you to buy the home you want—and in the most tax-advantaged way. Your equity and assets will help you secure a good mortgage on terms beneficial to you. That means you can buy the smart way—making sure that you don't overextend yourself financially. And, finally, you can make sure you have asset protection on your home by using an LLC to hold the title, instead of holding it personally.

Get Money Out of Your House! Maximize Your Cash Flow with Home Loopholes

In step six, you bought your home. In step seven, it's time to ask yourself this: How can I turn my house purchase from a liability (something that takes money from my pocket) into an asset (something that puts money into my pocket)? In step seven, you will discover some of the home loopholes available for the innovative homeowner.

Diane has clients that do nothing more than take advantage of one or more of these home loopholes to increase their wealth dramatically. One of Diane's clients takes advantage of the "two-out-of-five-year" rule to live in homes that he rehabilitates. He always chooses older neighborhoods that are "on their way up." He buys a house and fixes it up; then sells it and he collects proceeds—tax free! Of course, pulling off such a plan needs good financing, credit lines, or a cash reserve.

The point is, your home can be an asset if you are prepared to look at home ownership just a little bit differently than you may have done in the past.

Have you noticed that throughout this book, we've already covered steps one through three? That's because having a business is, in Diane's eyes, critical to your overall success. The business is the first step, because it allows you to begin to move away from your status as a W-2 wage earner and the onerous taxation burden that goes along with that status.

Jump-Start Your Wealth with eBay

If you use your eBay business profits to invest in rental real estate, you accomplish two things: First, you create another source of income for yourself. Even if your properties are barely cash-flow positive, as long as at the end of the day you have a few more dollars coming in than going out, you have created another income source. Second, you create another powerful source of deductions. The depreciation and other expenses that come with rental real estate can create paper losses, and all of those paper losses can flow back against your income, reducing, or maybe even eliminating, your tax bill entirely.

Perhaps the most important element of rental real estate, though, is the appreciation that these properties are going to experience over time. You can leverage that appreciation by refinancing, pulling equity out, and reinvesting that equity in additional properties. You can thus create a self-sustaining income portfolio that is going to continue to grow over time.

Make no mistake about it. There is a finite supply of real estate in the United States and an increasing population. Everyone needs to live somewhere. Real estate is a potent source of income, wealth, and financial security for millions of people around the world. Your eBay business can help you get there, no matter what the size of your operation.

Next Steps—Advanced Loophole Strategies to Increase Your Income

As business owners, we're always looking for ways to make our businesses work better and more efficiently. After all, that's how our business expands and our profits grow. But, what if you could also make some money by packaging and selling your business methods?

1. What intellectual property have you consciously or subconsciously created with your business? Could it be trademarked, copyrighted, or patented?
2. Document and protect through trademark or copyright as appropriate.
3. Review the Jump Start Your Wealth plan. What commitment do you have to take your wealth even higher with real estate investing and/or home loopholes? What is your next step?
4. What additional asset protection is needed for the wealth you are building for you and your family? Are new business structures needed?

13

The Future of
eBay Tax Issues

I f you are already an eBay seller, you've probably heard the rumblings. Local businesses in every state are complaining, long and loud, about having to pay sales taxes while eBay operators are flying under the radar.

There is no denying the impact online sales are having on commerce in the United States and around the world. The Department of Commerce reported that total online sales in 2004 reached $69.2 billion, just shy of 2 percent of all retail sales in the country. There's also no denying the impact that eBay has had on online commerce. eBay's 2004 financial statements (as filed with the Securities and Exchange Commission) show that sales in 2004 increased from $2.17 billion worldwide to $3.27 billion, a 51 percent increase.

With all of this money at stake, it is inconceivable that governments around the world won't recognize the implications of trying to tax Internet sales and won't act to implement some form of tax. The only reason it hasn't already happened is that the Internet is still a relatively new form of commerce, and the rules haven't yet been defined.

Sales Tax Is Coming to the Internet

Here in the United States, eBay sellers and business owners are looking at three possible tax scenarios:

If you aren't familiar with the term *SSTP*, go to www.stream linedsalestax.org to learn more about this major issue facing Internet retailers.

1. The IRS will impose a requirement for eBay sellers to collect and remit sales tax on all eBay sales in the same way a brick-and-mortar store would. In other words, all sales made by an eBay business would be taxed as though the purchasers were from that business's home state.
2. The IRS will act to impose an "Internet Tax" on all businesses operating on the Internet. This may not trickle down to an individual eBay seller, but if a tax were levied on eBay itself, for example, that tax would be passed on to the eBay seller community. This type of tax could also affect businesses that transact sales through eBay or through the Internet generally.
3. States will move to impose the *Streamlined Sales Tax Project* (SSTP) legislation originally enacted in 2000. Under this plan, Internet sellers would be required to collect taxes based on the purchaser's jurisdiction and remit those taxes to the purchaser's taxation authorities.

The Streamlined Sales Tax Project

Of these three possibilities, the one of most concern to the eBay community is the SSTP. The difference between this tax and the tax collection requirements of an offline store is that, in this case, businesses are effectively considered to have a *nexus* in all 50 states instead of the state where the business is located. If you sell an item to a customer in Indiana, for example, you would be responsible for collecting Indiana sales tax and remitting it to the Indiana authorities, all at your own business's expense and no matter where your business operates. The requirement for an out-of-state customer to declare his or her purchases and remit use tax to local tax authorities would disappear, as that responsibility was shifted instead to the online retailer.

The major arguments against the SSTP are that it doesn't apply to brick-and-mortar businesses, and that it will have serious negative consequences to small businesses operating on the Internet. Meg Whitman, the founder of eBay, had the following to say about enacting SSTP when speaking to the National Press Club in May 2004:

Were SSTP adopted, it would double, or even triple, the nation's taxing jurisdictions. SSTP would force businesses that operate over the Internet to collect and remit taxes in thousands of cities and counties across the country...the red tape for small businesses would be enormous.

Some 44 states have signed on to the SSTP in principle or have enacted legislation agreeing to bring state tax regulations in line with the SSTP, should it be enacted by Congress. However, eBay and other Internet retailers have not given up the fight, and the battle over a fair standard of taxation for online businesses continues.

What You Can Do About It

We believe that the taxation of Internet sales is inevitable. There's just too much money at stake and too many cash-strapped state governments for the issue to go away.

So what can you, as a beginning eBay business owner, do about it?

First, you can accept the inevitability of taxation, and plan your business operations accordingly. That means running your eBay operation through a proper business structure, so that you can offset the increased tax burden against your business income as much as possible.

Second, stay informed! Most state governments hold seminars on taxation for small business owners, often for free or for a nominal fee. Keep your eye on changes, and if you get the chance to speak out—take it!

Income Tax

Ask any eBay University teacher and he or she will likely tell you the same thing: Everyone wants to know about income tax requirements. Does eBay report to the IRS? At this juncture, eBay does not report sales to the IRS. However, if eBay or PayPal receives a legal subpoena, both have stated they would comply with the request.

Of course, that leads to what the question is really about. Is the income you make from selling items on eBay taxable? And, for some people, the question might be, "How can I get away with not paying tax?"

Some people try to hide under the radar by not registering in their own name, by using fake ID numbers, or by using a shell corporation. *That is tax fraud.* The legal method to pay less tax is the tax loopholes method. Go ahead and report the full amount of your sales. Then, correctly report the costs associated with these sales. Find your hidden business deductions. Use the right business structures, and above all, practice good recordkeeping. You'll pay less tax *and* sleep at night.

Next Steps—Get Informed to Stay Ahead of the Game

Tax law changes quickly. The IRS alone produces thousands of pages of new tax rulings each year. While we aren't suggesting that you try to become an expert in tax law, you can help yourself by keeping an eye on what's happening in this important area.

1. Stay informed. Regularly review the eBay web site for news.
2. Be proactive. Talk to your advisors regularly and ask for updates as and when tax laws affecting you and your eBay business change. You can also

use this as a measuring stick to gauge the effectiveness of your tax advisors. If you find you're constantly ahead of your advisor, it may be time to look for a new advisor.

3. Stay informed. Watch the Tax Loopholes web site and register by going to www.taxloopholes.com/ebaysellers.

Conclusion

Creating Your Own eBay Strategy

Now is when the real question comes into play. What will you do with the information you've received? Chances are you were at least intrigued with the idea of finding treasure from what you might now consider trash in your garage. Or, maybe you already have a business and are looking for a way to expand your product line into new markets and reduce costs at the same time. eBay can do all of that and more!

The plain and simple fact is that now is the time for all of us to take responsibility for our own financial future. It's estimated that 96 out of 100 Americans will need to significantly decrease their lifestyle or be dependent on someone else when they retire. If you're one of those 4 out of 100 Americans who want something better for their future, then eBay selling might just be the way to do it.

It all starts with you, though. You see, we know a lot of people will read this book and then just put it away. In fact, one of Diane's favorite reader stories came from someone who had discovered one of her books under a friend's couch. Diane's first best-selling book, *Loopholes of the Rich*, had been thumbed through but never really read. The person who discovered the book under the couch went on to apply the money making, tax saving techniques and now, years later, has been able to quit her job. The friend who originally bought the book lives in the same apartment and basically has the same life.

If you want more for your life, don't just file this book away. Keep it and refer to it, again and again. But, more importantly than that even: Take action! Go back through the chapters and photocopy the Next Steps. Make a commitment to keep moving. Take small steps at first, if you need to, but whatever you do, make some movement.

Take some kind of action today. It might be something as small as picking up a notebook and pen and committing to writing down an action step each week, or maybe it means turning on your computer and going to www.taxloopholes.com/ebaysellers to start downloading all the free information available to you. Whatever that first step means to you, do it today.

The Chinese have a saying. When is the best time to plant a tree? Answer: 10 years ago. When is the second best time to plant a tree? Answer: Today.

Plant your tree today and change the future of your family.

Part 5

Appendixes

Appendix A

The IRS Nine Steps to Business Quiz

Are you operating a business or a hobby? Take this quick test to find out!
Instructions:

1. **Line one**—Fill in the name of your company.
2. **Line two**—Fill in the type of business your company does.
3. **Questions**—Answer the questions with yes or no. Each no answer weakens your position as a business.

Name of Company: _____

Type of Business: _____

Factor One: Businesslike Manner

1. Do you have a separate bank account for your business? Yes ❏   No ❏
2. Do you (or your CPA or bookkeeper) keep
   accounting records for your business? Yes ❏   No ❏
3. Do you keep copies of receipts in a filing system? Yes ❏   No ❏
4. Do you make an effort to collect accounts receivable? Yes ❏   No ❏
5. Do you review profit and loss statements regularly? Yes ❏   No ❏

Factor Two: Time and Effort

1. Do you keep track of time spent in your
   business activity? Yes ❏   No ❏
2. Do you keep track of business appointments in a
   schedule or diary? Yes ❏   No ❏

3. Do you have notes of conversations you have had
   with consultants or experts to enhance your business? Yes ❑ No ❑
4. Do you keep evidence from business seminars that
   you have attended? Yes ❑ No ❑

Factor Three: Dependence on Income

1. Do you need the income from your business for
   your lifestyle? Yes ❑ No ❑
2. Do you intend to replace your current job with
   this business? Yes ❑ No ❑

Factor Four: Reasonable Losses

If you have losses, do you have documentation that:

1. They are normal for the type of business you
   are in at the beginning? Yes ❑ No ❑
2. Shows that other similar businesses have
   experienced the same type of downturn? Yes ❑ No ❑

Factor Five: Effort to Make Money

If you have losses, do you have evidence that:

1. You have made changes to try and improve
   your business? Yes ❑ No ❑
2. You have investigated ways to make your
   business more profitable? Yes ❑ No ❑
3. You have consulted with experienced business
   owners or other advisors regarding your business? Yes ❑ No ❑

Factor Six: Experienced Advisors

1. Have you identified the advisors you need
   for your business? Yes ❑ No ❑
2. Do your advisors have the business experience
   needed to give you good advice? Yes ❑ No ❑

Factor Seven: Your Experience

1. Have you been successful in this type of
   business before? Yes ❑ No ❑
2. Have you been successful in a similar business? Yes ❑ No ❑

Factor Eight: Past Profit

1. Has your business been profitable in previous years? Yes ❑ No ❑
2. If your business has been profitable, has the
   profit been enough to make a reasonable decision
   to continue your business? Yes ❑ No ❑

Factor Nine: Asset Appreciation

1. Is your business building assets that will have
   future appreciation?   Yes ❏   No ❏

Scoring the Test

For each of the nine sections above, rate how strong your case is as to business purpose on a scale of 1 to 5, with 5 being the strongest.

Businesslike manner	1	2	3	4	5
Time and effort	1	2	3	4	5
Dependence on income	1	2	3	4	5
Reasonable losses	1	2	3	4	5
Effort to make money	1	2	3	4	5
Experienced advisors	1	2	3	4	5
Your experience	1	2	3	4	5
Past profit	1	2	3	4	5
Asset appreciation	1	2	3	4	5

For your weakest elements, what can you do to strengthen your point score?

_____

_____

_____

Note: Don't underestimate yourself! For example, you may have shown a slight profit in your business and answered *yes* to both questions in Factor Eight, but you don't feel totally confident in this area so you rate the Factor Eight questions as only 3.

Appendix B

Asset Valuation Worksheet

(To be transferred into [NAME OF BUSINESS ENTITY])

Description of Asset	Business (B) or Inventory (I) Use	Original Purchase Date (Estimated)	Original Purchase Price (Estimated)	Present Value (Estimated)
TOTAL VALUE OF PERSONAL ASSETS AND INVENTORY TO BE TRANSFERRED INTO BUSINESS			$	

Appendix C

Resolution for Transfer of Assets, Second Promissory Note to Document Loan

U se this form to transfer personal property into the name of your corporation. Three methods of payment are set out here. Choose a method and delete the other two sections. Note that you must take taxes and other considerations into account when transferring property or assets into a corporate entity. See your attorney, CPA, or tax advisor before proceeding.

Consent Resolution of the Directors of [Name of Entity]

[FOR C OR S CORPORATIONS]

I, being the sole Director/We, being all or a quorum of the directors of *[Name of Corporation]* ("Corporation") hereby WAIVE notice of the time and place of a Meeting of the Directors of the Corporation and DO HEREBY CONSENT to the adoption of the following resolutions:

RESOLVED that *[Name of Entity]* purchase from *[Name of Person or Company Transferring Assets]* the assets set out on the attached Exhibit "A," Asset Valuation Sheet, for the following consideration:

- **CHOICE 1:** The sum of $*[amount]*, to be paid by way of the issuance of a total of *[number of share]* shares of common stock of *[Name of Entity]*, at a deemed value of $*[value per share]* per share;

- **CHOICE 2:** The sum of $[amount]$, to be paid by way of the issuance of a Promissory Note in favor of *[Name of Person Transferring in Assets or Property]* in the amount of $[value of promissory note— i.e., value of assets or property being transferred in]*, in the form attached as Exhibit "B";
- **CHOICE 3:** The sum of $[amount]$, to be paid by way of the issuance of *[number of shares]* shares of common stock in *[Name of Entity]*, at a deemed value of $[value per share] per share, together with and a Promissory Note in favor of *[Name of Person Transferring in Assets or Property]* in the amount of $[value of promissory note]$, in the form attached as Exhibit "B";

(end of choices—don't delete anything below this line)

RESOLVED that *[Name of Entity]* purchase from *[Name of Person or Company Transferring Assets]* the assets set out on the attached Exhibit "A," Asset Valuation Sheet, for the following consideration:

RESOLVED FURTHER that the shares to be issued as set out above shall, upon issuance, be fully paid and nonassessable, and shall be issued immediately upon execution of these resolutions in the following denominations and registered as follows:

Name and Address	Number of Shares/ Interests to Be Issued	Certificate No.

RESOLVED FURTHER that the President and Secretary of *[Name of Entity]* be and are hereby authorized to sign such documents and perform such deeds as are required to fully carry out and implement the corporate decisions set out in these Resolutions.

Date:_____

_____

Signature line(s) for each Director. All Directors should sign and print their names below their signatures.

Promissory Note

[A Promissory Note is written evidence of a loan. In this instance, we are using it to document the value of the assets—personal property, inventory, and any cash—that you are loaning to your corporation to get started. You may want to consult with an attorney to make sure this document is complete and does not contradict any of your state's laws. Delete any optional words or choices you are not using.]

Promissory Note

$*[AMOUNT]*   *[DATE OF NOTE]*

For value received, *[Name of Your Corporation]* of *[Address of Your Corporation]*, (hereinafter the "Promisor"), a *[State of Incorporation]* corporation, promises to pay upon demand to *[Your Name, or Name of Whoever Is Loaning Your Corporation Money or Transferring Assets]*, of *[Your Address or Other Lender's Address]* (hereinafter the "Promisee"), the principal sum of *[amount being loaned—e.g., the total value of the assets and any cash you or someone else are transferring into the corporation]* of lawful money of the United States of America on:

- **CHOICE 1:** The date that is *[due date, in months/weeks, etc.]* from the date of this Promissory Note,
- **CHOICE 2:** Demand,

together with interest on the principal sum set out above at the rate of ___% per annum, compounded annually.

[Charging interest on the loan is optional. If you don't want to charge interest, delete this sentence. If you do want to charge interest, don't charge a rate higher than current market conditions.]

The Promisor reserves the right to prepay without penalty.

As security for the repayment of this Promissory Note the Promisor agrees to grant to the Promisee a lien over all of the real and personal property now or hereafter belonging to the Promisor *[Or such other security as is being put up as collateral for the loan]*. At the request of the Promisee the Promisor shall also provide evidence of such lien in a form registerable under the Uniform Commercial Code.

All remedies hereunder or by law afforded shall be cumulative and all shall be available to the Promisee in connection with this Note until the liability of the Promisor herein created has been paid in full. In the event of any dispute, the prevailing party shall be entitled to attorneys fees and costs. Exclusive venue shall be the *[District, County, State, etc.]*.

IN WITNESS WHEREOF, the Promisor has executed this Note the day and year first above written.

PROMISOR

_____

Signature

Appendix D

State Tax Resources

These links are current as of Fall 2005, however web sites do change frequently. If you find that the link for your state doesn't work, try an Internet search for the terms "Department of Revenue <Your State>."

State Department of Revenue Web Site Links

State	Department of Revenue Web Link
Alabama	www.ador.state.al.us/
Alaska	www.tax.state.ak.us/
Arizona	www.revenue.state.az.us
Arkansas	www.state.ar.us/dfa/
California	www.boe.ca.gov
Colorado	www.revenue.state.co.us/main/home.asp
Connecticut	www.ct.gov/drs
Delaware	www.state.de.us/revenue
District of Columbia	http://www.brc.dc.gov/
Florida	http://sun6.dms.state.fl.us/dor/taxes/
Georgia	http://www.etax.dor.ga.gov/

State	Department of Revenue Web Link
Hawaii	www.state.hi.us/tax/tax.html
Idaho	http://tax.idaho.gov
Illinois	www.revenue.state.il.us
Indiana	www.ai.org/dor/
Iowa	www.state.ia.us/government/drf/index.html
Kansas	www.ink.org/public/kdor
Kentucky	www.state.ky.us/agencies/revenue/
Louisiana	www.rev.state.la.us
Maine	www.state.me.us/revenue/
Maryland	www.comp.state.md.us/
Massachusetts	www.state.ma.us/dor/
Michigan	www.michigan.gov/treasury
Minnesota	www.taxes.state.mn.us
Mississippi	www.mstc.state.ms.us/
Missouri	http://dor.state.mo.us
Montana	www.state.mt.us/revenue/
Nebraska	www.revenue.state.ne.us/index.html
Nevada	http://tax.state.nv.us
New Hampshire	www.state.nh.us/revenue/
New Jersey	www.state.nj.us/treasury/taxation
New Mexico	www.state.nm.us/tax
New York	www.tax.state.ny.us/
North Carolina	www.dor.state.nc.us
North Dakota	www.state.nd.us/taxdpt
Ohio	www.state.oh.us/tax/
Oklahoma	www.oktax.state.ok.us
Oregon	www.dor.state.or.us
Pennsylvania	www.revenue.state.pa.us
Rhode Island	www.info.state.ri.us/admin.htm
South Carolina	www.sctax.org/
South Dakota	www.state.sd.us/drr2/revenue.html
Tennessee	www.state.tn.us/revenue
Texas	www.cpa.state.tx.us/taxinfo/salestax.html
Utah	http://tax.utah.gov/
Vermont	www.state.vt.us/tax/

State	Department of Revenue Web Link
Virginia	www.tax.state.va.us/
Washington	http://dor.wa.gov/
West Virginia	www.state.wv.us/taxdiv/
Wisconsin	www.dor.state.wi.us/
Wyoming	http://revenue.state.wy.us

BOE-401-A2 (S1) REV. 96 (10-04)

STATE OF CALIFORNIA
BOARD OF EQUALIZATION

STATE, LOCAL and DISTRICT SALES and USE TAX RETURN

BOARD USE ONLY		
RA-TT	LOC	REG
RA-BTR	AACS	REF
EFF		

DUE ON OR BEFORE	FOR	PERIOD	YEAR

IMPORTANT:
Your account number and reporting period are required.

SELLER'S PERMIT ACCOUNT NUMBER (i.e., SRY XX-XXXXXXX)
Select one

Mail To:
BOARD OF EQUALIZATION
PO BOX 942879
SACRAMENTO CA 94279-7072

NAME

BUSINESS ADDRESS

CITY   STATE   ZIP

READ RETURN INSTRUCTIONS 04-2 BEFORE PREPARING THIS RETURN

1. TOTAL (gross) SALES	1.	$ .00
2. PURCHASES SUBJECT TO USE TAX	2.	.00
3. TOTAL (add lines 1 and 2)	3.	.00

PLEASE COMPLETE LINES 4 THRU 10(f) ON THE BACK PAGE OF THIS RETURN.

11. TOTAL NONTAXABLE TRANSACTIONS REPORTED (Enter total deductions from line 11 on the back page)	11.	.00
12. TRANSACTIONS SUBJECT TO STATE TAX (subtract line 11 from line 3)	12.	.00
12.(a) ENTER AMOUNT FROM TAX ADJUSTMENT WORKSHEET LINE 12, COLUMN C 12.(a)		.00
13. STATE TAX 6% (multiply line 12 by .06 OR enter line 13, Column D from the Tax Adjustment Worksheet)	13.	.00 <
14. (a) TRANSACTIONS SUBJECT TO COUNTY TAX [add amount in box 61 (back) and line 12 above]	14.(a)	.00
(b) COUNTY TAX 1/4% [multiply line 14(a) by .0025]	14.(b)	.00 <
15. ADJUSTMENTS FOR LOCAL TAX (see line 15 instructions)	15.	.00
16. TRANSACTIONS SUBJECT TO LOCAL TAX [add or subtract line 15 to/from line 14(a)]	16.	.00
17. COMBINED STATE AND LOCAL TAX 1% (multiply line 16 by .01)	17.	.00 <
18. DISTRICT TAX (from Schedule A, line A11) YOU MUST COMPLETE FORM BOE-531-A, SCHEDULE A IF YOU ARE ENGAGED IN BUSINESS IN A TRANSACTIONS AND USE TAX DISTRICT	18.	.00 <
19. TOTAL STATE, COUNTY, LOCAL AND DISTRICT TAX [add lines 13, 14(b), 17, & 18]	19.	.00
20. DEDUCT SALES OR USE TAX IMPOSED BY OTHER STATES AND PAID ON THE PURCHASE PRICE OF TANGIBLE PERSONAL PROPERTY. THE PURCHASE PRICE MUST BE INCLUDED IN LINE 2 ABOVE.	20.	.00
21. NET TAX (subtract line 20 from line 19)	21.	.00
22. LESS-TAX PREPAYMENTS 1st prepayment (Tax only) $ 2nd prepayment (Tax only) $	22.	.00
23. REMAINING TAX (subtract line 22 from line 21)	23.	.00
24. PENALTY of 10% (.10) is due if your tax payment is made, or your return is filed, after the due date shown above. (see line 24 instructions) PENALTY	24.	.00
25. INTEREST: One month's interest is due on tax for each month or fraction of a month that payment is delayed after the due date. The adjusted monthly interest rate is .00583 (7% divided by 12.) INTEREST	25.	.00
26. TOTAL AMOUNT DUE AND PAYABLE (add lines 23, 24, and 25)	26.	$ .00

REC. NO

PM

RE

IF YOU PAID BY CREDIT CARD AS DESCRIBED ON PAGE 1 OF THE INSTRUCTIONS, CHECK HERE [ ].

I hereby certify that this return, including any accompanying schedules and statements, has been examined by me and to the best of my knowledge and belief is a true, correct and complete return.

YOUR SIGNATURE AND TITLE	TELEPHONE NUMBER ( )	DATE	I/F
PAID PREPARER'S USE ONLY PAID PREPARER'S NAME	PREPARER'S TELEPHONE NUMBER ( )		

Make a copy for your records.

Figure D.1 State of California sales and use tax return.

BOE-401-A2 (S2) REV. 96 (10-04)

STATE OF CALIFORNIA
BOARD OF EQUALIZATION

STATE, LOCAL and DISTRICT SALES and USE TAX RETURN

YOUR ACCOUNT NO.	REPORTING PERIOD

Deductions/Exemptions Schedule

4. SALES TO OTHER RETAILERS FOR PURPOSES OF RESALE	50	$ .00
5. NONTAXABLE SALES OF FOOD PRODUCTS	51	.00
6. NONTAXABLE LABOR (repair and installation)	52	.00
7. SALES TO THE UNITED STATES GOVERNMENT	53	.00
8. SALES IN INTERSTATE OR FOREIGN COMMERCE	54	.00
9. SALES TAX (if any) INCLUDED ON LINE 1 ON THE FRONT OF THE RETURN	55	.00
10. (a) (1) BAD DEBT LOSSES ON TAXABLE SALES	56	.00
(2) BAD DEBT LENDER LOSSES	62	.00
(b) COST OF TAX-PAID PURCHASES RESOLD PRIOR TO USE	57	.00
(c) RETURNED TAXABLE MERCHANDISE	58	.00
(d) CASH DISCOUNTS ON TAXABLE SALES	59	.00

(e) PARTIAL STATE TAX EXEMPTION - IF YOU ARE REPORTING ANY TRANSACTIONS THAT OCCURRED PRIOR TO 7-1-04, YOU MUST COMPLETE THE PARTIAL STATE TAX EXEMPTION WORKSHEET, PAGE 3 OF BOE-531-T, SCHEDULE T, BEFORE YOU CLAIM ANY OF THESE DEDUCTIONS.

(1) AMOUNT SUBJECT TO THE MANUFACTURER'S EQUIPMENT EXEMPTION [If you are completing Schedule T, enter the amount from Partial State Tax Exemption Worksheet, Column D, line 10(e)(1)] (discontinued 12-31-03) — 63 — .00

(2) AMOUNT SUBJECT TO THE TELEPRODUCTION EQUIPMENT EXEMPTION [If you are completing Schedule T, enter the amount from Partial State Tax Exemption Worksheet, Column D, line 10(e)(2)] — 64 — .00

(3) AMOUNT SUBJECT TO FARM EQUIPMENT EXEMPTION [If you are completing Schedule T, enter the amount from Partial State Tax Exemption Worksheet, Column D, line 10(e)(3)] — 65 — .00

(4) AMOUNT SUBJECT TO THE DIESEL FUEL USED IN FARMING AND FOOD PROCESSING EXEMPTION [If you are completing Schedule T, enter the amount from Partial State Tax Exemption Worksheet, Column D, line 10(e)(4)] — 66 — .00

(5) AMOUNT SUBJECT TO THE TIMBER HARVESTING EQUIPMENT AND MACHINERY EXEMPTION [If you are completing Schedule T, enter the amount from Partial State Tax Exemption Worksheet, Column D, line 10(e)(5)] — 67 — .00

(6) AMOUNT SUBJECT TO THE RACEHORSE BREEDING STOCK EXEMPTION [If you are completing Schedule T, enter the amount from Partial State Tax Exemption Worksheet, Column D, line 10(e)(6)] — 68 — .00

TOTAL PARTIAL STATE TAX EXEMPTIONS - If you are required to complete the Tax Adjustment and Partial State Tax Exemption Worksheet, enter the amount from page 3, Column D, box 60. If you are not required to complete the Worksheet, enter the sum of boxes 63 through 68. — 60 — .00

STATE TAX EXEMPTION FACTOR - Only for use if Partial State Tax Exemption Worksheet is NOT required. — .8750

TOTAL ADJUSTED PARTIAL EXEMPTIONS - If you completed BOE-531-T, Schedule T, enter the amount from page 1, Column D, box 61. If you did not complete Schedule T, multiply the amount in box 60 by the State Tax Exemption Factor shown above and enter the result in box 61. — 61 — .00

(f) OTHER (clearly explain) — 90 — .00

11. TOTAL NONTAXABLE TRANSACTIONS [Add lines 4 thru 10(d), box 61 and line 10(f), then enter here and on the front page line 11] — 11 — $ .00

Figure D.1 continued

BOE-531-A (FRONT) REV. 8 (1-05)

STATE OF CALIFORNIA
BOARD OF EQUALIZATION

SCHEDULE A - COMPUTATION SCHEDULE FOR DISTRICT TAX

DUE ON OR BEFORE

[FOID   ]   YOUR ACCOUNT NO.

A1.	AMOUNT ON WHICH LOCAL TAX APPLIES (Enter amount from line 16 on the front of your Sales and Use Tax return)	$	.00
A2./A3.	DEDUCT sales delivered to any location not in a district tax area 000	-	.00
A4.	AMOUNT OF DISTRICT TRANSACTIONS (Subtract line A2/A3 from line A1) (Allocate this amount to the correct district tax areas in Column A5)	$	.00

READ RETURN INSTRUCTIONS 05-1 BEFORE PREPARING THIS SCHEDULE
Please round cents to the nearest whole dollar

DISTRICT TAX AREAS		A5. ALLOCATE LINE A4 TO CORRECT DISTRICT(S)	A6./A7. ADD (+) / DEDUCT (-) ADJUSTMENTS	A8. TAXABLE AMOUNT A5 plus/minus A6/A7	A9. TAX RATE	A10. DISTRICT TAX DUE Multiply A8 by A9
ALAMEDA Co. Bay Area Rapid Transit 087	020				.005	$ .00
ALAMEDA Co. Transportation Improvement Authority (Effective 4-1-02)	079				.005	.00
ALAMEDA Co. Essential Health Care Services	086				.005	.00
ALAMEDA Co. Transportation Authority (Expires 3-31-02)	010	Discontinued			.005	.00
*CONTRA COSTA Co.	025				.01	.00
CITY OF PLACERVILLE (El Dorado Co.)	070				.0025	.00
*FRESNO Co. 074	072				.00625	.00
CITY OF CLOVIS (Fresno Co.) Public Safety Transactions & Use Tax	073				.003	.00
CITY OF TRINIDAD (Humboldt Co.)	092				.01	.00
*IMPERIAL Co. Local Transportation Authority 046	029				.005	.00
*CITY OF CALEXICO Heffernan Hospital District	045				.005	.00
INYO Co.	014				.005	.00
CITY OF CLEARLAKE (Lake Co.)	058				.005	.00
*LOS ANGELES Co. 078	036				.01	.00
*CITY OF AVALON Avalon Municipal Hospital and Clinic	077				.005	.00
MADERA Co.	034				.005	.00
MARIPOSA Co. (Expired 6-30-04)	076	Discontinued			.005	.00

Continue to back of form

A11(a)	TOTAL DISTRICT TAX (FRONT) Add Column A10.	.00
A11(b)	TOTAL DISTRICT TAX (BACK) Enter total from Column A10, Schedule A (Back).	.00
A11	TOTAL DISTRICT TAX Add lines A11(a) and A11(b). (Enter here and on line 18 on front of your Sales and Use Tax return.)	$ .00

*This district tax area includes more than one transactions and use tax district. (See Instructions 05-1 for Schedule A)

Figure D.1   continued

BOE-531-A (BACK) REV. 8 (1-05)

SCHEDULE A - COMPUTATION SCHEDULE FOR DISTRICT TAX

READ RETURN
INSTRUCTIONS 05-1
BEFORE PREPARING
THIS SCHEDULE
Please round cents to the
nearest whole dollar

ACCOUNT NUMBER		REPORTING PERIOD				

DISTRICT TAX AREAS		A5. ALLOCATE LINE A4 TO CORRECT DISTRICT(S)	A6./A7. ADD (+) / DEDUCT (-) ADJUSTMENTS	A8. TAXABLE AMOUNT A5 plus/minus A6/A7	A9. TAX RATE	A10. DISTRICT TAX DUE Multiply A8 by A9
CITY OF WILLITS (Mendocino Co.)	084				.005	$ .00
CITY OF POINT ARENA (Mendocino Co.)	085				.005	.00
CITY OF FORT BRAGG (Mendocino Co.)	094				.005	.00
NAPA Co.	065				.005	.00
*NEVADA Co. Public Library Transactions & Use Tax 069	067				.00125	.00
·TOWN OF TRUCKEE Road Maintenance Transactions & Use Tax	068				.005	.00
ORANGE Co.	037				.005	.00
RIVERSIDE Co.	026				.005	.00
SACRAMENTO Co.	023				.005	.00
SAN BERNARDINO Co.	031				.005	.00
SAN DIEGO Co.	013				.005	.00
*SAN FRANCISCO Co.	052				.0125	.00
SAN JOAQUIN Co.	038				.005	.00
*SAN MATEO Co.	019				.01	.00
SANTA BARBARA Co.	030				.005	.00
*SANTA CLARA Co.	064				.01	.00
*SANTA CRUZ Co. 090	062				.0075	.00
CITY OF SANTA CRUZ (Santa Cruz Co.)	089				.0025	.00
SOLANO Co.	066				.00125	.00
SONOMA Co. 083	039				.0025	.00
CITY OF SEBASTOPOL	082				.00125	.00
STANISLAUS Co.	059				.00125	.00
CITY OF VISALIA (Tulare Co.)	091				.0025	.00
CITY OF SONORA (Tuolumne Co.)	093				.005	.00
CITY OF WOODLAND (Yolo Co.)	075				.005	.00
CITY OF WEST SACRAMENTO (Yolo Co.)	081				.005	.00
CITY OF DAVIS (Yolo Co.)	088				.005	.00
A11(b)	TOTAL DISTRICT TAX (BACK) Add Column A10. Enter here and on front of Schedule A, line A11(b).					$ .00

*This district tax area includes more than one transactions and use tax district. (See Instructions 05-1 for Schedule A)

Figure D.1   continued

New York State Department of Taxation and Finance

Quarterly ST-100

New York State and Local Quarterly Sales and Use Tax Return

1st Quarter

March April May

Tax period
March 1, 2005 – May 31, 2005

June 2005
S M T W T F S
1 2 3 4
5 6 7 8 9 10 11
12 13 14 15 16 17 18
19 20 21 22 23 24 25
26 27 28 29 30

106

Sales tax identification number ▶

Legal name *(if no label, print legal name as it appears on the Certificate of Authority)*

DBA (doing business as) name

Number and street

City, state, ZIP code

Due date:
20 Monday,
June 20, 2005
You will be responsible for penalty and interest if your return is not postmarked by this date.

No tax due? If so, check the box to the right and complete Step 1; in Step 3 on page 3, enter *none* in boxes 13, 14, and 15; and complete Step 9. You **must** file by the due date even if no tax is due. **There is a $50 penalty for late filing of a no-tax-due return.** See ❶ in instructions. ...

Multiple locations? If you are reporting sales tax for more than one business location **and** your identification number does not end in *C*, check the box to the right and attach a list of your locations. ....

Final return? Check the box to the right if you are discontinuing your business and this is your final return; complete this return and the back of your *Certificate of Authority.* Attach the *Certificate of Authority* to the return. See ❷ in instructions. ....

Has your address or business information changed? If so, call the Business Tax Information Center (see *Need help?* on page 4) to update address information or check the box to the right and enter new mailing address on preprinted label above. See ❸ in instructions.

Step 1 of 9   Gross sales and services

Enter total **gross sales and services** in box 1 .... ▶ 1 .00

Do not include sales tax in the gross sales and services amount. See ❹ in instructions.

Step 2 of 9   Identify required schedules

Check the box(es) on the right below, then complete the schedule(s) if necessary and proceed to Step 3. **Need to obtain schedules?** See *Need help?* on page 4 of this form.

Quarterly schedule	Description	Check the box for each schedule you are attaching
SCHEDULE **A**	Use Form ST-100.2, *Quarterly Schedule A,* to report tax and taxable receipts from sales of food and drink (restaurant meals, takeout, etc.) and from hotel/motel room occupancy **in Nassau or Niagara County,** as well as admissions, club dues, and cabaret charges in Niagara County.	☐
SCHEDULE **B**	Use Form ST-100.3, *Quarterly Schedule B,* to report tax due on **nonresidential utility services** in certain counties where school districts or cities impose tax, and on **residential energy sources and services** subject to local taxes. Reminder: Use Form ST-100.3-ATT, *Quarterly Schedule B-ATT,* to report sales of these nonresidential utility services made to QEZEs.	☐
SCHEDULE **FR**	Use Form ST-100.10, *Quarterly Schedule FR,* to **report retail sales of motor fuel or diesel motor fuel,** and fuel taken from inventory, as explained in the schedule's instructions.	☐
SCHEDULE **H**	Form ST-100.7, *Quarterly Schedule H,* (used to report sales of clothing and footwear eligible for exemption) is **not applicable for the quarterly period March 1, 2005, through May 31, 2005.** For this period, vendors must collect and remit the total New York State and local sales and use taxes on sales of clothing, footwear, and items used to make or repair such clothing regardless of the price, and must report these sales on the appropriate jurisdiction line on Form ST-100.	N/A
SCHEDULE **N**	Use Form ST-100.5, *Quarterly Schedule N,* to report taxes due and sales of certain **services in New York City.** Reminder: Use Form ST-100.5-ATT, *Quarterly Schedule N-ATT,* if you are a provider of parking services in New York City.	☐
SCHEDULE **Q**	Use Form ST-100.9, *Quarterly Schedule Q,* to report **sales of tangible personal property or services to Qualified Empire Zone Enterprises (QEZEs) eligible for exemption** from New York State and some local sales and use tax.	☐
SCHEDULE **T**	Use Form ST-100.8, *Quarterly Schedule T,* to report taxes due on **telephone services, telephone answering services, and telegraph services** imposed by certain counties, school districts, and cities. Reminder: Use Form ST-100.8-ATT, *Quarterly Schedule T-ATT,* to report sales of these services made to QEZEs.	☐

Schedules CT and NJ: For reciprocal tax agreement filing requirements, see ❺ in instructions.

Refer to instructions (Form ST-100-I) if you have questions or need help. Please be sure to keep a completed copy of your return for your records.

For office use only

ST-100 (3/05) **Page 1** of 4

Proceed to Step 3, page 2 ▶

Figure D.2   State of New York quarterly sales and use tax return.

State Tax Resources 227

Page 2 of 4   ST-100 (3/05) — Sales tax identification number — 106 Quarterly

Step 3 of 9   Calculate sales and use taxes
Refer to instructions (Form ST-100-I) if you have questions or need help.

Column C — Taxable sales and services + Column D — Purchases subject to tax × Column E — Tax rate = Column F — Sales and use tax (C + D) × E

Enter total from Form ST-100.10 (if any) in box 2 **FR**   [2]

Enter totals from: [A] + [B] + [B-ATT] + [N] + [Q] + [T] + [T-ATT] =   [3] .00   [4] .00   [5]

Column A — Taxing jurisdiction	Column B — Jurisdiction code			Tax rate	
New York State only	NE 0011	.00	.00	4¼%	
Albany County	AL 0171	.00	.00	8¼%	
Allegany County	AL 0201	.00	.00	8¾%	
Broome County	BR 0311	.00	.00	8¼%	
Cattaraugus County (outside the following)	CA 0491	.00	.00	8¼%	
Olean (city)	OL 0411	.00	.00	8¼%	
Salamanca (city)	SA 0421	.00	.00	8¼%	
Cayuga County (outside the following)	CA 0501	.00	.00	8¼%	
Auburn (city)	AU 0551	.00	.00	8¼%	
Chautauqua County	CH 0611	.00	.00	8½%	
Chemung County	CH 0701	.00	.00	8¼%	
Chenango County (outside the following)	CH 0821	.00	.00	8¼%	
Norwich (city)	NO 0841	.00	.00	8¼%	
Clinton County	CL 0901	.00	.00	8%	
Columbia County	CO 1001	.00	.00	8¼%	
Cortland County	CO 1121	.00	.00	8¼%	
Delaware County	DE 1211	.00	.00	8¼%	
Dutchess County	DU 1301	.00	.00	8¼%	
Erie County	ER 1401	.00	.00	8¼%	
Essex County	ES 1511	.00	.00	8%	
Franklin County	FR 1601	.00	.00	7¼%	
Fulton County (outside the following)	FU 1701	.00	.00	7¼%	
Gloversville (city)	GL 1761	.00	.00	7¼%	
Johnstown (city)	JO 1771	.00	.00	7¼%	
Genesee County	GE 1801	.00	.00	8¼%	
Greene County	GR 1901	.00	.00	8¼%	
Hamilton County	HA 2001	.00	.00	7¼%	
Herkimer County	HE 2101	.00	.00	8¼%	
Jefferson County	JE 2211	.00	.00	8%	
Lewis County	LE 2311	.00	.00	8%	
Livingston County	LI 2401	.00	.00	8¼%	
Madison County (outside the following)	MA 2501	.00	.00	8¼%	
Oneida (city)	ON 2531	.00	.00	8¼%	
Monroe County	MO 2601	.00	.00	8¼%	
Montgomery County	MO 2791	.00	.00	8¼%	
Nassau County	NA 2801	.00	.00	8¾%	
Niagara County	NI 2901	.00	.00	8¼%	
Oneida County (outside the following)	ON 3011	.00	.00	9¾%	
Rome (city)	RO 3031	.00	.00	9¾%	
Sherrill (city)	SH 3071	.00	.00	9¾%	
Utica (city)	UT 3061	.00	.00	9¾%	
Onondaga County	ON 3111	.00	.00	8¼%	
Ontario County (outside the following)	ON 3271	.00	.00	7¼%	
Canandaigua (city)	CA 3231	.00	.00	7¼%	
Geneva (city)	GE 3241	.00	.00	7¼%	
Orange County	OR 3311	.00	.00	8¼%	
Orleans County	OR 3471	.00	.00	8¼%	
Oswego County (outside the following)	OS 3581	.00	.00	8¼%	
Fulton (city)	FU 3531	.00	.00	8¼%	
Oswego (city)	OS 3521	.00	.00	8¼%	

Column subtotals; also enter on page 3, boxes 10, 11, and 12:   [6] .00   [7] .00   [8]

Figure D.2   continued

Quarterly 106 | Sales tax identification number | **ST-100** (3/05) **Page 3** of 4

Column A Taxing jurisdiction	Column B Jurisdiction code	Column C Taxable sales and services +	Column D Purchases subject to tax ×	Column E Tax rate =	Column F Sales and use tax (C + D) × E
Otsego County	OT 3611	.00	.00	8¼%	
Putnam County	PU 3701	.00	.00	7½%	
Rensselaer County	RE 3871	.00	.00	8¼%	
Rockland County	RO 3901	.00	.00	8⅛%*	
St. Lawrence County	ST 4081	.00	.00	7¼%	
Saratoga County (outside the following)	SA 4101	.00	.00	7¼%	
Saratoga Springs (city)	SA 4121	.00	.00	7¼%	
Schenectady County	SC 4231	.00	.00	8¼%	
Schoharie County	SC 4311	.00	.00	8¼%	
Schuyler County	SC 4401	.00	.00	8¼%	
Seneca County	SE 4501	.00	.00	8¼%	
Steuben County (outside the following)	ST 4681	.00	.00	8¼%	
Corning (city)	CO 4601	.00	.00	8¼%	
Hornell (city)	HO 4631	.00	.00	8¼%	
Suffolk County	SU 4701	.00	.00	8¾%	
Sullivan County	SU 4801	.00	.00	7¾%	
Tioga County	TI 4911	.00	.00	8¼%	
Tompkins County (outside the following)	TO 5091	.00	.00	8¼%	
Ithaca (city)	IT 5011	.00	.00	8¼%	
Ulster County	UL 5101	.00	.00	8¼%	
Warren County (outside the following)	WA 5291	.00	.00	7¼%	
Glens Falls (city)	GL 5201	.00	.00	7¼%	
Washington County	WA 5301	.00	.00	7¼%	
Wayne County	WA 5411	.00	.00	8¼%	
Westchester County (outside the following)	WE 5591	.00	.00	7½%	
Mount Vernon (city)	MO 5511	.00	.00	8½%	
New Rochelle (city)	NE 6851	.00	.00	8½%	
White Plains (city)	WH 5551	.00	.00	8%	
Yonkers (city)	YO 6501	.00	.00	8½%	
Wyoming County	WY 5601	.00	.00	8¼%	
Yates County	YA 5711	.00	.00	8¼%	
Taxes in New York City [includes counties of Bronx, Kings (Brooklyn), New York (Manhattan), Queens, and Richmond (Staten Island)]					
New York City/State combined tax	NE 8011	.00	.00	8⅝%*	
New York State/MCTD (fuel and utilities)	NE 8041	.00	.00	4½%	
New York City - local tax only *(enter box 9 amount in Step 7B)*	NE 8021	9 .00	.00	4⅛%*	
		.00	.00		
Column subtotals from page 2, boxes 6, 7, and 8:		10 .00	11 .00		12
If the total of box 13 + box 14 = $300,000 or more, see page 1 of instructions. **Column totals:**		13 .00	14 .00		15
Credit summary — Enter the **total** amount of credits claimed in Step 3 above, and on any attached schedules *(see 12c).*					

Step 4 of 9 **Calculate special taxes**	*Internal code*	Column G Taxable receipts ×	Column H Tax rate =	Column J Special taxes due (G × H)
Passenger car rentals	PA 0003	.00	5%	
Information & entertainment services furnished via telephony and telegraphy	IN 7009	.00	5%	
Total special taxes:				16

Step 5 of 9 **Calculate tax credits and advance payments**	*Internal code*	Column K Credit amount
Credit for prepaid sales tax on cigarettes	CR C8888	
Credits against sales or use tax *(see 16 in instructions)*	C	
Advance payments (made with Form ST-330)	A	
Unclaimed vendor collection credit *(attach Form TR-912)*	UN 7804	
Total tax credits and advance payments:		17

***8⅛% = 0.08125; 8⅝% = 0.08625; 4⅛% = 0.04125**

Proceed to Step 6, page 4

Figure D.2 continued

Page 4 of 4   ST-100 (3/05)

Sales tax identification number

106   Quarterly

Step 6 of 9   Calculate taxes due

Add *Sales and use tax* column total (box 15) to *Total special taxes* (box 16) and subtract *Total tax credits and advance payments* (box 17).

Taxes due

Box 15 amount $ _____ + Box 16 amount $ _____ − Box 17 amount $ _____ =

18

Step 7 of 9   Calculate vendor collection credit or pay penalty and interest

You are eligible for **vendor collection credit ONLY** if you file by **June 20, 2005, and** you pay the full amount due with the return. If you are not eligible, enter *0* in box 19 and go to **7D.**

7A If you are not required to file any schedules, start at the asterisk (★) in 7B.

Schedule B, Part 4, box 3 _____
Schedule B-ATT + _____
Schedule N + _____
Schedule Q + _____
Schedule T-ATT + _____

Total adjustment = _____

7B Schedule FR, Step 3, box 7 _____
★Form ST-100, page 3, box 13 + _____
Total adjustment from **7A** − _____
Form ST-100, page 3, box 9 − _____

Eligible sales amount *(move to 7C)* = _____

7C
Eligible sales amount from *7B* above
$ _____ × 4¼% = $ _____

State tax rate

Credit rate
× 3½% = $ _____ ★★

Vendor collection credit VE 7704

19

★★ In box 19, enter the amount calculated, but not more than $150

OR   Pay penalty and interest if you are filing late

Penalty and interest

7D Penalty and interest are calculated on the amount in box 18, *Taxes due.* See ㉒ on page 3 in the instructions.

20

Step 8 of 9   Calculate total amount due

Make check or money order payable to **New York State Sales Tax.** Write on your check your sales tax ID#, **ST-100,** and **5/31/05.**

Total amount due

Final calculation: **Taking vendor collection credit?** Subtract box 19 from box 18. **Paying penalty and interest?** Add box 20 to box 18.

Step 9 of 9   Sign and mail this return
Please be sure to keep a completed copy for your records.

Must be postmarked by **Monday, June 20, 2005,** to be considered filed on time. See below for complete mailing information.

Printed name of taxpayer _____   Title _____

Signature of taxpayer _____   Date ___ / ___ / ___   Daytime telephone (___)

Printed name of preparer, if other than taxpayer _____

Preparer's address _____

Signature of preparer, if other than taxpayer _____   Daytime telephone (___)

Where to mail your return and attachments
If using a private delivery service rather than the U.S. Postal Service, see ㉔ in instructions for the correct address.

Do you participate in the New Jersey/New York or the Connecticut/New York reciprocal tax agreement?

No
Address envelope to:
NYS SALES TAX PROCESSING
JAF BUILDING
PO BOX 1205
NEW YORK NY 10116-1205

Yes
Address envelope to:
NYS SALES TAX PROCESSING
RECIPROCAL TAX AGREEMENT
JAF BUILDING
PO BOX 1209
NEW YORK NY 10116-1209

☑ Make check payable to *New York State Sales Tax.*

David Sample   2971
100 Elm Street
Albany, NY 12203   DATE June 10, 2005

PAY TO THE ORDER OF New York State Sales Tax $ 1,050.32

One thousand fifty and 32/100   DOLLARS

First State Bank

00-0000000   ST-100   5/31/05

Don't forget to write your sales tax ID#, *ST-100*, and *5/31/05*

Don't forget to sign your check

Need help?

Internet access: www.nystax.gov (for information, forms, and publications)

Fax-on-demand forms: Forms are available 24 hours a day, 7 days a week.   1 800 748-3676

Telephone assistance is available from 8:00 A.M. to 5:00 P.M. (eastern time), Monday through Friday.
To order forms and publications: 1 800 462-8100
Business Tax Information Center: 1 800 972-1233
From areas outside the U.S. and outside Canada: (518) 485-6800

Hotline for the hearing and speech impaired:
If you have access to a telecommunications device for the deaf (TDD), contact us at 1 800 634-2110. If you do not own a TDD, check with independent living centers or community action programs to find out where machines are available for public use.

Persons with disabilities: In compliance with the Americans with Disabilities Act, we will ensure that our lobbies, offices, meeting rooms, and other facilities are accessible to persons with disabilities. If you have questions about special accommodations for persons with disabilities, please call 1 800 972-1233.

Refer to the instructions (Form ST-100-I) if you have questions or need further help.

Figure D.2   continued

Sales and Use Tax Return

DR-15CS
R. 01/05

Please complete this return.
Attach your check or money order and mail to:

Florida Department of Revenue
5050 W. Tennessee Street
Tallahassee, FL 32399-0120

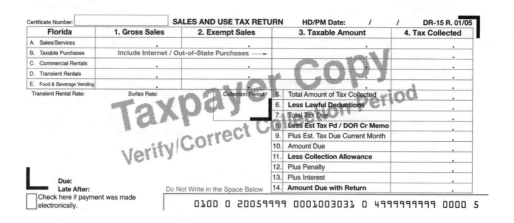

Figure D.3 State of Florida sales and use tax report.

DUE DATE OF RETURN — Your return and payment are **due on the 1st and late after the 20th day of the month** following each collection period. If the 20th falls on a Saturday, Sunday, or state or federal holiday, your return must be postmarked or hand delivered on the first business day following the 20th. **You must file a return even if no tax is due.**

SIGNATURE REQUIREMENT — Sign and date your return. For corporations, the authorized corporate officer must sign. If someone else prepared the return, the preparer also must sign and date the return in the space provided.

Fraud Penalties
FRAUDULENT CLAIM OF EXEMPTION; PENALTIES — Section 212.085, Florida Statutes (F.S.), provides that when any person fraudulently, for the purpose of evading tax, issues to a vendor or to any agent of the state a certificate or statement in writing in which he or she claims exemption from sales tax, such person, in addition to being liable for payment of the tax plus a mandatory penalty of 200% of the tax, shall be liable for fine and punishment as provided by law for a conviction of a felony of the third degree, as provided in s. 775.082, s. 775.083, or s. 775.084, F.S.

SPECIFIC FRAUD PENALTY — Any person who makes a false or fraudulent return with a willful intent to evade payment of any tax or fee imposed under Ch. 212, F.S., in addition to the other penalties provided by law, will be liable for a specific penalty of 100% of the tax bill or fee and, upon conviction, for fine and punishment as provided in s. 775.082, s. 775.083, or s. 775.084, F.S.

FAILURE TO COLLECT AND PAY OVER TAX OR AN ATTEMPT TO EVADE OR DEFEAT TAX — Any person who is required to collect, truthfully account for, and pay over any tax enumerated in Ch. 201, Ch. 206, or Ch. 212, F.S., and who willfully fails to collect such tax or truthfully account for and pay over such tax or willfully attempts in any manner to evade or defeat such tax or the payment thereof; or any officer or director of a corporation who has administrative control over the collection and payment of such tax and who willfully directs any employee of the corporation to fail to collect or pay over, evade, defeat, or truthfully account for such tax will, in addition to other penalties provided by law, be liable to a penalty equal to twice the total amount of the tax evaded or not accounted for or paid over, as provided in s. 213.29, F.S.

I hereby certify that this return has been examined by me and to the best of my knowledge and belief is a true and complete return.

_____   _____   _____   _____
Signature of Taxpayer   Date   Signature of Preparer   Date

Discretionary Sales Surtax (Lines 15(a) through 15(d))

15(a). Exempt Amount of Items Over $5,000 (included in Column 3)	15(a).
15(b). Other Taxable Amounts **NOT** Subject to Surtax (included in Column 3)	15(b).
15(c). Amounts Subject to Surtax at a Rate Different Than Your County Surtax Rate (included in Column 3)	15(c).
15(d). **Total Amount of Discretionary Sales Surtax Collected** (included in Column 4)	15(d).
16. Total **Enterprise Zone Jobs Credits** (included in Line 6)	16.
17. Taxable Sales/Purchases/Rentals of **Farm Equipment** — 2.5% Rate (included in Line A)	17.
18. Taxable Sales/Purchases of **Electric Power or Energy** — 7% Rate (included in Line A)	18.
19. Taxable Sales/Purchases of **Dyed Diesel Fuel** — 6% Rate (included in Line A)	19.
20. Taxable Sales from **Amusement Machines** (included in Line A)	20.

I hereby certify that this return has been examined by me and to the best of my knowledge and belief is a true and complete return.

_____   _____   _____   _____
Signature of Taxpayer   Date   Signature of Preparer   Date

Discretionary Sales Surtax (Lines 15(a) through 15(d))

15(a). Exempt Amount of Items Over $5,000 (included in Column 3)	15(a).
15(b). Other Taxable Amounts **NOT** Subject to Surtax (included in Column 3)	15(b).
15(c). Amounts Subject to Surtax at a Rate Different Than Your County Surtax Rate (included in Column 3)	15(c).
15(d). **Total Amount of Discretionary Sales Surtax Collected** (included in Column 4)	15(d).
16. Total **Enterprise Zone Jobs Credits** (included in Line 6)	16.
17. Taxable Sales/Purchases/Rentals of **Farm Equipment** — 2.5% Rate (included in Line A)	17.
18. Taxable Sales/Purchases of **Electric Power or Energy** — 7% Rate (included in Line A)	18.
19. Taxable Sales/Purchases of **Dyed Diesel Fuel** — 6% Rate (included in Line A)	19.
20. Taxable Sales from **Amusement Machines** (included in Line A)	20.

Figure D.3 continued

Appendix E

List of Department of Labor and Employment-Related Web Sites

These links are current as of Fall 2005, however, web sites do change frequently. If you find that the link for your state doesn't work, try an Internet search for the terms "Department of Labor <Your State>."

State	Web Site Link
Alaska	www.labor.state.ak.us/home.htm
Alabama	http://dir.alabama.gov/business/
Arkansas	http://asbdc.ualr.edu/
Arizona	www.revenue.state.az.us/
California	www.edd.ca.gov/taxrep/taxloc.htm
Colorado	www.revenue.state.co.us/main/wrap.asp?incl=contactus
Connecticut	www.ct.gov/drs/site/default.asp
Delaware	www.state.de.us/revenue/services/BusServices.shtml
District of Columbia	http://does.dc.gov/does/site/default.asp
Florida	http://www.myflorida.com/dbpr/
Georgia	www.dol.state.ga.us/em/
Hawaii	http://pahoehoe.ehawaii.gov/portal/business/government.html
Idaho	http://cl.idaho.gov/portal/go/jobservice/3742/DesktopDefault.aspx

State	Web Site Link
Illinois	www.revenue.state.il.us/Businesses/
Indiana	http://www.in.gov/dwd/employers/employer_svcs.html
Iowa	www.iowaworkforce.org/files/contiwd.htm
Kansas	www.dol.ks.gov/home/html/contact_ALL.html
Kentucky	www.des.ky.gov/des/office/office.asp
Louisiana	www.ldol.state.la.us/qm_orgchart.asp
Maine	www.maine.gov/labor/
Maryland	www.dllr.state.md.us/employment/
Massachusetts	www.detma.org/DETCustService.htm
Michigan	www.michigan.gov/treasury/0,1607,7-121-4313-8483—,00.html
Minnesota	www.deed.state.mn.us/ContactUs.htm
Mississippi	www.mstc.state.ms.us/info/offices/withinfo.htm
Missouri	www.dolir.state.mo.us/es/ui-tax/phonenum.htm
Montana	http://uid.dli.state.mt.us/uid/contact.asp
Nebraska	www.dol.state.ne.us/nwd/index.cfm
Nevada	http://detr.state.nv.us/es/esd_employers.htm
New Hampshire	www.nhes.state.nh.us/esb/eb/esr.htm
New Jersey	www.state.nj.us/treasury/taxation/
New Mexico	http://www.dol.state.nm.us/dol_emsv.htm Yes it does
New York	www.labor.state.ny.us/business_ny/unemployment_insurance/uiemplyr/uihlplst.htm
North Carolina	www.ncesc.com/business/faqs/contactMain.asp?init=true
North Dakota	www.jobsnd.com/
Ohio	http://jfs.ohio.gov/ouc/uctax/compliance_phone.stm
Oklahoma	www.oesc.state.ok.us/contact.shtm
Oregon	http://findit.emp.state.or.us/offices/
Pennsylvania	www.state.pa.us/papower/taxonomy/taxonomy.asp?DLN=29888&papowerNav=|29888|
Rhode Island	www.dlt.state.ri.us/
South Carolina	www.sces.org/Contacts.htm
South Dakota	www.state.sd.us/dol/dolui/tax/TX_home.htm
Tennessee	www.state.tn.us/labor-wfd/email.html
Texas	www.twc.state.tx.us/twcinfo/contactus.html
Utah	http://jobs.utah.gov/ui/contact.asp

State	Web Site Link
Vermont	www.det.state.vt.us/contact.cfm
Virginia	www.vec.state.va.us/vecportal/field/field_offices.cfm
Washington	http://dor.wa.gov/content/contactus/default.aspx
West Virginia	www.wvbep.org/bep/
Wisconsin	www.dor.state.wi.us/html/business.html
Wyoming	http://wydoe.state.wy.us/

Appendix F

Jenny's State and Federal Tax Forms for Treasure Trove, Inc.

Form 1120S

Department of the Treasury
Internal Revenue Service

U.S. Income Tax Return for an S Corporation

► Do not file this form unless the corporation has timely filed
Form 2553 to elect to be an S corporation.

► See separate instructions.

OMB No. 1545-0130

2004

For calendar year 2004, or tax year beginning _____ , 2004, and ending _____ , 20 ___

A Effective date of S election	Use the IRS label. Other-wise, print or type.	Name	C Employer identification number
01-09-05		TREASURE TROVE, INC.	20 : 0010007
B Business code number (see pages 36–38 of the Insts.)		Number, street, and room or suite no. (If a P.O. box, see page 12 of the instructions.)	D Date incorporated
		1832 Montemarte Avenue, Ste. 206	January 9, 2005
		City or town, state, and ZIP code	E Total assets (see page 12 of instructions)
		Dallas, TX 76767	$ 15,715	00

F Check applicable boxes: (1) ☑ Initial return (2) ☐ Final return (3) ☐ Name change (4) ☐ Address change (5) ☐ Amended return
G Enter number of shareholders in the corporation at end of the tax year . . . . ►

Caution: *Include only trade or business income and expenses on lines 1a through 21. See page 13 of the instructions for more information.*

Income

1a	Gross receipts or sales	25,750	00	b Less returns and allowances	200	00	c Bal ►	1c	25,550	00
2	Cost of goods sold (Schedule A, line 8)			2	7,250	00
3	Gross profit. Subtract line 2 from line 1c			3		
4	Net gain (loss) from Form 4797, Part II, line 17 (attach Form 4797)			4		
5	Other income (loss) (attach schedule)			5		
6	**Total income (loss).** Add lines 3 through 5. . . . . ►			6	18,300	00

Deductions (see page 14 of the instructions for limitations)

7	Compensation of officers		7		
8	Salaries and wages (less employment credits)		8	4,225	00
9	Repairs and maintenance		9		
10	Bad debts		10		
11	Rents		11		
12	Taxes and licenses		12		
13	Interest		13		
14a	Depreciation (attach Form 4562)	14a	700	00			
b	Depreciation claimed on Schedule A and elsewhere on return .	14b					
c	Subtract line 14b from line 14a		14c	700	00
15	Depletion **(Do not deduct oil and gas depletion.)**		15		
16	Advertising		16	100	00
17	Pension, profit-sharing, etc., plans		17		
18	Employee benefit programs		18		
19	Other deductions (attach schedule)		19	8410	00
20	**Total deductions.** Add the amounts shown in the far right column for lines 7 through 19 ►		20	13,435	00
21	Ordinary business income (loss). Subtract line 20 from line 6		21	4,865	00

Tax and Payments

22	**Tax: a** Excess net passive income tax (attach schedule) . . .	22a				
	b Tax from Schedule D (Form 1120S)	22b				
	c Add lines 22a and 22b (see page 18 of the instructions for additional taxes)		22c		
23	**Payments: a** 2004 estimated tax payments and amount applied from 2003 return	23a				
	b Tax deposited with Form 7004	23b				
	c Credit for Federal tax paid on fuels (attach Form 4136) . . .	23c				
	d Add lines 23a through 23c		23d		
24	Estimated tax penalty (see page 18 of instructions). Check if Form 2220 is attached . . ►☐		24		
25	**Tax due.** If line 23d is smaller than the total of lines 22c and 24, enter amount owed . . .		25		
26	**Overpayment.** If line 23d is larger than the total of lines 22c and 24, enter amount overpaid .		26		
27	Enter amount of line 26 you want: **Credited to 2005 estimated tax** ►_____ Refunded ►		27		

Sign Here

Under penalties of perjury, I declare that I have examined this return, including accompanying schedules and statements, and to the best of my knowledge and belief, it is true, correct, and complete. Declaration of preparer (other than taxpayer) is based on all information of which preparer has any knowledge.

► Signature of officer _____ Date _____ ► Title **Preident** _____

May the IRS discuss this return with the preparer shown below (see instructions)? ☑ Yes ☐ No

Paid Preparer's Use Only

Preparer's signature ►		Date	Check if self-employed ☐	Preparer's SSN or PTIN 012-34-5678
Firm's name (or yours if self-employed), address, and ZIP code	Olivia Acostas, CPA 2225 Kennedy Drive, Dallas, TX 77777		EIN 99 : 1234567	
			Phone no. (206) 125-3456	

For Privacy Act and Paperwork Reduction Act Notice, see the separate instructions.   Cat. No. 11510H   Form **1120S** (2004)

Figure F.1 Treasure Trove, Inc.'s Federal 1120S tax return (first four pages).

Form 1120S (2004)   Page **2**

Schedule A   Cost of Goods Sold (see page 18 of the instructions)

1	Inventory at beginning of year	**1** 6,000	00
2	Purchases	**2** 8,750	00
3	Cost of labor	**3**	
4	Additional section 263A costs *(attach schedule)*	**4**	
5	Other costs *(attach schedule)*	**5**	
6	**Total.** Add lines 1 through 5	**6** 14,750	00
7	Inventory at end of year	**7** 7,500	00
8	**Cost of goods sold.** Subtract line 7 from line 6. Enter here and on page 1, line 2	**8** 7,250	00

9a Check all methods used for valuing closing inventory: *(i)* ☐ Cost as described in Regulations section 1.471-3

   (ii) ☐ Lower of cost or market as described in Regulations section 1.471-4

   (iii) ☐ Other (specify method used and attach explanation) ▶ ....

  b Check if there was a writedown of subnormal goods as described in Regulations section 1.471-2(c) . . . . . ▶ ☐

  c Check if the LIFO inventory method was adopted this tax year for any goods (if checked, attach Form 970) . . . . . ▶ ☐

  d If the LIFO inventory method was used for this tax year, enter percentage (or amounts) of closing inventory computed under LIFO . . . . | **9d** |

  e If property is produced or acquired for resale, do the rules of Section 263A apply to the corporation? . . . . ☐ Yes ☐ No

  f Was there any change in determining quantities, cost, or valuations between opening and closing inventory? . . ☐ Yes ☐ No
    If "Yes," attach explanation.

Schedule B   Other Information (see page 19 of instructions)

		Yes	No
1	Check method of accounting: (a) ☐ Cash (b) ☑ Accrual (c) ☐ Other (specify) ▶....................		
2	See pages 36 through 38 of the instructions and enter the:		
	(a) Business activity ▶............................. (b) Product or service ▶....................		
3	At the end of the tax year, did the corporation own, directly or indirectly, 50% or more of the voting stock of a domestic corporation? (For rules of attribution, see section 267(c).) If "Yes," attach a schedule showing: (a) name, address, and employer identification number and (b) percentage owned		
4	Was the corporation a member of a controlled group subject to the provisions of section 1561?		
5	Check this box if the corporation has filed or is required to file **Form 8264,** Application for Registration of a Tax Shelter ▶ ☐		
6	Check this box if the corporation issued publicly offered debt instruments with original issue discount . . ▶ ☐		
	If checked, the corporation may have to file **Form 8281,** Information Return for Publicly Offered Original Issue Discount Instruments.		
7	If the corporation: (a) was a C corporation before it elected to be an S corporation **or** the corporation acquired an asset with a basis determined by reference to its basis (or the basis of any other property) in the hands of a C corporation **and (b)** has net unrealized built-in gain (defined in section 1374(d)(1)) in excess of the net recognized built-in gain from prior years, enter the net unrealized built-in gain reduced by net recognized built-in gain from prior years . . . . ▶ $		
8	Check this box if the corporation had accumulated earnings and profits at the close of the tax year . . ▶ ☐		
9	Are the corporation's total receipts (see page 19 of the instructions) for the tax year **and** its total assets at the end of the tax year less than $250,000? If "Yes," the corporation is not required to complete Schedules L and M-1.		

Note: *If the corporation had assets or operated a business in a foreign country or U.S. possession, it may be required to attach Schedule N (Form 1120), Foreign Operations of U.S. Corporations, to this return. See Schedule N for details.*

Schedule K   Shareholders' Shares of Income, Deductions, Credits, etc.

		Shareholders' Pro Rata Share Items		Total amount
Income (Loss)	1	Ordinary business income (loss) (page 1, line 21)		**1**
	2	Net rental real estate income (loss) *(attach Form 8825)* . . .		**2**
	3a	Other gross rental income (loss)	**3a**	
	b	Expenses from other rental activities *(attach schedule)* . .	**3b**	
	c	Other net rental income (loss). Subtract line 3b from line 3a . .		**3c**
	4	Interest income		**4**
	5	Dividends: a Ordinary dividends		**5a**
		b Qualified dividends	**5b**	
	6	Royalties		**6**
	7	Net short-term capital gain (loss)		**7**
	8a	Net long-term capital gain (loss)		**8a**
	b	Collectibles (28%) gain (loss)	**8b**	
	c	Unrecaptured section 1250 gain *(attach schedule)* . . .	**8c**	
	9	Net section 1231 gain (loss) (attach Form 4797)		**9**
	10	Other income (loss) *(attach schedule)*		**10**

Form **1120S** (2004)

Figure F.1   continued

Form 1120S (2004) Page **3**

	Shareholders' Pro Rata Share Items (continued)		Total amount
Deductions	**11** Section 179 deduction *(attach Form 4562)*	**11**	
	12a Contributions	**12a**	
	b Deductions related to portfolio income *(attach schedule)*	**12b**	
	c Investment interest expense	**12c**	
	d Section 59(e)(2) expenditures **(1)** Type ▶ .... **(2)** Amount ▶	**12d(2)**	
	e Other deductions *(attach schedule)*	**12e**	
Credits & Credit Recapture	**13a** Low-income housing credit (section 42(j)(5))	**13a**	
	b Low-income housing credit (other)	**13b**	
	c Qualified rehabilitation expenditures (rental real estate) *(attach Form 3468)*	**13c**	
	d Other rental real estate credits	**13d**	
	e Other rental credits	**13e**	
	f Credit for alcohol used as fuel *(attach Form 6478)*	**13f**	
	g Other credits and credit recapture *(attach schedule)*	**13g**	
Foreign Transactions	**14a** Name of country or U.S. possession ▶		
	b Gross income from all sources	**14b**	
	c Gross income sourced at shareholder level	**14c**	
	Foreign gross income sourced at corporate level:		
	d Passive	**14d**	
	e Listed categories *(attach schedule)*	**14e**	
	f General limitation	**14f**	
	Deductions allocated and apportioned at shareholder level:		
	g Interest expense	**14g**	
	h Other	**14h**	
	Deductions allocated and apportioned at corporate level to foreign source income:		
	i Passive	**14i**	
	j Listed categories *(attach schedule)*	**14j**	
	k General limitation	**14k**	
	Other information:		
	l Foreign taxes paid	**14l**	
	m Foreign taxes accrued	**14m**	
	n Reduction in taxes available for credit *(attach schedule)*.	**14n**	
Alternative Minimum Tax (AMT) Items	**15a** Post-1986 depreciation adjustment	**15a**	
	b Adjusted gain or loss	**15b**	
	c Depletion (other than oil and gas)	**15c**	
	d Oil, gas, and geothermal properties—gross income	**15d**	
	e Oil, gas, and geothermal properties—deductions.	**15e**	
	f Other AMT items *(attach schedule)*	**15f**	
Items Affecting Shareholder Basis	**16a** Tax-exempt interest income	**16a**	
	b Other tax-exempt income	**16b**	
	c Nondeductible expenses	**16c**	
	d Property distributions	**16d**	
	e Repayment of loans from shareholders	**16e**	
Other Information	**17a** Investment income	**17a**	
	b Investment expenses	**17b**	
	c Dividend distributions paid from accumulated earnings and profits	**17c**	
	d Other items and amounts *(attach schedule)*		
	e Income/loss reconciliation. (Required only if Schedule M-1 must be completed.) Combine the amounts on lines 1 through 10 in the far right column. From the result, subtract the sum of the amounts on lines 11 through 12e and lines 14l or 14m, whichever applies	**17e**	

Form **1120S** (2004)

Figure F.1 continued

Form 1120S (2004)   Page **4**

Note: The corporation is not required to complete Schedules L and M-1 if question 9 of Schedule B is answered "Yes."

Schedule L   Balance Sheets per Books

		Beginning of tax year		End of tax year	
Assets		(a)	(b)	(c)	(d)
1	Cash				3,725
2a	Trade notes and accounts receivable . . .			450	
b	Less allowance for bad debts				450
3	Inventories				7,500
4	U.S. government obligations.				
5	Tax-exempt securities				
6	Other current assets (attach schedule) . .				
7	Loans to shareholders				
8	Mortgage and real estate loans . . .				
9	Other investments (attach schedule) . . .				
10a	Buildings and other depreciable assets . .			4,740	
b	Less accumulated depreciation			700	4,040
11a	Depletable assets				
b	Less accumulated depletion.				
12	Land (net of any amortization)				
13a	Intangible assets (amortizable only) . . .				
b	Less accumulated amortization. . . .				
14	Other assets (attach schedule)				
15	Total assets				15,715
	Liabilities and Shareholders' Equity				
16	Accounts payable				1,410
17	Mortgages, notes, bonds payable in less than 1 year .				
18	Other current liabilities (attach schedule) .				2,730
19	Loans from shareholders.				5,710
20	Mortgages, notes, bonds payable in 1 year or more				
21	Other liabilities (attach schedule)				
22	Capital stock				1,000
23	Additional paid-in capital.				
24	Retained earnings				4,865
25	Adjustments to shareholders' equity (attach schedule).				
26	Less cost of treasury stock		( )		( )
27	Total liabilities and shareholders' equity . . .				15,715

Schedule M-1   Reconciliation of Income (Loss) per Books With Income (Loss) per Return

1	Net income (loss) per books.		5	Income recorded on books this year not included on Schedule K, lines 1 through 10 (itemize):	
2	Income included on Schedule K, lines 1, 2, 3c, 4, 5a, 6, 7, 8a, 9, and 10, not recorded on books this year (itemize):		a	Tax-exempt interest $	
3	Expenses recorded on books this year not included on Schedule K, lines 1 through 12, and 14I or (14m) (itemize):		6	Deductions included on Schedule K, lines 1 through 12, and 14I or (14m), not charged against book income this year (itemize):	
a	Depreciation $		a	Depreciation $	
b	Travel and entertainment $				
			7	Add lines 5 and 6.	
4	Add lines 1 through 3.		8	Income (loss) (Schedule K, line 17e). Line 4 less line 7	

Schedule M-2   Analysis of Accumulated Adjustments Account, Other Adjustments Account, and Shareholders' Undistributed Taxable Income Previously Taxed (see page 32 of the instructions)

		(a) Accumulated adjustments account	(b) Other adjustments account	(c) Shareholders' undistributed taxable income previously taxed
1	Balance at beginning of tax year			
2	Ordinary income from page 1, line 21 . .			
3	Other additions.			
4	Loss from page 1, line 21	( )		
5	Other reductions	( )	( )	
6	Combine lines 1 through 5			
7	Distributions other than dividend distributions			
8	Balance at end of tax year. Subtract line 7 from line 6			

Form **1120S** (2004)

Figure F.1   continued

Comptroller 05-142 (Rev.1-05/13)

Do Not Staple or Paper Clip

1111
INTERNET

TEXAS CORPORATION
FRANCHISE TAX REPORT - Page 1

a. ☐ ■ 13100 Franchise
   ☐ ■ 16100 Bank   e. ■

d. REPORT YEAR
■ 04

FRANCHISE TAX QUESTION?
CALL US
1-800-252-138

Please do not write in space above

i. ● Blacken box to indicate
  your accounting method ..... GAAP 1 ● ■   FIT 2 ■ ☐

● If Close and/or "S," blacken
  the applicable box(es) .... Close 3 ■ ☐   "S" 4 ■ ☐

c. Taxpayer number	f. Due date	g. Privilege period covered by this report
■ 20-0010007	May 16, 2005	Jan 1, 2004 through Dec 31, 2004

j.

h.   Taxpayer name and mailing address

TREASURE TROVE, INC.
1832 Montemarte Avenue, Ste. 206
Dallas, TX 76767

k. ■   ■   l. ■

☐ Check this box if your
  address has changed.

READ DETAILED INSTRUCTIONS BEFORE COMPLETING THIS REPORT
SCHEDULE A - COMPUTATION OF TAX DUE ON NET TAXABLE CAPITAL

Print your numerals in boxes as shown
0 1 2 3 4 5 6 7 8 9

1. Is this corporation the survivor of a merger? ☑ NO - Proceed to Item 2.
   ☐ YES - See instructions BEFORE proceeding to Item 2.

2. Enter the ending date of your accounting period.
   (See instructions for date to use) .... 2. ■

MONTH	DAY	YEAR
12	31	04

3. Gross receipts in Texas (Whole dollars only)
   (If you had "0" gross receipts in Texas, enter "0" in Item 11 and SKIP TO ITEM 13.) ... 3. ■   1,235.00

4. Gross receipts everywhere (Whole dollars only) .... 4. ■   25,750.00

5. Apportionment factor (Item 3 divided by Item 4) 5.   0.048

6. Stated capital (See instructions for determining stated capital) .... 6. ■   1,000.00

7. Surplus (See instructions for determining surplus) .... 7. ■   4,865.00

8. Total taxable capital (Item 6 plus Item 7) (If less than "0," enter "0") .. 8. ■   5,865.00

9. Apportioned taxable capital (Multiply Item 8 by Item 5) .... 9. ■   282.00

10. Allowable deductions (See instructions) .... 10. ■   0.00

11. Net taxable capital (Item 9 minus Item 10) (If less than "0," enter "0") ... 11.   282.00

12. Tax due on net taxable capital (Multiply Item 11 by .00250) ...... 12. ■   0.71

Complete SCHEDULE B (Items 13-35) on Page 2, then complete SCHEDULE C below.

SCHEDULE C - TOTAL AMOUNT DUE AND PAYABLE

FOR ALL REPORT YEARS, if the amount in Item 35 is LESS THAN $100, you do not owe tax. FOR REPORTS ORIGINALLY DUE ON OR AFTER JANUARY 1, 2000, if Item 4 and Item 17 are each less than $150,000 you do not owe any tax. Enter zero (0) in Item 36, sign on Page 2, and file the report even if no tax is due. If tax is due, complete Schedule C, sign on Page 2, and file the report.

36. Total tax due on this report (Enter the amount from Item 35.) 36.   0.00

37. Enter prior payments (Credit available $ 0.00 as of ___) 37.   0.00

38. Net tax due (Item 36 minus Item 37) 38.   0.00

39. PENALTY: 1-30 days late-5% of Item 38. More than 30 days late-10% of Item 38.
    (See instructions for calculating penalty if an extension was filed.) 39.   0.00

40. INTEREST: (See instructions) 40.   0.00

41. TOTAL AMOUNT DUE AND PAYABLE - (Item 38 plus Item 39 plus Item 40)
    Make amount payable to STATE COMPTROLLER .... 41. ■ $ 0.00

TREASURE TROVE, INC.

c. T.Code   Taxpayer number   Period

Form 05-142 (Rev.1-05/13)

Figure F.2 Treasure Trove, Inc.—Texas Franchise Tax Return.

Form 05-142 (Back)(Rev.1-05/13)

DO NOT SEND IRS FORMS

READ DETAILED INSTRUCTIONS
BEFORE COMPLETING THIS REPORT

You have certain rights under Ch. 559, Government Code, to review,
request, and correct information we have on file about you. Contact us
at the address or toll-free number listed on this form.

WHO MUST FILE: All Texas corporations and all foreign corporations doing business in Texas are liable for Texas franchise tax.
The term "corporation" includes a bank, a state limited banking association, a savings and loan association, a limited liability
company, a corporation that elects to be an S corporation for federal income tax purposes, and a professional corporation.

FOR ASSISTANCE: If you have any questions regarding franchise tax, you may contact the Texas State Comptroller's field office
in your area or call 1-800-252-1381, toll free, nationwide. The Austin number is 512/463-4600. From a Telecommunications
Device for the Deaf (TDD), call 1-800-248-4099, toll free, or in Austin, 512/463-4621.

GENERAL INSTRUCTIONS:
- Please do not write in shaded areas.
- TYPE OR PRINT information in the heading of this form.
- To assist the Comptroller's office in processing your report more quickly and ➔
  accurately, please print all your numbers in the boxes, as shown, using black ink.
- If typing, numbers may be typed consecutively, as shown. ————————➔
- Complete all applicable items that are not preprinted.
- Correct any preprinted information that is not correct by marking it out and writing in the correct information.
- NEGATIVE NUMBERS: On this report, Items 7, 19, 22, 23, 24, and 25 may be negative numbers. If any of these numbers
  are negative, enclose them in brackets < >.
- MAIL TO: COMPTROLLER OF PUBLIC ACCOUNTS
                111 E. 17th Street
                Austin, Texas 78774-0100

DETAILED INSTRUCTIONS: To complete this report for annual franchise tax originally due May 16, 2005, see Form 05-386. For
instructions to complete initial reports originally due 1992 through 2005 and annual reports originally due 1992 through 2004,
see Form 05-364.

Figure F.2   continued

05-143
(Rev.6-04/9)

Comptroller
of Public
Accounts
FORM

Do Not Staple or Paper Clip

TEXAS CORPORATION
FRANCHISE TAX REPORT - Page 2   *INTERNET*

a. ☑ ■ 13120 Franchise
   ☐ ■ 16120 Bank   e. ■

Please do not write in space above.

g. ■   h. ■   ■   i. ■

d. REPORT YEAR
■ 04

c. Taxpayer number
■ 20-0010007

f. Taxpayer name
TREASURE TROVE, INC.

FRANCHISE TAX QUESTION?
CALL US
1-800-252-1381

SCHEDULE B - COMPUTATION OF SURTAX ON NET TAXABLE EARNED SURPLUS

	MONTH	DAY	YEAR		MONTH	DAY	YEAR
13. Enter beginning and ending date of your accounting period (See instructions for dates to use) — Beginning date ■	01	01	04	Ending date ■	12	31	04

14. If you do not have a Texas Charter and PL 86-272 applied during the period shown in Item 13, enter the effective date. .... 14. ■   [MONTH DAY YEAR]

15. Business loss carryover from prior years (See instructions) (NOTE: An amount cannot be entered for the 1st initial report.) .... 15. ■   0 .00

16. Gross receipts in Texas (Whole dollars only) (If you had "0" gross receipts in Texas, enter "0" in Item 23 and complete the remainder of the report.) .... 16. ■   1,235 .00

17. Gross receipts everywhere (Whole dollars only) .... 17. ■   25,750 .00

18. Apportionment factor (Item 16 divided by Item 17) 18.   0.048

19. Federal taxable income (Before net operating loss deduction and special deductions. See instructions) .... 19. ■   18,300 .00

20. Special deductions (See instructions)
   a. I.R.S. Form 1120, Schedule C, Special Deductions .... 20a. ■   .00

   b. Other authorized deductions .... 20b. ■   13,435 .00

21. Officer and director compensation (See instructions) .... 21. ■   4,225 .00

22. Earned surplus (Item 19 minus Items 20a and 20b plus Item 21) .... 22. ■   9,090 .00

23. Apportioned earned surplus (Dollars and cents) (Multiply Item 22 by Item 18) .... 23. ■   43.63

24. Allocated earned surplus (Does not include dividends and interest, AND does not apply to 1992 or 1993 report years.) .... 24. ■   0.00

25. Apportioned plus allocated earned surplus (Item 23 plus Item 24) .... 25. ■   43.63

26. Allowable deductions (See instructions) .... 26. ■   0.00

27. Business loss carryover used this year (See instructions) (NOTE: An amount cannot be entered for the 1st initial report.) .... 27. ■   0.00

28. Net taxable earned surplus (Item 25 minus Item 26 and Item 27) (If less than "0," enter "0") .... 28. ■   43.63

29. Tax due on net taxable earned surplus (Multiply Item 28 by .04500) .... 29. ■   1.96

30. Temporary credit (See instructions) .... 30. ■   0.00

31. Net tax due on net taxable earned surplus (Item 29 minus Item 30) (If less than "0," enter "0") .... 31. ■   1.96

32. Net tax due (Enter the greater of Item 12 on Page 1 or Item 31) .... 32. ■   1.96

33. Additional tax due if temporary credit has been claimed on this or previous reports (Multiply Item 11 by .00200) .... 33. ■   0.00

34. Tax credits (If credits are claimed, Schedule D must be completed and submitted--see instructions.) (NOTE: Please do not enter extension payments, penalty, interest, or prior payments on this line.) .... 34. ■   0.00

35. Total tax due (Item 32 plus Item 33 minus Item 34. Enter here and in Item 36 on Page 1.) (NOTE: If less than $100, or if Item 4 and Item 17 are each less than $150,000, you do not owe tax. Enter 0 (zero) in Item 36.) .... 35. ■   1.96

COMPLETE SCHEDULE C on Page 1.

I declare that the information in this document and any attachments is true and correct to the best of my knowledge and belief.

sign here ►
Officer, director or authorized agent   Print or type name   Date

Daytime phone (Area code and no.)

Figure F.2   continued

Appendix G

Discover Your Own Loopholes

To discover your own loopholes, you need two things: an understanding of what constitutes a qualified business expense, and complete and accurate records. Take the test, "Where Does Your Personal Income Go," to see where you are spending your money. Then, review the "300+ Possible Business Deductions," to see how many of those expenses can become qualified business expenses. Use the "Expense Report" to keep track of your expenses, and don't forget to attach your receipts and notes to the report as back-up.

Expense Sheet to Track Your Own Expenses

Expense Report

(Give one of these to each employee or other person who spends personal funds on company-related business. At the end of each month, collect these and provide them to your bookkeeper for posting to your company's accounts.)

Date	Vendor Name	Amount	Purpose	Paid by	Receipt Provided?	Reimbursement Date

For Bookkeeper Use:

Date Posted: _____

Date Reimbursed: _____

Check No. _____

Where Does Your Personal Income Go? Quiz

Instructions: For each of the items below, enter the *average amount* you pay in a month. Please note that these are expenses you currently *do not deduct* in a business. *Do not include business expenses.* **Note:** You can substitute a personal expense list from a software package, if applicable.

Auto & Truck Expenses		Entertainment Expenses	
Auto insurance*		Computer games	
Auto lease		Event tickets	
Gas/oil/tires		Hotel	
Insurance deduction		Music	
Payments		Other games	
Registration		RV	
Repairs		Travel	
Security		Vacations	
TOTAL		Videos	
Charities/Donations		Wine/liquor	
Church		TOTAL	
Other		**Equipment Expenses**	
TOTAL		Art/sculpture	
Children Expenses		Computer	
Child care		Computer software	
Child support		Furniture	
Clothing		Home entertainment center	
Education/tuition		Home office	
Education savings		TOTAL	
Private school		**Gift Expenses**	
Religious training		Birthday	
Toys		Holiday	
Sports		Weddings/anniversary	
Wedding		Other	
TOTAL		TOTAL	
Clothing Expenses		**Hobby Expenses**	
Altering/repair		Boat	
Cleaning		Collectibles	
Purchasing		Hobbies/classes	
TOTAL		Pet food	

Education Expenses		Pets	
Books & tapes		Vacation homes	
Dues & subscriptions		Vet bills	
School loans		TOTAL	
Seminars		**Personal Care Expenses**	
Travel		Hair/nails	
Tuition		Personal items	
TOTAL		TOTAL	
Housing Expenses		**Supply Expenses**	
Assessments		Cleaning	
Garden tools		Home supplies	
Home Owner Association dues		Laundry	
Home security		Lawn & garden	
Insurance		Linen	
Janitorial/supplies		Office supplies	
Lawn services		Personal hygiene	
Mortgage		Postage	
Mortgage insurance		TOTAL	
Pool service		**Taxes**	
Rent		Federal	
Repairs/improvements		Payroll	
Snow removal		Property	
TOTAL		State	
Legal Expenses		Other	
Wills & Trust		TOTAL	
Other		**Utility Expenses**	
TOTAL		Telephone	
Miscellaneous Expenses		Cable TV	
Alimony		Cell phone	
Bank fees		Utilities	
Gambling		Internet	
TOTAL		TOTAL	
Personal Health Expenses		**Additional Personal Expenses**	
Dental work		Medical co-pays	
Exercise equipment		Medical insurance	
Glasses/eye-exam		Prescriptions	

Health club dues		Therapy	
Hearing aids		Vitamins	
Massage		TOTAL	

* If your business pays for your auto insurance, it would not be listed in this chart.

What other personal expenses do you foresee in the next 12 months?

Item	Amount $

Once you've completed this sheet, compare it against the next section, "300+ Business Deductions." You might find it surprising how many expenses you have right now that can become legitimate business deductions!

300+ Business Deductions

Here they are! How many of these deductions can you fit into your business tax strategy plan? Use this guide to spark your imagination. Check off items and add additional ones as you think of them. Then, go over the list with your tax advisor to discover how you can legitimately take these deductions.

A

____ Abandonment of property used for business purposes
____ Accounting and auditing expenses, such as:
____ Auditing of your books and accounts
    ____ Costs of bookkeeping
    ____ Costs of tax strategy preparation
    ____ Costs of preparing and filing any tax returns
    ____ Costs of investigation of any tax returns
    ____ Costs of defense against any IRS or state agency audits or challenges
____ Accounts receivable, worthless
____ Achievement awards—requires plan
    ____ Longevity award
    ____ Safety award
    ____ Sales award
____ Advances made to employees or salespeople where repayment is not expected
____ Advances to employees calculated as bonus
____ Advertising expenses, such as:
    ____ Premiums given away
    ____ Advertising in
        ____ Newspaper
        ____ Magazine
        ____ Radio
        ____ Other media
    ____ Prizes and other expenses in holding contests or exhibitions
    ____ Contributions to various organizations for advertising purposes
    ____ Costs of displays, posters, etc., to attract customers
    ____ Publicity—generally speaking, all costs including entertainment, music, etc.
    ____ Christmas present to customers or prospects—(to a maximum of $25 per gift)
____ Alterations to business property, if minor

____ Amortization

____ Attorney's fees and other legal expenses involving:

   ____ Tax strategy

   ____ Drafting of agreements, resolutions, minutes, etc.

   ____ Defense of claims against you

   ____ Collection actions taken against others

   ____ Any other business related legal activity

____ Auto expenses for business purposes, such as:

   ____ Damage to auto not covered by insurance

   ____ Gasoline

   ____ Oil

   ____ Repairs and replacements

   ____ Washing and waxing

   ____ Garage rent

   ____ Interest portion of payments

   ____ Insurance premiums such as fire, theft, collision, liability, etc.

   ____ Lease payment

   ____ License plates

   ____ Driver's license fee

   ____ Depreciation

   ____ Wages of chauffeur

   ____ Section 179 deduction (for qualified vehicle)

B

____ Bad debts—if previously taken into income

____ Board and room to employee:

   ____ All meals and lodging if for employer's benefit

   ____ Temporary housing assignment

____ Board meetings

____ Bonuses as additional compensation to employees

____ Bookkeeping services

____ Building expenses, used for business, such as:

   ____ Repairs to building

   ____ Janitorial service

   ____ Painting

   ____ Interest on mortgage

   ____ Taxes on property

   ____ Water

   ____ Rubbish removal

   ____ Depreciation of building

   ____ Heating

   ____ Lighting

____ Landscaping
____ Burglary losses not covered by insurance
____ Business, cost of operating office
____ Business taxes—except federal income taxes

C

____ Cafeteria plan—requires written plan
____ Capital assets sale—losses
____ Car and taxi fares
____ Charitable contributions
____ Casualty damages, such as:
    ____ Bombardment
    ____ Fire
    ____ Storm
    ____ Hurricane
    ____ Drought
    ____ Forest fire
    ____ Freezing of property
    ____ Impairment or collapse of property
    ____ Ice
    ____ Heat
    ____ Wind
    ____ Rain
____ Checking account bank charges
____ Child care—requires written plan
____ Children's salaries
____ Christmas presents to employees, customers, and prospects for advertising, publicity purposes, goodwill, or if customary in the trade (to a maximum of $25 per gift)
____ Collection expenses, including attorney's charges
____ Commissions on sales of securities by dealers in securities
____ Commissions paid to salesmen
____ Commissions paid to agents
____ Commissions paid to employees for business purposes
____ Condemnation expenses
____ Contributions deductible if made to organization founded for the following purposes, subject to some limitations:
    ____ Religious
    ____ Charitable
    ____ Scientific
    ____ Literary
    ____ Educational

____ Prevention of cruelty to children and animals
____ Convention expenses, cost of attending conventions
____ Cost of goods
____ Credit report costs

D

____ Day care facility
____ Depletion
____ Depreciation
____ Discounts allowed to customers
____ Dues paid to:
    ____ Better Business Bureau
    ____ Chamber of Commerce
    ____ Trade associations
    ____ Professional societies
    ____ Technical societies
    ____ Protective services association

E

____ Education assistance—requires written plan
____ Embezzlement loss not covered by insurance
____ Employees' welfare expenses, such as:
    ____ Dances
    ____ Entertainment
    ____ Outings
    ____ Christmas parties
    ____ Shows or plays
____ Endorser's loss
____ Entertainment expenses
____ Equipment purchases—may require capitalization and depreciation
____ Equipment repairs
____ Equipment, minor replacements
____ Exhibits and displays, to publicize your products
____ Expenses of any kind directly chargeable to business income, such as:
    ____ Renting of storage or space
    ____ Safe deposit boxes
    ____ Upkeep of property
    ____ Books to record income and expenses or investment income
____ Experimental and research expenses

F

____ Factoring

_____ Fan mail expenses
_____ Fees for passports necessary while traveling on business
_____ Fees to accountants
_____ Fees to brokers
_____ Fees to agents
_____ Fees to technicians
_____ Fees to professionals for services rendered
_____ Fees to investment counsel
_____ Fire loss
_____ Forfeited stock
_____ Freight charges

G

_____ Gifts to customers—limit of $75
_____ Gifts to organized institutions, such as:
    _____ Charitable
    _____ Literary
    _____ Educational
    _____ Religious
    _____ Scientific
_____ Group term insurance on employees' lives
_____ Guarantor's loss

H

_____ Health insurance
_____ Heating expense
_____ Hospitals, contributions to

I

_____ Improvements, provided they are minor
_____ Insurance premiums paid
_____ Interest on loans of all kinds for business purposes, such as:
    _____ On loans
    _____ On notes
    _____ On mortgages
    _____ On bonds
    _____ On tax deficiencies
    _____ On installment payments of auto, furniture, etc.
    _____ On margin account with brokers
    _____ Bank discount on note is deductible as interest
_____ Inventory loss due to damages
_____ Investment counsel fees

L

____ Lawsuit expenses
____ Legal costs
     ____ In defense of your business
     ____ In settlement of cases
     ____ Payment of damages
____ License fees
____ Lighting
____ Living quarter furnished employees for business's benefit
____ Lobbying costs
____ Losses, deductible if connected with your business or profession, such as:
     ____ Abandoned property
     ____ Accounts receivable
     ____ Auto damages caused by fire, theft, heat, storm
     ____ Bad debts
     ____ Bank closed
     ____ Bonds
     ____ Buildings—damaged
     ____ Burglary
     ____ Business ventures
     ____ Capital assets
     ____ Casualties caused by fire, theft, heat, storm
     ____ Damages to property or assets
     ____ Deposit forfeiture, on purchase of property
     ____ Drought
     ____ Embezzlements
     ____ Equipment abandoned
     ____ Forced sale or exchange
     ____ Foreclosures
     ____ Forfeitures
     ____ Freezing
     ____ Goodwill
     ____ Loans not collectible
     ____ Theft
     ____ Transactions entered into for profits

M

____ Maintenance of business property
____ Maintenance of office, store, warehouse, showroom, etc.
____ Maintenance of rented premises
____ Management costs

_____ Materials
_____ Meals, subject to limitation
_____ Membership dues
_____ Merchandise
_____ Messenger service
_____ Moving cost
_____ Musician expenses

N

_____ Net operating loss—may be carried back to previous years' income for refund and/or forward against future years' income
_____ Newspapers

O

_____ Office expenses, including:
  _____ Wages
  _____ Supplies
  _____ Towel service
  _____ Heating and lighting
  _____ Telephone and telegraph
  _____ Repairs
  _____ Refurnishing, minor items
  _____ Decorating
  _____ Painting
_____ Office rent
_____ Office rent—portion of home used for business
_____ Office stationery and supplies

P

_____ Passport fees
_____ Pension plans—must be properly drawn
_____ Periodicals
_____ Physical fitness center
_____ Plotting of land for sale
_____ Postage
_____ Professional society dues
_____ Property maintenance
_____ Property repairs
_____ Property depreciation
_____ Publicity expenses

R

____ Real estate expenses of rental or investment property, including:
    ____ Taxes of property
    ____ Insurance
    ____ Janitorial services
    ____ Repairing
    ____ Redecorating
    ____ Painting
    ____ Depreciation
    ____ Supplies
    ____ Tools
    ____ Legal expenses involving leases, tenants, or property
    ____ Bookkeeping
    ____ Property management
    ____ Utilities
    ____ Commissions to secure tenants
    ____ Maintenance—heating, lighting, etc.
    ____ Advertising for tenants
    ____ Cost of manager's unit, if on-site and at employer's convenience
____ Rebates on sales
____ Refunds on sales
____ Rents paid, such as:
    ____ Business property
    ____ Parking facilities
    ____ Safe deposit boxes
    ____ Taxes paid by tenant for landlord
    ____ Warehouse and storage charges
____ Rent settlement—cancel lease
____ Rent collection expense
____ Rental property expense, such as:
    ____ Advertising of vacant premises
    ____ Commissions to secure tenant
    ____ Billboards and signs
____ Repairing of business property, such as:
    ____ Alterations, provided they are not capital additions
    ____ Casualty damages replaced, provided they are not capital additions
    ____ Cleaning
    ____ Minor improvements
    ____ Painting

_____ Redecorating

_____ Repairing of furniture, fixtures, equipment, machinery, and buildings

_____ Roof repairs

_____ Royalties

S

_____ Safe deposit box rental

_____ Safe or storage rental

_____ Salaries (including bonuses, commissions, pensions, management fees)

_____ Sample room

_____ Selling expenses, such as:

_____ Commissions and bonuses as prized

_____ Discounts

_____ Entertainment

_____ Prizes offered in contests

_____ Publicity and promotion costs

_____ Rebates

_____ Services, professional or other necessary for conduct of business

_____ Social Security taxes paid by employers

_____ Sports team equipment for business publicity

_____ Stationery and all other office supplies used

_____ Subscriptions to all trade, business, or professional periodicals

_____ Supplies, office or laboratory

T

_____ Taxes, all taxes paid except federal income taxes, such as:

_____ City gross receipts tax

_____ City sales tax

_____ State gross receipts tax

_____ State sales tax

_____ State unemployment insurance tax

_____ Federal Social Security tax

_____ State income tax

_____ State unincorporated business tax

_____ Real estate tax

_____ Tangible property tax

_____ Intangible property tax

_____ Custom, import or tariff tax

_____ License tax

_____ Stamp taxes

____ Any business tax, as a rule
____ Auto registration tax
____ Safe deposit tax
____ Membership dues tax
____ Gasoline tax
____ Admission tax
____ Telephone and telegraphs
____ Traveling expenses (includes meals, taxi fare, rail fare, airfare, tips, telephone, telegrams, laundry and cleaning, entertainment for business purposes)

U

____ Unemployment compensation taxes paid by employer
____ Uniforms furnished to employees

W

____ Wages
____ Workmen's Compensation Fund contributions

Appendix H

Glossary of Accounting Terms

accelerated depreciation

Depreciation taken in excess of the straight line method.

account

A section in a ledger devoted to a single aspect of a business (bank accounts, rent expense account).

accountant's opinion

Signed statement regarding the financial status of an entity from an independent public accountant after examination of that entity's records and accounts.

accounting

A general term that refers to the overall process of tracking your business's income and expenses, and then using these numbers in various calculations and formulas to answer specific questions about the financial and tax status of the business.

accounting equation

The accounting equation represents both the relationship among the assets, liabilities, and equity of the business, as well as the double-entry system of financial statement presentation:

A = Assets, L = Liabilities, O/E = Owner's Equity

Assets = Liability + Equity

To increase: Accounts on the left side of the equation are increased through a debit entry (DR), whereas accounts on the right side of the equation are increased by a credit entry (CR).

To decrease: Accounts on the left side of the equation are decreased by a credit entry, whereas accounts on the right side of the equation are decreased by a debit entry

accounting period
Time period over which account reports cover.

accounts payable
The amount due, but not yet paid, by the business.

accounts receivable
The amount due to, but not yet received by, the business.

accruals (or accrued expenses)
Expenses that have been incurred by the business but no invoice has been received. Typical accrued expense items are accrued interest or accrued property taxes. This is a balance sheet account.

accrual method of accounting
A method of accounting whereby accounts payable and accrued expenses are recorded, so that the resulting expense reduces the income and accounts receivable are recorded, so that the unpaid, but due, receipt is counted as income.

accrued assets
Assets from revenues earned but not yet received.

accrued expenses
Expenses incurred during an accounting period for which payment is postponed.

accrued income
Income earned during a fiscal period but not paid by the end of the period.

accrued interest
Interest earned but not paid since the last due date.

accrued liability
Liabilities that are incurred, but for which payment is not yet made.

accumulated depreciation account
A balance sheet account that holds the depreciation of a fixed asset until the end of the asset's useful life. It is credited each year with that

year's depreciation; hence, the balance will increase, or accumulate, over time.

ACRS depreciation

Accelerated Cost Recovery System. A system of depreciation authorized by Congress for tax purposes. Rapid write-off of the cost of assets.

adjusted gross income (AGI)

Annualized total income prior to exclusions and deductions.

adjusting journal entries (AJE)

Accounting entries that are made to correct or record activities to your journals (the records of your company).

ADR (The Class Life Asset Depreciation Range System)

A flexible set of government guidelines for depreciation that sets up an "asset depreciation period" rather than using the useful life.

AICPA

American Institute of Certified Public Accountants.

amortization

The gradual reduction of an amount by means of equal periodic payments. This could include amortization of debt, where the periodic payments of principal and interest reduce the debt. The term *amortization* is also used to describe the spreading of an intangible item over its expected useful life. The amortization is similar to depreciation in this second definition.

annual percentage rate (APR)

The effective interest rate required to be disclosed under the Truth in Lending Act.

annualize

To convert anything into a yearly figure. For example, if profit is $1,000 per month, then the annualized profit would be $12,000.

appreciation

Increase in the value of an asset in excess of its depreciable cost, which is due to economic and other conditions, as distinguished from increases in value due to improvements or additions made to it.

assets

A balance sheet that shows what a business owns or is due. This includes bank accounts, equipment, vehicles and buildings. Typical breakdown would include fixed assets, current assets, and noncurrent assets. The fixed assets are equipment, buildings, and vehicles. The current assets are cash and accounts receivable. Noncurrent assets are the "other" items of assets.

audit

Inspection of the accounting records and procedures of a business, government unit, or other reporting entity by a trained accountant for the purpose of verifying the accuracy and completeness of the records. It could be conducted by a member of the organization (internal audit) or by an outsider (independent audit).

audit trail

A list of transactions in the order in which they occurred.

bad debts account

Account used with the accrual method of accounting. It is an income statement that shows the write-off of unrecoverable debts from customers.

balance sheet

A summary of the assets, liabilities, and equity accounts of the business. It typically reflects the historic cost of items (not their current value) as of a specific point in time.

balloon payment

The final installment on a loan that is greater than the prior payments and pays any remaining amount outstanding under the loan.

bank reconciliation

Verification of a bank statement balance and the depositor's checkbook balance.

beneficiary

(1) One for whose benefit a trust is created. (2) In states in which deeds of trust are commonly used instead of mortgages, the lender is called the beneficiary.

bookkeeping

The art, practice, or labor involved in the systematic recording of the transactions affecting a business.

business entity

Selection of the legal form under which a business is to operate: sole proprietorship, general partnership, C corporation, S corporation, limited partnership, or limited liability company.

capital

An amount of money, goods, or services that have been contributed into the company in exchange for ownership.

capital account
Term usually applied to the owner's equity in the business.

capital asset
Assets of a permanent nature used to produce income, such as machinery, buildings, equipment, land, and so on.

capital gains
When a fixed asset is sold at a value more then the depreciable basis (original asset minus accumulated depreciation), the difference is called capital gains. These gains are either short term (assets had been held less then one year) or long term (asset had been held one year or more).

capitalization
Adding costs, such as improvements, to the basis of assets. It is then depreciated or amortized over time.

cash basis accounting
Accounting basis in which revenue and expenses are recorded in the period they are actually received or expended in cash. It does not include accounts payable or accounts receivable.

cash flow
The flow of money in and out of a project or business over a period of time, usually monthly.

cash from financing
Sum of all individual financing activity cash flow line items. This is part of the statement of cash flows.

cash from investing
Sum of all individual investing activity cash flow line items. This is part of the statement of cash flows.

cash from operations
Sum of all individual operating activity cash flow line items, less cash realized from the sale of extraordinary items (fixed assets). This is part of the statement of cash flows.

certified financial statements
Financial statements that have undergone a formal audit by a certified public accountant.

chart of accounts
A list of all of the accounts.

common stock

The most frequently issued class of stock. It usually provides a voting right but is secondary to preferred stock in dividend and liquidation rights.

contra account

An account created to offset another account. An example would be accumulated depreciation offsetting the equipment account.

cook the books

To falsify a set of accounts.

corporation

Type of business organization chartered by a state and given many of the legal rights as a separate entity.

credit

As used in double-entry bookkeeping, a credit will decrease assets, increase income, decrease expenses, or increase liabilities. See *accounting equation*.

creditors

Entities to which a debt is owed by another entity.

current assets

Those assets of a company that are reasonably expected to be realized in cash, or sold, or consumed during the normal operating cycle of the business (usually one year). Such assets include cash, accounts receivable and money due usually within one year: short term investments, government bonds, inventories, and prepaid expenses.

current liabilities

Liabilities to be paid within one year of the balance sheet date.

debit

As used in bookkeeping, a debit increases an asset or expense. It records a reduction from revenue, net worth, or a liability account.

depreciation

Amount of expense charged against earnings by a company to write off the cost of an asset over its useful life. The depreciation is a current period expense and is accumulated as a contra asset account under accumulated depreciation.

depreciation recapture

When tangible personal property is sold, the tax gain is based on the difference between the asset's adjusted basis and the selling price. Any gain up to the amount of depreciation taken is deemed depreciation recapture and is generally taxed as ordinary income.

double-entry accounting
System of recording transactions in a way that maintains the equality of the accounting equation. The accounting technique records each transaction as both a credit and a debit. Double-entry bookkeeping was developed during the fifteenth century and was first recorded in 1494 as a system by the Italian mathematician Luca Pacioli. Also see *accounting equation*.

earned income
Income earned within a trade or business. Depending on the business structure, the net earned income may be subject to self-employment tax in addition to regular income tax.

equity
The value of a business in excess of all liabilities against the business.

expense
Cost incurred in the normal course of business to generate revenue. This is recorded on the income statement.

extraordinary item
Nonrecurring event that must be explained to shareholders in an annual or quarterly report of financial or operational results.

fair market value
The highest price offered in a competitive market. It is determined by negotiation between an informed, willing, and capable buyer and an informed, willing, and capable seller.

financial statement
An accounting statement showing assets and liabilities of a person or company.

fiscal
Accounting period of 12 months.

fiscal year
Declared accounting year end for a company. Typically, this is December 31 for all business entities except the C corporation.

fixed assets
Those assets of a permanent nature required for the normal conduct of a business, and which will not normally be converted into cash during the ensuring fiscal period. For example, furniture, fixtures, land, and buildings are all fixed assets. Cash is not.

fixed assets (net)

All fixed assets net of accumulated depreciation.

G & A

Refers to the indirect overhead costs contained within the general and administrative expense.

general ledger

Accounting records that show all the financial statement accounts of a business.

going concern value

The additional value that attaches to property because the property is an integral part of an ongoing business activity. It includes value based on the ability of a business to continue to function and generate income even though there is a change in ownership.

gross income

The total amount of income received. Also see *gross profit*.

gross profit

Refers to the gross income less the costs related to the items sold.

hard money

A hard money loan refers to a loan that has higher than normal interest rates and is frequently from a lender of last resort.

installment sale

Created when property is sold and the sales price is received over a series of payments, instead of all at once at the close of the sale.

intangibles (net)

This includes intangible assets such as goodwill, trademarks, patents, brands, copyrights, formulas, franchises, and mailing lists, net of accumulated amortization.

investor

A person who purchases property with the intention of retaining that property for long-term investment purposes.

joint return

US federal income tax filing status that can be used by a married couple. The married couple must be married as of the last day of their tax year in order to qualify for this filing status. A married couple can also elect to file as married, filing separate returns.

K-1

The information form received from a partnership, S corporation, trust, or estate, which provides the flow-through income and losses to be reported on an investor's individual return.

lease

An agreement by which an owner of real property (lessor) gives the right of possession to another (lessee), for a specified period of time (term) and for a specified consideration (rent).

lease option

Also known as lease with option to purchase. A lease under which the lessee has the right to purchase the property. The price and terms of the purchase must be set forth for the option to be valid. The option may run for the length of the lease or only for a portion of the lease period.

legal entity

Person or organization that has the legal standing to enter into contracts and may be sued for failure to perform as agreed in the contract.

lessee

The tenant.

lessor

The landlord.

letter of credit

Legal document issued by a buyer's bank that guarantees that upon presentation of required documents, payment would be made by the bank.

leverage

The use of debt financing. Also, the use of borrowed money to increase the return on investment. For leverage to be positive, the rate of return on the investment must be higher than the cost of the money borrowed.

liability

A claim on the assets of an entity that must be paid or otherwise honored by that entity.

loan to value

The ratio of the loan amount divided by the total value of the property.

long-term debt

Debt that is due to be paid after one year, including bonds, debentures, bank debt, mortgages, and capital lease obligations.

long-term liabilities

Liabilities of a business or a legal entity that are due in more than one year. An example of a long-term liability would be a mortgage payable.

MACRS depreciation

Modified Accelerated Cost Recovery System. A system of depreciation used for property purchased after 1986.

net income

Difference between total revenue and total expenses. Also see *net profit*.

net operating loss (NOL)

The loss experienced by a business when business deductions exceed business income for the fiscal year. For income tax purposes, a net operating loss can be used to offset income in a prior year, or a taxpayer can elect to forego the carry back and carry the net operating loss forward.

nexus

Taxpayer's base of operations for state income tax purposes.

nonrecourse financing

Financing that does not require the personal guarantees of owners or others. The collateral is sufficient to secure the loan.

operating expenses

The cost of operating an income property. More narrowly defined as those costs that fluctuate with the rate of occupancy.

operating lease

Short term, cancelable lease.

option

A right to buy an asset, such as property, that is granted by the owner of the asset named in the option agreement. The option holder has the right to purchase but not the obligation to purchase.

organizational costs

Amounts spent to begin a business entity. This would include filing fees, franchise acquisition, and legal fees. Organizational expenses may be capitalized and amortized over a period of 60 months or more.

passive income
   Income that comes from real estate investment.

personal residence
   See *principal residence*.

phantom income
   Taxable income where no cash is produced from the transaction.

portfolio income
   Income that is earned by money invested—typically, interest, dividends, and capital gains.

preferred stock
   Nonvoting (typically) capital stock that pays dividends at a specified rate and has preference over common stock in the payment of dividends and the liquidation of assets.

prepaid expenses
   Amounts that are paid in advance to a vender or creditor for goods and services.

principal residence
   An IRS designation for a taxpayer's primary residence. Used to determine taxpayer's nexus for personal income tax and is the only residence where taxpayer is entitled to take gain exclusion on its sale.

property tax
   Generally, a tax levied on both real and personal property. The amount of the tax is dependent on the value of the property.

realized income
   The amount of gain that is earned but due to exceptions in the tax law may or may not be taxable.

recapture
   The portion of a depreciation taken in excess of straight line rates that has previously escaped taxation and is returned, or recaptured, to the category of ordinary income when the property is sold.

recognized income
   That portion of gain on the disposition of an asset that is taxable.

retained earnings
   Profits of the business that have not been paid out to the owners as of the balance sheet date for a corporation. Retained earnings is an account in the equity section of the balance sheet.

reverse mortgage

A type of loan that increases in balance as the owner takes draws against it. It is typically used with older homeowners looking for a way to tap into their equity and is not due to be paid off until their death.

reversing entry

A debit or credit bookkeeping entry made to reverse a prior bookkeeping entry.

short-term asset

An asset expected to be converted into cash within the normal operating cycle (usually one year).

short-term liability

A liability that will come due within one year or less.

sole proprietor

An individual who owns a business. A sole proprietor has unlimited liability for business debts and obligations. This is also known as a Schedule C business.

sole proprietorship

A form of business organization that has only one owner and unincorporated status.

straight line depreciation

Depreciation expense computed at an equal annual rate so that the cost (or other basis) will be expensed over its useful life.

tax bracket

The highest percentage of income tax that you pay, based on graduated tax tables.

tax credit

A tax credit directly reduces the amount of tax you pay.

tax deduction

A tax deduction reduces your taxable income.

tax deferred

Taxes will be deferred to a later time but not eliminated.

tax free

No taxes will ever be assessed.

total assets

Total of all assets, both current and fixed.

total current assets

Total of cash and equivalents, trade receivables, inventory, and all other current assets.

total current liabilities

Total of notes payable-short term, current maturities-LTD, trade payable, income taxes payable, and all other current liabilities.

trial balance (also known as a working trial balance or WTB)

A listing of all accounts from the general ledger and their balances as of a specified date. A trial balance is usually prepared at the end of an accounting period and is used to see if additional adjustments are required to any of the balances. Since the basic accounting system relies on double-entry bookkeeping, a trial balance will have the same total debit amount as it has total credit amount.

unearned revenue

Represents money you have received in advance of providing a service to your customer. It is actually a liability of your business, because you still owe the service to the customer.

unrealized income

Profit that has been made but not yet realized or collected through a transaction.

Index

Note: Boldface numbers indicate illustrations, italic *t* indicates a table.

payroll taxes *(continued)*
  W4, W2, and 1099 forms in, 56–57
  worker's compensation and, 53
pension. *See* retirement savings and
  pensions
permanent files, 71–72
personal income tax withholding, 50
phantom loss, 161–162
portfolio income, 146–148
Prince, Dennis, 17
profit, 10–11, 41–42, 84
profit and loss statement as. *See*
  income statement, 83
profit margin ratio, 91

quarterly payment of taxes, 141
  Form 941 Employer's Quarterly
  Federal Tax Return, **54–55**
QuickBooks software, 95–122
  access control and passwords in,
  101, **102**
  Accounting Assistant eBay tool
  for, 76–77
  asset accounts in, 118, **119, 120**
  bank accounts in, 116–118, **118**
  bill payment in, 103–104, **105**
  business type selection in,
  100–101, **101**
  cash vs. accrual-based accounting
  in, 105, **106**
  chart of accounts in, 101, **102**
  chart of accounts in, 133–134, **134**
  checks and deposit slips in, 118,
  119
  classes of income selection, 103,
  104
  company name in, 98, **99**
  cost of goods sold in, 136–137,
  137, 138
  credit card accounts in, 116
  customer accounts in, 114–115,
  115
  deduction tracking in, 107–108
  depreciation in, 118–119
  Easy Step Interview process to set
  up, 98–122, **99–122**

QuickBooks software *(continued)*
  eBay business and, 122
  equity account in, 119–120, **120,
  121**
  estimates selection, 103
  expense account in, 139, **139**
  finish screen, **122**
  Income and Expenses in, 105–107,
  107, 108
  income tax form selection in, 99,
  100
  inventory account in, 134–135, **135**
  inventory in, 109, 112–113, **113, 114**
  inventory purchases in, 137–138,
  138
  invoice type selection in, 103
  liability accounts in, 116, **116,
  117**
  Loans and Notes Payable in, 116,
  116, 117
  noninventory parts in, 109, **110**
  other charges items in, 109–111,
  110, 111, 112
  Preferences setting for, 101–102
  receipt of payments in, 109, **109**
  sales receipts in, 135–136, **136**
  sales tax in, 102–103, **104**
  shipping and handling charges in,
  109–112, **110, 111, 112**
  start date for, 98, 105, **106**
  tax ID number in, 98, **100**
  vendor accounts in, 115, **115**
  Welcome screen in, 98, **99**
  What's Next recommendations in,
  121, **121**

ratio analysis, 89–91
real estate investment, 193–195,
  197
  corporation as holding company
  for, 194–195
  LLC or LP as holding company
  for, 193–195
recordkeeping, 65–78. *See also*
  accounting and bookkeeping
  systems; financial statements

About the Authors

Diane Kennedy, the nation's preeminent tax strategist, is the owner of D Kennedy & Associates, a leading tax strategy and accounting firm, and the author of *The Wall Street Journal* and *BusinessWeek* best-sellers, *Loopholes of the Rich* and *Real Estate Loopholes*.

Diane's extensive teachings have empowered people throughout the country to minimize their tax liabilities through the use of legal tax loopholes.

Diane has written for *The Tax Savings Report*, *Investment Advisor Magazine*, *Personal. Excellence*, the Money & Finance Section of *Balance* magazine, and *Healthy Wealthy 'n Wise*, where she has a regular column. She's been featured in *Kiplinger's Personal Finance*, *The Wall Street Journal*, *USA Today*, and the Associated Press, and on CNN, CNNfn, Bloomberg TV and Radio, CNBC and StockTalkAmerica, and numerous regional TV and radio shows.

A highly sought-after international speaker and educator, Diane has dedicated her career to empowering and educating others about financial investments and the tax advantages that are available. Through Diane's knowledge and execution of legal tax loopholes in her business and real estate investments, she and her husband, Richard Cooley, are able to contribute to special, life-changing projects and charities in the United States and third-world countries.

Diane provides critical tax law updates, advice on the latest tax loopholes as well as tax-advantaged wealth building resources on her web site, www.taxloopholes.com. Her business office is located at 821 North 5th Avenue, Phoenix, AZ 85003 (Tel: 1-888-592-4769).

Janelle Elms is a lead instructor touring nationwide with eBay University. A Silver PowerSeller on eBay (http://www.JanelleElms.com), she has recently wrapped up production on a new training video for eBay called *Beyond the Basics*. Janelle's work with eBay has extended to teaching pilot training programs, including a leading-edge program initiated by Senator Hillary Rodham Clinton that is designed to help small towns understand how to sell globally instead of just locally.

Creator of the exclusive eBay 101 and 102 classes taught throughout the United States, Janelle has helped numerous individuals build successful businesses on eBay. To date, she has trained more than 2,030,000 people in eBay sales, marketing, customer service, and customer-retention strategies. Janelle specializes in corporate consulting designed to teach companies how to develop or maximize an eBay sales channel.

Co-author of the best-selling *eBay Your Business: Maximize Sales and Get Results* (McGraw-Hill, 2004), Janelle also self-published two eBay how-to books, *Don't Throw It Away Sell It On eBay!*, and *No Seriously, What Do You Really Do For a Living?* She has also started several eBay community groups in the Pacific Northwest, including the eBay for Beginners, and eBay PowerSellers groups and a new women's entrepreneurial group in her hometown of Seattle. As a national and corporate speaker and educator, Janelle believes that the eBay opportunity is available for all who seek to become a part of this global community.

Best-Selling Author, Educator, & Speaker

Learn How to Increase your eBay Sales and Profit Margins by 20-50%!

Speaker

A national speaker and lead eBay University instructor, Janelle has taught over 30,000 individuals and businesses how to build a successful eBay enterprise.

Educator

As a corporate and individual trainer, Janelle teaches her clients how to optimize their eBay sales and realize an increase in profit margins by 20-50%.

Author

Janelle is author of several eBay books, including the best-selling, "eBay Your Business" published by McGraw Hill.

To learn more about Janelle's consulting and speaking services, go to http://www.janelleelms.com/ebayexpert

"Janelle Elms is a dynamic, motivational speaker! She has the ability to engage the audience and teach the strategies required to grow an eBay business, while at the same time inspiring people to see the vision of what their eBay business can become."

--S. Grayson

"Janelle, just wanted to thank you for our consulting meeting yesterday. My head has been spinning with ideas of ways I can better advertise my eBay business and increase my revenue! Your branding suggestions have put me on the right track towards building a strong, unique presence on eBay."

--T. Lee

FREE Special Report!

Did you know that 99% of eBay Stores are not set-up correctly? Get your free eBay Store report and discover 5 quick fixes to make your Store part of the 1% at: www.JanelleElms.com/eBayExpert